CONSUMER SALES REMEDIES IN US AND EU COMPARATIVE PERSPECTIVE

CONSUMER SALES REMEDIES IN US AND EU COMPARATIVE PERSPECTIVE

Sanne Jansen

intersentia
Cambridge – Antwerp – Chicago

Intersentia Ltd
Sheraton House | Castle Park
Cambridge | CB3 0AX | United Kingdom
Tel.: +44 1223 370 170 | Fax: +44 1223 370 169
Email: mail@intersentia.co.uk
www.intersentia.com | www.intersentia.co.uk

Distribution for the UK and Ireland:
NBN International
Airport Business Centre, 10 Thornbury Road
Plymouth, PL6 7PP
United Kingdom
Tel.: +44 1752 202 301 | Fax: +44 1752 202 331
Email: orders@nbninternational.com

Distribution for Europe and all other countries:
Intersentia Publishing nv
Groenstraat 31
2640 Mortsel
Belgium
Tel.: +32 3 680 15 50 | Fax: +32 3 658 71 21
Email: mail@intersentia.be

Distribution for the USA and Canada:
Independent Publishers Group
Order Department
814 North Franklin Street
Chicago, IL 60610
USA
Tel.: +1 800 888 4741 (toll free) | Fax: + 1312 337 5985
Email: orders@ipgbook.com

Consumer Sales Remedies in US and EU Comparative Perspective

ISBN 978-1-78068-651-6
D/2018/7849/67
NUR 828

British Library Cataloguing in Publication Data. A catalogue record for this book is available from the British Library.

PREFACE

The primary purpose of this book is to provide an in-depth study of the US and EU approaches towards the organization of consumer sales remedies. Chapter 2 treats the comparison of the hierarchy of consumer sales remedies in a multitude of EU instruments, in US contract law, and the Uniform Commercial Code. In addition, the latest developments in EU law, namely the amended Proposal for a Directive on (online and other distance) sales of goods of 31 October 2017, are briefly discussed. In a Chapters 3 and 4, the (extra)judicial application of remedies and notification duties are examined in the same EU/US instruments.

This book aims to contribute to the discussion of what the organization of remedies should look like to best protect consumers. Should we adopt the US system favoring the remedy of damages? Or is specific performance preferred? Or, is there another valuable alternative? How should we define 'consumer protection'? All these questions are raised at a time when the EU is considering a 'new' consumer sales directive, and US scholars have drafted a restatement of consumer contract law, which is intended for discussion at the Annual Meeting Agenda in 2019 (although, regrettably, it will not include all possible aspects of consumer contract law).

This book is designed for EU civil (and common) lawyers and US common lawyers to gain a better understanding of the remedial system and the logic behind it. Due to the differences between those systems, it is sometimes dangerous to use certain terms such as 'termination', 'damages' and 'specific performance'. Therefore, specific attention is paid to terminology. By giving a terminological overview, the most commonly used terms are framed and explained within their respective legal systems.

There is inevitably more work to be done in this area and it is ripe for further research by other scholars. The interaction of the remedies is fascinating, but also very complex, and many factors have to be taken into account. Not only their original set hierarchy, but their (extra)judicial application and the notification duties have an important role to play. Therefore, further research is required to unravel the correlation with examination duties, limitation rules, and the relation remedy and the nature of the shortcoming, for example. In addition, the theoretical underpinning of the 'best' organization of remedies could be further food for thought. How should one, for example the EU lawmaker, deal with the spread of the law and economics logic and behavioral approaches? Which political ends are furthered by adopting one or the other policy? Should we, and if so how, take into account the emotions of consumers?

This book was mainly written during a postdoctoral research stay in the United States. This project has been made possible by a generous fellowship (2016–2017) from the Belgian American Educational Foundation (BAEF) and, more specifically, the Cabeaux-Jacobs Fund. Professor Boulpaep (Yale School of Medicine and President of the BAEF) and Ms Hayoit de Termicourt (Program Manager of the BAEF) deserve, in this regard, a special mention for combining their amazing organizational skills and enthusiastic commitment to helping and supporting young scholars and students. During this year, I was warmly welcomed by the East Coast BAEF community, and the staff and students of Yale Law School and Columbia Law School. More specifically, I must thank Professor Kronman for letting me attend his animated contract law course at Yale Law School and Professor Garro for being my sponsor at Columbia Law School. Without Professor Allemeersch's (KU Leuven) enthusiasm, kind recommendation and advice, the Yale experience would not have been possible. Also, Professor Wéry (UCL) and Professor Samoy (KU Leuven), mentors from the very beginning of my career, have to be thanked. Without their unremitting faith in my projects, this book would not have existed. Last, but not least, Professor Stijns (KU Leuven) deserves my deepest gratitude. She has guided me through this academic adventure from the very first moment. Patient and with eye for detail, she taught me every step. She encouraged me to push my limits and to broaden my academic horizon abroad. Therefore, I dedicate this book to her.

Sanne Jansen, April 2018

CONTENTS

LIST OF CASES*

BELGIUM

COURT OF JUSTICE OF THE EUROPEAN UNION

FRANCE

* References are to page numbers.

GERMANY

ITALY

THE NETHERLANDS

UNITED STATES OF AMERICA

CHAPTER 1

INTRODUCTION*

1 *Introductory examples revealing confusion and dissatisfaction.* A couple bought a couch. After delivery, they noticed that the legs of the couch were not rectangular, as they ordered, but circular. After angry phone calls and letters to the retailer, they introduced an action before a Belgian court seeking to terminate the contract in order to get their money back. Against all expectations, the Court of Appeal of Ghent decided completely against the couple.[1] According to the court, the couple had disregarded the consumer sales rules in the Civil Code, implementing the EU Consumer Sales Directive (CSD).[2] They did not respect the strict hierarchy of remedies which favors repair or replacement over termination and price reduction: the buyers should have sued for repair or replacement instead of trying to terminate the contract.[3] Moreover, they transgressed the

---

* 'He' and 'him' is often used throughout the book for convenience. It is not intended to be a particular gender choice.

1 Ghent 20 October 2010, *DCCR* 2012, 124, note S. Jansen.

2 Directive 1999/44/EC of 25 May 1999 on certain aspects of the sale of consumer goods and associated guarantees, OJ L 1999 171/12.

3 This national case law should also be read in the light of the *Duarte Hueros* decision of the Court of Justice of the EU: CJEU Judgement of 3 October 2012, *Soledad Duarte Hueros v. Autociba SA, Automóviles Citroën España SA*, C-32/12, ECLI:EU:C:2013:637 (national law is precluded insofar that it 'does not allow hearing the dispute to grant of its own motion an appropriate reduction in the price of goods which are the subject of a contract of sale in the case where a consumer who is entitled to such a reduction brings proceedings which are limited to seeking only rescission of that contract and such rescission cannot be granted because the lack of conformity in those goods is minor, even though that consumer is not entitled to refine his initial application or to bring a fresh action to that end'). EU law thus probably requires that national law allows the judge to grant by his own motion the alternative (and correct) remedies and/or should give the consumer the opportunity to refine his claim or to bring a fresh action. Also under Belgian law, the Court of Cassation would require a judge to raise of his own motion the legal grounds of the dispute, at least if they result from the facts directly invoked by the claimant and the defendant (without, of course, breaching the *ultra petita* – prohibition, which a judge can counter by using his right to ask questions): see e.g. Cass. 14 April 2005, *Arr. Cass.* 2005, 868, concl. P. De Koster, JT 2005, 659, note J. Van Compernolle, err. *JT* 2005, 796, *JLMB* 2005, 856,

notification rules: they should have notified the seller about the shortcoming, before calling upon a remedy (such as termination). This case shows that *confusion* reigns in the area of the hierarchy of consumer sales remedies.

Not only *confusion* reigns in this area, but also *dissatisfaction*. Think about the Volkswagen (VW) scandal: the car giant admitted in September 2015 that it had cheated on the emission tests of its diesel cars.[4] The cars appear to be multiple times more polluting than measured in the emission tests. Both in the EU and in the US, VW has been obliged to remedy the shortcomings to the cars.[5] In the US a huge product recall has taken place and VW announced that a certain number of VW owners would be eligible to receive $1,000 in vouchers.[6] VW also considered real 'compensation' measures for the affected US VW car owners. The final outcome was even more generous for consumers. From October 2016 until May 2017, several settlements were approved by the United States District Court for the District of Northern California.[7] The settlement provided consumers with the choice between a buyback or a modification ('repair').[8] All owners will also be entitled to an additional cash payment, depending on the model, mileage, and features of the car. In Europe, the car giant merely offered free 'reparations' (software and sometimes hardware updates).[9] The Belgian consumers have not accepted this 'dissatisfying remedy', and have argued in a Test-Aankoop led (class) action they should also be entitled

---

note G. De Leval, *Pas.* 2005, I, 862, concl. P. De Koster, *RABG* 2005, 1663, note R. Verbeke, *Soc. Kron.* 2008, 497 and *P&B* 2005, 300, concl. O.M., note.

4 See for a timeline https://www.theguardian.com/business/2015/dec/10/volkswagen-emissions-scandal-timeline-events.

5 When talking about remedies for non-conformity, the important aspect of fraud has been deliberately omitted (along with other important aspects, such as criminal litigation and procedural differences between the EU and US systems).

6 See e.g.: http://finance.yahoo.com/news/vw-diesel-owners-1-000-205314161.html; https://www.theguardian.com/business/2015/dec/10/volkswagen-emissions-scandal-timeline-events.

7 See (2.0 liter partial settlement) *In re Volkswagen 'Clean Diesel' Mktg., Sales Practices, & Prods. Liab. Litig.*, 2016 U.S. Dist. LEXIS 148374 (N.D. Cal. 25 October 2016); (3.0 liter partial settlement) *In re Volkswagen 'Clean Diesel' Mktg., Sales Practices & Prods. Liab. Litig.*, 2017 U.S. Dist. LEXIS 76092 (N.D. Cal. 17 May 2017). See also https://www.epa.gov/enforcement/volkswagen-clean-air-act-civil-settlement; https://www.justice.gov/opa/pr/volkswagen-ag-agrees-plead-guilty-and-pay-43-billion-criminal-and-civil-penalties-six.

8 At least for the 2.0 liter models. See for more detail the official website of the settlement: https://www.vwcourtsettlement.com/en.

9 http://moneytalk.knack.be/geld-en-beurs/rechten/strijd-van-test-aankoop-tegen-volkswagen-aansluiten-of-niet/article-normal-762583.html.

to compensation.[10] Class actions[11] and individual actions[12] have also been undertaken in other countries.[13] Might this difference in outcomes (damages versus reparation) in the US and in the EU be influenced by the current organization of the (consumer) sales remedies? Might this be one element influencing the proposals that Volkswagen makes for compensating its betrayed costumers?

2 *State of the art.* These cases, and many others, show at least that *confusion* and *dissatisfaction* reigns in the area of the organization of EU consumer sales remedies. The strict hierarchy of remedies proposed by the EU Consumer Sales Directive might offer insufficient protection for consumers. As Jeloschek points out: 'It becomes clear that the hierarchy of remedies is a double-edged sword capable of curtailing the interests of both parties: in some cases the buyer may be protected, in others the seller will benefit'.[14] Moreover, after withdrawing the Common European Sales Law (CESL)[15] proposal,[16] the EU Commission issued new proposals, addressing, among other issues, contractual remedies in the e-commerce sector, including one proposal relating to online sales.[17] The EU Parliament,

10 http://moneytalk.knack.be/geld-en-beurs/rechten/strijd-van-test-aankoop-tegen-volkswagen-aansluiten-of-niet/article-normal-762583.html. See also: Test-Aankoop/Test-Achat, March 2017, n° 617, p. 30 and http://www.test-aankoop.be/auto-fiets/auto-s/dossier/dieselgate-wij-zijn-allemaal-bedrogen.

11 See for an admission of a Volkswagen class action in Italy: Tribunale Ordinario di Venezia, 25 May 2017, RG n.3711/2016.

12 See for an overview of German individual actions: *infra*, para. 15.

13 See for an overview up until May 2016: EP Briefing May 2016, *Lawsuits Triggered by the Volkswagen Emission Case* http://www.europarl.europa.eu/RegData/etudes/BRIE/2016/583793/EPRS_BRI(2016)583793_EN.pdf. See also: https://www.nytimes.com/2017/03/10/business/volkswagen-europe-diesel-car-owners.html?_r=0 ('As VW Pleads Guilty in U.S. Over Diesel Scandal, Trouble Looms in Europe').

14 Jeloschek, Christoph, *Examination and Notification Duties in Consumer Sales Law* (Munich: Sellier, 2006), p. 213.

15 Proposal of the European Commission of 11 October 2011 for a regulation of the European Parliament and the Council on a Common European Sales Law, COM(2011) 635 final.

16 http://eur-lex.europa.eu/legal-content/EN/TXT/?uri=celex:52011PC0635.

17 See Proposal for a directive of the EP and the Council on certain aspects concerning contracts for the online and other distance sales of goods, COM(2015) 635 final, http://eur-lex.europa.eu/legal-content/EN/TXT/?uri=COM%3A2015%3A635%3AFIN; Proposal for a directive of the EP and the Council on certain aspects concerning contracts for the supply of digital content, COM(2015) 634 final. See also (but not about the remedies) the adopted Regulation (EU) 2017/1128 of the European Parliament and of the Council of 14 June 2017 on cross-border portability of online content services in the internal market, OJ L 168, 30 June 2017, pp. 1–11, http://eur-lex.europa.eu/legal-content/ENG/TXT/ELI/?eliuri=eli:reg:2017:1128:oj.

however, issued amendments to include also offline sales contracts, making the current Consumer Sales Directive superfluous. This would counter the critiques that the introduction of a separate directive for online sales contracts would lead to more fragmentation.[18] On 31 October 2017 the European Commission issued an 'amended Proposal for a Directive on (online and other distance) sales of goods'.[19] This proposal would repeal Directive 1999/44[20] and merge the rules on offline and online consumer sales contracts. On 22 February 2018, the Committee on Internal Market and Consumer Protection ('IMCO committee') adopted its report on the proposal.[21] It proposes substantial amendments to the latest proposal. Finally, on the European side it is interesting to note that some scholars are increasingly interested in behavioral sciences and their potential influence on consumer contract law (see also *infra*, para. 84 and 168).[22] This is a

---

18 EU Parliament Committee on the Internal Market and Consumer Protection, Draft report on the proposal for a directive of the European Parliament and of the Council on certain aspects concerning contracts for the online and other distance sales of goods, 18 November 2016, http://www.europarl.europa.eu/sides/getDoc.do?pubRef=-//EP//NONSGML+COMPARL+PE-593.817+03+DOC+PDF+V0//EN&language=EN. See also the studies on the amendments: Milieu Ltd. and Europe Economics, Impact assessment of proposed substantial EP amendments extending the scope of the Commission proposal on online sales of goods to offline sales, presented at the EP IMCO Committee Meeting, 8 June 2017.

19 See amended Proposal for a Directive of the European Parliament and of the Council on certain aspects concerning contracts for the online and other distance sales of goods, amending Regulation (EC) No 2006/2004 of the European Parliament and of the Council and Directive 2009/22/EC of the European Parliament and of the Council and repealing Directive 1999/44/EC of the European Parliament and of the Council, COM(2017) 637 final (it is currently being discussed within the Council and its preparatory bodies; https://eur-lex.europa.eu/legal-content/EN/TXT/?uri=COM%3A2017%3A637%3AFIN). For more information, see Mańko, Rafał, 'Briefing Consumer Sale of Goods, EU Legislation in Progress', March 2018, http://www.europarl.europa.eu/RegData/etudes/BRIE/2018/614744/EPRS_BRI(2018)614744_EN.pdf.

20 See Art. 21 of the amended Proposal.

21 See http://www.europarl.europa.eu/sides/getDoc.do?type=REPORT&mode=XML&reference=A8-2018-0043&language=EN.

22 See e.g. Bar-Gill, Oren, *Seduction by Contract: Law, Economics and Psychology in Consumer Markets* (Oxford: Oxford University Press, 2012), 280p.; Engels, Martin, and Stark, Johanna, 'Buttons, Boxes, Ticks, and Trust' in Mathis, Klaus (ed.), *European Perspectives on Behavioural Law and Economics* (Heidelberg: Springer International Publishing Switzerland, 2015), pp. 107–23; Sibony, Anne-Lise, and Helleringer, Geneviève, 'EU Consumer Protection and Behavioural Sciences: Revolution or Reform?' in Alemanno, Alberto, and Sibony, Anne-Lise (eds.), *Nudge and the Law: A European Perspective* (London: Hart Publishing, 2015), pp. 209–34; Sibony, Anne-Lise, 'Can EU Consumer Law Benefit from Behavioural Insights?' in Mathis, Klaus (ed.), *European Perspectives on Behavioural Law and Economics* (Heidelberg: Springer International Publishing Switzerland, 2015), pp. 71–106. See also more generally: Sibony, Anne-Lise, and Alemanno, Alberto, 'The Emergence of Behavioural

recent development in the EU but American scholars have already applied social sciences and empirical analysis in the domain of contract law (see *infra*, para. 54).[23] While this book is not based on a fully fledged behavioral research method, it might be connected to this trend. When discussing the 'best organization of remedies', references are often made to the emotions and feelings of consumers, such as confusion, frustration, trust, and good faith (see also *infra*, paras. 4 and 168).

In both the EU and the US there is an ongoing debate about the organization of remedies in general contract law and in the Uniform Commercial Code (UCC) regarding sales law. Also, work is currently being undertaken on a restatement of US consumer contract law.[24] Moreover, in the last few decades, many publications have discussed the 'irreparable injury' rule and the 'adequacy' rule.[25] This is the rule that basically favors damages over specific performance in situations where there has been breach of contract. It has drawn the attention of law and economics specialists,[26] legal philosophers, and others. And as mentioned earlier, more recently, behaviorists have also expressed their interest in the topic.[27] Of course, behind this scholarship lie deep policy choices and ideologies (see e.g. *infra*, para. 53).

Indeed, it is interesting to note at the very beginning of this research that the differences in approach towards (consumer sales) remedies might be connected to the differences in the socio-economic systems in the US and the EU. Whitman described these differences between common and

---

Policy Making: A European Perspective' in Alemanno, Alberto, and Sibony, Anne-Lise (eds.), *Nudge and the Law: A European Perspective* (Oxford: Hart Publishing, 2015), pp. 1–25.

23 See White, Alan M., 'Behavior and Contract', 27 *Law & Inequality: A Journal of Theory and Practice* 1 (2009), pp. 135–79. See also with regard to disclosure requirements and reading requirements: Ayres, Ian, and Schwartz, Alan, 'The No-Reading Problem in Consumer Contract Law', 66 *Stan. L. Rev.* 3 (2014), pp. 545–610; Schwartz, Alan, 'Regulating for Rationality', 67 *Stan. L. Rev.* 6 (2015), pp. 1373–1410. See also in general: Jolls, Christine, et al., 'A Behavioral Approach to Law and Economics', *Stan. L. Rev.* (1998), pp. 1471–550.

24 https://www.ali.org/projects/show/consumer-contracts.

25 See e.g. Laycock, Douglas, 'The Death of the Irreparable Injury Rule', 103 *Harv. L. Rev.* 3 (1990), p. 696. See recently Bray, Samuel L., 'The Supreme Court and the New Equity', 68 *Vand. L. Rev.* 4 (2015), pp. 997–1054.

26 See *infra*, para. 53 and e.g. Schwartz, Alan, 'The Case for Specific Performance', *Yale L.J.* (1979), pp. 271–306 (pro specific performance). See e.g. pro status quo: Kronman, Anthony T., 'Specific Performance', 45 *U. Chi. L. Rev.* (1978), pp. 351–82; Yorio, Edward, 'In Defense of Money Damages for Breach of Contract', 82 *Colum. L. Rev.* (1982), pp. 1365–424.

27 See *infra*, para. 54.

civil law as the 'consumerism' versus the 'producerism' paradox.[28] The US is thought to be more consumer oriented: the interest of the consumers is considered the highest good in society and this is protected by introducing antitrust laws, class actions, triple damages, competitive prices, and warranties of quality and safety. The EU is considered more producer oriented since it has introduced rules to protect artisanal products, workers, competitors, distributors, and small retailers.[29] Whitman observes that continental law is slowly growing towards more 'paternalistic guarantees' of safety and quality of the goods (i.e. consumer *protection* interest), which is still reconcilable with the protection of the producers. Nevertheless, sharp price competition (i.e. consumer *economic* interest) is making slower headway compared to the US.[30] One of the questions this raises is whether we can explain the different approach towards the hierarchy of remedies, (extra)judicial approach and notification duties by the consumerism/producerism paradox? Perhaps some basic choices such as the European attachment to the performance of the contract and the 'right to cure' can be explained by the producer-friendly approach of the EU socio-economic system (see also *infra*, paras. 79 and 81). This will be discussed in more detail later. Nevertheless, both systems, in the EU and in the US, have evolved over time to find a complex and unique equilibrium which cannot entirely be explained by the consumerism/producerism paradox.

3 *Novelty and necessity of the undertaken research.* As previously mentioned, the organization of remedies is a widely discussed topic, both in the US and in the EU. Admittedly, efforts have already been made to compare common and civil law with regard to contractual remedies. However, often only national common contract law and (commercial) sales law (bearing in mind the United Nations Convention on Contracts for the International Sale of Goods (CISG)[31]) were the topics of these comparisons.[32] A thorough cross-examination of the EU consumer sales

---

28 Whitman, James Q., 'Consumerism Versus Producerism: A Study in Comparative Law', 177 *Yale L.J.* (2007), pp. 340–406.

29 Of course, the author nuances the sharp delimitation between consumer and producer interest, which can coincide or differ according to which kind of producer is meant (existence of different classes of producers and internal conflicts): ibid, p. 347.

30 Ibid., p. 348.

31 United Nations Convention on Contracts for the International Sale of Goods (Vienna, 1980) (CISG).

32 See e.g. Miller, Lucinda, 'Specific Performance in the Common and Civil Law' in Giliker, Paula (ed.), *Re-examining Contract and Unjust Enrichment* (Leiden: Martinus Nijhoff, 2007), pp. 281–310 and Musgrave, Thomas D., 'Comparative Contractual Remedies',

law system (mainly based on the civil law tradition) and the US common law system is missing in the current debate. Therefore, this book will address the organization of consumer sales remedies on the basis of in-depth comparative research. Chapter 2 assesses the so-called 'hierarchy' of remedies that is prescribed by law. Chapter 3 deals with the ability (or not) of consumers to invoke remedies 'extrajudicially'. It is assumed that the easier it is for the consumer to invoke a remedy, the more protection this regime will provide for consumers. Chapter 4 examines the so-called 'notification duties' of the contracting parties. Is there an obligation for the consumer to put his debtor (the seller) 'in default' ('*mise en demeure/ ingebrekestelling*') or has the consumer an obligation to notify the non-conformity or the remedy he wants to invoke? Stringent notification duties will often limit the ability of consumers to invoke their remedies. The main question is: what would be the best possible organization of remedies in order to protect consumers?[33] This proposed organization of remedies could then be used as an inspiration for any project aiming at harmonization of transnational/transatlantic consumer sales law.

Consumer protection as the main yardstick. Because 'consumer protection' is the main yardstick to measure the appropriateness of the organization of remedies, its meaning should be made clear. In the EU, one of the important goals is to protect consumers. Article 38 of the EU Charter of Fundamental Rights[34] and Articles 12[35] and 169[36] of the Treaty on the Functioning of the EU (TFEU) guarantee and define a high standard of consumer protection in the EU. An important area of protection is the protection of the '*economic* interests' of the consumers. This entails that consumers, when contracting with traders, should be treated in such a way that their economic interests are not impaired. Along with the purely economic interests of the consumer (e.g. competitive pricing), the 4

U.W. Austl. L. Rev. (2008–09), pp. 300–72. See also Mak, Vanessa, *Performance-oriented Remedies in European Sale of Goods Law* (Oxford: Hart Publishing, 2009), 222p.

33 By examining the hierarchy of remedies, the (extra)judicial application of the remedies and notification duties (of breaches and remedies).

34 Art. 38 Charter: 'Union policies shall ensure a high level of consumer protection'.

35 Art. 12 TFEU: 'Consumer protection requirements shall be taken into account in defining and implementing other Union policies and activities.'

36 Art. 169 TFEU: '1. In order to promote the interests of consumers and to ensure a high level of consumer protection, the Union shall contribute to protecting the health, safety and economic interests of consumers, as well as to promoting their right to information, education and to organize themselves in order to safeguard their interests.'

procedural 'protection' of the consumer is also, in the view of the present author, taken into account by EU consumer contract law.[37] This would include issues such as product safety, guaranties of quality, and remedies. A remedial system protecting these consumer interests should be a fairly easy system to apply, supporting fast and generous solutions for consumers. Of course, the interests of the sellers cannot be totally disregarded. Both parties will win if a system supports solutions enhancing legal certainty. This implies that some safeguards must exist to avoid consumers abusing the system. It cannot be the intention to burden sellers to the point that trade will be hampered. Indeed, one of the main goals of the EU is to create a functioning and efficient internal market.[38]

Questions remain: how does one assess the ease of use of a system and the generosity of its remedies? How does one assess the consumer-friendliness of a system? As previously mentioned, it may be possible to refer to the behaviorist sciences to provide a partial answer. Indeed, when discussing the 'best organization of remedies', this will inevitably include references to the emotions and feelings of consumers and sellers such as confusion, frustration, (dis)trust, and good faith (see also *supra*, para. 2 and *infra*, para. 168). Secondly, lessons will be learned from a legal comparison with the US, in order to assess the current system in the EU and evaluate its logic and coherence.

5 *Delimitation: modest approach.* By choosing to discuss three key elements of the organization of the remedies – the hierarchy of remedies, their (extra)judicial application and the notification duties – a deliberate choice has been made to leave out other important elements that might enhance and influence consumer protection. Therefore, this book has to be understood as a modest attempt to approach this problem. It has to be understood *as one of the elements* that might enhance consumer protection, and maybe not even the most important solution. The limitations of the discussion in this book can be found at three different levels.

First, this book will focus upon (consumer) *contract* law. This means that some mechanisms and tools of other legal branches are not considered. In the context of the Volkswagen case, one might also think about the importance of procedural law and enforcement law.[39] It is

---

[37] See also Whitman, James Q., 'Consumerism Versus Producerism: A Study in Comparative Law', 177 *Yale L.J.* (2007), pp. 341–406.

[38] See Arts. 26 *et seq.* and 114 TFEU.

[39] For recent works about EU enforcement law, see Cafaggi, Fabrizio, and Micklitz, Hans-Wofgang (eds.), *New Frontiers of Consumer Protection: The Interplay Between*

indeed essential to assess whether or not class actions are allowed and to what extent. In times of mass consumption, a system allowing a generous system in relation to class actions[40] might be considered more consumer-friendly when compared to a system that lacks such mechanisms. Also private enforcement mechanisms – such as jurisdiction and arbitration clauses – are on the rise and influence heavily (and may undermine) the position of the consumer.[41] The same is true for the criminal law system, for example.[42] One should not underestimate the importance of the willingness and resources available to prosecute white collar crimes. A more active prosecution policy, not afraid to provide for severe fines and jail sentences to be imposed on lying and cheating managers, is more likely to be experienced as consumer-friendly. Evidence law can also play an important role with regard to the protection of consumers. Evidence rules may make it harder or easier for consumers to secure their claims.

Secondly, this book focuses on the possible ways in which the contractual *remedies* could be 'organized'. Consequently, it does not deal with other contractual issues that might influence the consumer-friendliness of the

Private and Public Enforcement (Cambridge: Intersentia, 2009), 451 p.; Micklitz, Hans-W, and Wechsler, Andrea (eds.), *The Transformation of Enforcement: European Economic Law in a Global Perspective* (Oxford: Hart Publishing, 2016), 424 p.

40 For the EU, see e.g. Hodges, Christopher, 'Collective Redress: A Breakthrough or a Damp Sqibb', 37 *J. Consum. Pol.* 1 (2013), 67–89; Voet, Stefaan, 'European Collective Redress Developments: A Status Quaestionis', *SSRN Working Paper*, https://ssrn.com/abstract=2318809 (2013), s.p; see also, for a joint collaboration between Stefaan Voet and Christopher Hodges: https://www.law.ox.ac.uk/sites/files/oxlaw/1710_policy_on_collective_redress_3.pdf. For an EU–US comparison, see Strong, S.I., 'Regulatory Litigation in the European Union: Does the U.S. Class Action Have a New Analogue?', *SSRN, University of Missouri School of Law Legal Studies Research Paper No. 2012-25* (2012), 1–77.

41 E.g. Reich, N., 'Negotiation and Adjudication. Class Actions and Arbitration Clauses in Consumer Contracts' in Cafaggi, Fabrizio, and Micklitz, Hans-Wofgang (eds.), *New Frontiers of Consumer Protection* (Cambridge: Intersentia, 2009), pp. 345–58; Riefa, Christine, 'Uncovering the Dangers Lurking below the Surface of European Consumer Arbitration', *SSRN Working Paper* (2010), pp. 1–9; Cole, Tony, Ortolani, Pietro, et al., 'Legal Instruments and Practice of Arbitration in the EU', *SSRN Working Paper* (2015), p. 204 *et seq*.

42 For the US, see e.g. Geis, Gilbert, and Edelhertz, Herbert, 'Criminal Law and Consumer Fraud: A Sociolegal View', 11 *Am. Crim. L. Rev.* (1973), pp. 989–1010. See also the work of Ralph Nader, e.g. Nader, Ralph, *Consumer and Corporate Accountability* (Boston: Houghton Mifflin Harcourt P, 1973), 368p. For the UK, see e.g. Cartwright, Peter, *Consumer Protection and the Criminal Law* (Cambridge: Cambridge University Press, 2001), 268p. For crime and business regulation in general, see also Braithwaite, John, *Regulation, Crime, Freedom* (Dartmouth: Ashgate, 2000), 360p; Sutherland, Edwin H., *White Collar Crime: The Uncut Version* (New Haven: Yale University Press, 1985), 328p.

systems. This means that important elements, such as the concept of 'fraud', the prescription and limitation periods, and the (objective or subjective) notion of a defect are not dealt with here. Nevertheless, all of these aspects undoubtedly have a very important influence on the protection of a consumer and the consumer-friendliness of a system.

Thirdly, the discussion in this book does not cover the study of the organization of remedies. Some remedies are not fully explored in this book, such as price reduction or cover damages[43]/execution in kind by a third party or by the contracting party. Moreover, the examination duties of the buyer and their relation with the notification duties are not sufficiently integrated in the research. Also, this book does not consider the question of whether a remedy is only applicable if certain breaches of the contract occur (such as 'non-conformity' of the goods, hidden defects, or late delivery) or whether a remedy is applicable for all 'non-performances' or breaches of the contract.

This book has to be understood as an invitation for further research. The claim made here is that the organization of the consumer remedies might have an influence on consumer protection. Three important elements of the organization of the remedies are: hierarchy, (extra)judicial character, and notification duties. Their mutual features, relationship, and interaction are currently underexplored in the literature. This book merely aims to make a contribution towards the way forward to a more consumer-friendly remedial system.

6 *Terminology and remedies.* Undertaking a legal comparison between EU consumer contract law and US sales law implies difficulties in terminology. In particular, the terms 'specific performance' and 'termination' require some clarification.

The first term that needs clarification is 'specific performance' or 'performance in kind'.[44] In US law the term 'specific performance' means the *exact performance* of the obligations, prescribed by the contract.[45]

---

[43] Cover damages of UCC §2-712 means that the buyer may obtain the goods himself and then gets damages for the difference between the cost of the substitute goods and the original contract price (together with any incidental or consequential damages).

[44] See also for a very broad definition in the UNIDROIT principles Art. 7.2.3.: 'The right to performance includes in appropriate cases the right to require repair, replacement, or other cure of defective performance'. See, for a very positive view about this definition: Heutger, Viola, and Oosterhuis, Janwillem, 'Specific Performance within the Hierarchy of Remedies in European Contract Law' in Smits, Jan, et al. (eds.), *Specific Performance in Contract Law: National and Other Perspectives* (Antwerp: Intersentia, 2008), p. 168.

[45] Miller, Lucinda, 'Specific Performance in the Common and Civil Law: Some Lessons for Harmonisation' in Giliker, Paula (ed.), *Re-examining Contract and Unjust Enrichment*,

If this is compared to e.g. Belgian/French contract law, the 'equivalent' term is *uitvoering in natura/exécution en nature*. It is in this regard important to stress that specific performance under US law does not imply an *indirect* form of *exécution en nature*, where the obligation is not performed by the debtor but by a third party (*exécution en nature par un tiers*), as is the case under French and Belgian contract law.[46] If this is compared to the EU consumer sales *acquis*, the terms 'repair and replacement' (by the seller) are often used to indicate specific performance, which excludes – similarly to the US terminology – (indirect) performance by a third party.[47] Secondly, specific performance under US law does not imply that an obligation is fulfilled by paying a fixed sum of money.[48] One has also to bear in mind that a US court can also order a party to refrain from doing something: this is called an 'injunction'.[49] Often the remedies of specific performance,

(Leiden: Martinus Nijhoff Publishers, 2007), p. 292. See also Szladits, Charles, 'The Concept of Specific Performance in Civil Law', 4 *Am. J. Comp. L.* (1955), footnote 20.

46 Miller, Lucinda, 'Specific Performance in the Common and Civil Law: Some Lessons for Harmonisation' in Giliker, Paula (ed.), *Re-examining Contract and Unjust Enrichment* (Leiden: Martinus Nijhoff Publishers, 2007), pp. 292–93; Musgrave, Thomas D., 'Comparative Contractual Remedies', *U.W. Austl. L. Rev.* (2008–09), p. 328. However, Shavell seems also to include (in the term specific performance) cases in which the seller would arrange for or pay for a covering contract, whereby another party would perform the contractual obligation: Shavell, Steven, 'Specific Performance Versus Damages for Breach of Contract: An Economic Analysis', 84 *Tex. L. Rev.* (2006), p. 839. Nevertheless, it must be noted that performance does not have to be exactly the same as that which was contracted for: Corbin, Arthur Linton, et al., *Corbin on Contracts* (New Providence, San Francisco: Matthew Bender & Co., Inc., 2016), §63.2.

47 See, for a detailed discussion about the differences and the similarities of the terms 'specific performance' and 'repair and replacement': Mak, Vanessa, *Performance-oriented Remedies in European Sale of Goods Law* (Oxford: Hart Publishing, 2009), p. 115 *et seq*.

48 Musgrave, Thomas D., 'Comparative Contractual Remedies', *U.W. Austl. L. Rev.* (2008–09), p. 328.

49 Farnsworth, E. Allan, *Farnsworth on Contracts* (New York: Kluwer, 2004), p. 168 ('Instead of ordering specific performance, a court may, by injunction, direct a party to refrain from doing a specified act'). See also Ferriell, Jeff, *Understanding Contracts* (New Providence, San Francisco: Matthew Bender & Co., Inc., 2009), p. 857. Cf. Corbin, Arthur Linton, Perillo, Joseph M., et al., *Corbin on Contracts* (New Providence, San Francisco: Matthew Bender & Co., Inc., 2016), §63.3 (a decree of specific performance to refrain from doing something is often called an injunction and specifies moreover: 'of course, there are innumerable duties of forbearance that are not created by contract. Therefore an injunction is very often not a decree for the specific performance of a contract'). Cf. Miller, Lucinda, 'Specific Performance in the Common and Civil Law: Some Lessons for Harmonisation' in Giliker, Paula (ed.), *Re-examining Contract and Unjust Enrichment* (Leiden: Martinus Nijhoff Publishers, 2007), p. 293 (specific performance does not comprise the remedy that one is ordered to refrain from

injunctions, and restitution of specific property or a fixed sum of money are also known under the common denominator of 'specific remedies'.[50] In this book the terms 'specific performance' and 'performance in kind' will be used interchangeably. There will also be references to the terms 'repair and replacement' where appropriate. This book will not focus upon performance of the contract by a third party, and hence this aspect will not be discussed here.

In EU and US law, there is no agreement about terminology when both parties are released from their obligations due to a breach of contract. Several terms are used, such as: 'recession', 'termination', 'cancellation', and 'resolution'. The term 'termination' will be used here, but sometimes references will be made to the exact term used in certain statutes for clarity.

7 *Structure*. This book is structured as follows. First, in Chapter 2, the *hierarchy* of remedies in the EU consumer sales *acquis* is compared with the system that is applicable to consumers in the US, which is mainly the UCC system. Here, the question arises which remedy is preferred over the others. Next, in Chapter 3, the ability of consumers to invoke their remedies without prior intervention by a judge (self-help or *extrajudicial* remedies) in the two systems will be compared. In Chapter 4 the consumer's *notification* duties will be examined. Chapter 5 provides the conclusion of this book.

---

doing a particular act (i.e. an injunction)). Cf. also Dobbs, Dan B., *Law of Remedies* (St. Paul: West Academic, 1993), §12.8(1) ('The specific performance remedy is a form of injunctive decree [...] Sometimes the order is in the form of a mandatory injunction to perform affirmative obligations of the contract [...]. Sometimes it is in the form of an ordinary prohibitory injunction'); similar: Fischer, James M., *Remedies* (New Providence, San Francisco: Matthew Bender & Co., Inc., 2014), §170.

50 Laycock, Douglas, 'The Death of the Irreparable Injury Rule', 103 *Harv. L. Rev.* 3 (1990), p. 696.

CHAPTER 2

HIERARCHY OF REMEDIES – SO DIFFERENT AND YET SO ALIKE

Meaning of hierarchy of remedies. The very concept of a 'hierarchy of remedies' might seem disturbing to a US scholar. Indeed, while EU scholars often refer to a hierarchy of sales remedies, US scholars almost never do. Does something like a 'hierarchy' of consumer sales remedies exist in case of breach of contract by a seller? The question that is asked is whether the legislator or case law consistently favors a certain remedy over another. If one remedy is favored over another – and one of the remedies is more readily available to the consumer – this implies a certain 'hierarchy' between them. On the other hand, it is also possible that the consumer is given a free choice between the remedies, if their respective conditions of application are fulfilled. In that case, there is no hierarchy between the remedies. 8

Of course, the mere examination of the 'hierarchy of remedies' in statutory law and case law, might give a distorted and rigid view of reality. This leaves out a lot of factors such as out-of-court negotiations, dispute resolution, and practical behavior that the seller and the buyer can adopt. One might think about a seller who agrees with the buyer to remedy a breach of contract in a certain way or a buyer informally asking a seller for the best solution. In this way, reality will be much more flexible than the theoretical rules that will be described and analyzed in this book.

Hierarchy of remedies as only a starting point towards an organization of remedies. Inquiring into the hierarchy of remedies is merely a starting point. When studying the 'hierarchy of remedies' only the 'intrinsic characteristics' of the remedy are taken into account: is the remedy subject to a seller's right to cure? Can it only be applied if another remedy is not adequate? Can it only be applied in case of a fundamental or substantial non-performance? The hierarchy of remedies is, of course, influenced by many other factors. Apart from the intrinsic factors, 'extrinsic factors' can also be taken into account. Two important factors that will be studied 9 are, as stated earlier, the notification duties and the possibility to invoke a remedy without prior intervention by a judge. When these 'extrinsic' factors are taken into account, the topic is broadened to the 'organization of remedies'.[51]

1. EU CONSUMER SALES *ACQUIS*

1.1. PRIORITY OF REPAIR AND REPLACEMENT UNDER THE CONSUMER SALES DIRECTIVE

10 *Priority of repair and replacement.* As already mentioned, Article 3(3) of the CSD introduces a clear *hierarchy*[52] between the different remedies of consumers in case of non-conformity of the delivered goods.[53] It states: '*In the first place*, the consumer may require the seller to repair the goods or he may require the seller to replace them, in either case free of charge,[54] unless this is impossible or disproportionate' (emphasis added). This means that the consumer and the seller are obliged to first invoke/execute the remedies of replacement or repair.

The choice for repair or replacement is 'disproportionate' (in comparison to the other specific remedy)[55] if the cost that the chosen

---

51 However, these additional factors do not make the research about the organization of remedies complete: *supra*, para. 5.

52 Bianca, Cesare Massimo, 'Article 3. Droits et remèdes du consommateur' in Bianca, Cesare Massimo, et al. (eds.), *La directive communautaire sur la vente, Commentaire* (Brussels/Paris: Bruylant-LGDJ, 2004), pp. 191 and 204; D'sa, Rose M., and Krummel, Thomas, 'Sale of Consumer Goods and Associated Guarantees: A Minimalist Approach to Harmonized European Union Consumer Protection', *E. L. Rev.* (2001), pp. 319–20; Zollers, Frances E., et al., 'Consumer protection in the European Union: An Analysis of the Directive on the Sale of Consumer Goods and Associated Guarantees', *U. Pa. J. Int'l. Econ. L.* (1999), p. 110, footnote 85. This principle of primary and secondary remedies and a hierarchy between them is more widely accepted: see Hawes, Cynthia, and Twigg-Flesner, Christian, 'Sales and Guarantees' in Howells, Geraint, et al. (eds.), *Handbook of Research on International Consumer Law* (Cheltenham: Edward Elgar Publishing Ltd, 2010), pp. 202–203; Schulze, Reiner, and Zoll, Fryderyk, *European Contract Law* (Munich: Beck, 2016), p. 255.

53 See also the following English author who wonders whether, after the implementation of the CSD, specific performance has become a regular remedy for consumers (also compared to damages) in English contract law: Harris, D.R., 'Specific performance – a regular remedy for consumers?', 119 *L.Q.R.* (2003), pp. 541–44.

54 The term 'free of charge' means the costs necessary to bring the goods into conformity, in particular the cost of postage, labour, and materials (Art. 3.4 CSD).

55 A detailed account of the relation between the two primary remedies, replacement and repair, which requires a detailed and lengthy survey of the case law of the CJEU will

remedy imposes on the seller is unreasonable compared to that of the other remedy. To consider the proportionality of a remedy, one can take into account: (1) the value of the goods if there had not been a lack of conformity; (2) the significance of the lack of conformity; and (3) whether the alternative remedy could be applied without significant inconvenience to the consumer. But also, generally, the remedies of repair and replacement must be completed without significant inconvenience to the consumer and within a reasonable time, taking into account the nature and purpose of the goods.

It should be noted that the *Weber/Putz*-cases of the Court of Justice of the EU (CJEU) allow a consumer to choose repair or replacement even in a context where the primary remedies would impose disproportionate costs to the seller, compared to the remedies of price reduction and termination.[56] The proportionality test is, as a consequence, only applicable between the two primary remedies, and not between the primary and the secondary remedies.

Only in a second phase can the consumer choose the remedy of price reduction or termination (rescission)[57] of the contract. Here, it is clear that these remedies are subsidiary to replacement and repair, because they can only be invoked in the following two situations: (1) if the consumer is entitled to neither repair nor replacement; or (2) if the seller has not completed the remedy within a reasonable time or without significant inconvenience to the consumer (Article 3(5) CSD). This means that the remedies of repair and replacement (specific remedies) are not only a right for the consumer, but also a right for the seller. It actually implies a certain 'right to cure' for the seller.[58] The seller has a second chance to perform the contract. Mak states it very clearly: the buyer's entitlement to specific performance (here in the form of repair or replacement) is a mirror image of the seller's right to cure. The fact that not only the seller, but also the buyer (by means of the seller's right to cure), has to respect the prevalence of repair and replacement makes it clear that there is a real

---

not be given here. The main point is that repair and replacement, both favoring specific performance of the contract, are preferred over price reduction and termination. See e.g. Mak, Vanessa, *Performance-oriented Remedies in European Sale of Goods Law* (Oxford: Hart Publishing, 2009), p. 127 *et seq*.

56 CJEU Judgement of 6 June 2011, *Gebruder Weber v. Jürgen Wittmer and Ingrid Putz v. Medianess Electronics GmbH*, C-65/09 and 87/09, ECLI:EU:C:2011:396.

57 The official term in the Directive is 'rescission' of the contract.

58 Mak, Vanessa, *Performance-oriented Remedies in European Sale of Goods Law* (Oxford: Hart Publishing, 2009), p. 150.

hierarchy between the remedies: a hierarchy in which performance-oriented remedies enjoy the pole position. Some authors claim that this hierarchy of remedies is not as such directed towards consumer protection; but more towards considerations of market efficiency and economic considerations.[59] Performance-oriented remedies are deemed to be more cost efficient.[60] Indeed, the most consumer protective organization of remedies is that the consumer would have a free choice between the remedies. Moreover, some authors applaud this hierarchy of remedies – favoring replacement and repair – because it would enhance and support the efforts of the EU to introduce a 'circular economy'.[61] Repair and replacement would play an important role in achieving this goal (from cradle-to cradle model). Repair would imply less waste and replacement would mean that primary materials would end up with the manufacturer, which would lead to recycling of these materials.[62] If this would be the purpose, this would be of course a very laudable goal of the legislator. However, the other remedies – termination and price reduction – are not necessarily less environmentally friendly. Termination would also mean that the primary materials would end up back with the manufacturer, who can recycle them. Price reduction would mean that the consumer would consider the goods still useful and would enjoy the defective goods without any negative effects on the circular economy.

---

59 Ibid., p. 201. See also Grundmann, Stefan, 'Consumer Law, Commercial Law, Private Law: How Can the Sales Directive and the Sales Convention Be So Similar?', 14 *EBLR* 3 (2003), p. 243. See also Proposal for European Parliament and Council Directive on the sale of consumer goods and associated guarantees, Brussels 18 June 1996, COM(95) 520 final, 96/0161 (COD) (this proposal provided for a free choice of remedies, but stressed the 'economic efficiency' of repair and replacement: p. 13 'to add the latter two [i.e. repair and replacement] would certainly help bring the law more into line with economic realities' and 'This [i.e. repair and replacement] corresponds to economic and social realities'). Cf. Cauffman, Caroline, 'The Principle of Proportionality and European Contract Law' in Rutgers, Jacobien, and Pietro Sirena (eds.), *Rules and Principles in European Contract Law* (Cambridge: Intersentia, 2015), p. 80 (the two-stage system does not necessarily enhance consumer protection).

60 See for this reasoning e.g. Mak, Vanessa, *Performance-oriented Remedies in European Sale of Goods Law* (Oxford: Hart Publishing, 2009), p. 201. However, for law and economic arguments in favor of and against the statement that specific performance is the most efficient remedy (compared to damages; which actually does not have a place in the CSD), see *infra*, para. 53.

61 Vandemaele, Sanne, 'Hiërarchie tussen de remedies bindt zowel de eindverkoper als de consument: focus op herstel en vervanging is en blijft essentieel', *DCCR* (2017), n° 8–9.

62 See also p. 20 of the Qualitative Eurobarometer Study, Sales Remedies, Conducted by TNS Qual+ at the request of the Directorate General for Health and Consumers, December 2009, http://ec.europa.eu/consumers/archive/rights/docs/aggregate%20report_dec2009_en.pdf ('a consumer wanted to have his shoes to be repaired instead of replaced [...] in the interest of sustainable development').

It also has to be noted that not all the versions of the Consumer Sales Directive Proposals implemented the current hierarchy of remedies. In the Proposal of 18 June 1996[63] Article 3.4 stated that the consumer could choose between repair within a reasonable period, or to replace the goods, when this was possible, or to demand an appropriate price reduction or rescission of the contract. The exercise of the remedies of replacement and rescission were only to be available for one year and Member States could rule out some remedies if the lack of conformity was minor. The Proposal of 31 March 1998[64] introduced the current hierarchy of remedies, without explaining the shift to this system.

Minimum harmonization. It has to be taken into account that the Consumer Sales Directive is a measure of 'minimum harmonization'. This means that EU Member States may adopt or maintain more stringent measures, ensuring a higher level of consumer protection (see Article 8 CSD). Consequently, Member States may derogate from the strict hierarchy of remedies, introduced by the Directive. Of course, the chosen hierarchy of remedies must be more favorable towards consumers, compared to the regime in the Consumer Sales Directive. This might include e.g. a regime which gives the consumer an absolute free choice between all four remedies. In the end, it will depend on the Member State which hierarchy of remedies is to be implemented. The minimum regime is provided by the Consumer Sales Directive; favoring the performance of the contract over termination and price reduction.[65] Belgium and Germany have, for example, maintained the priority of repair and replacement over price reduction and termination.[66] In France the consumer sales remedies, implying the priority of repair and replacement, do not prohibit the buyer from invoking other remedies.[67] In brief, most countries have chosen to 11

---

63 See Proposal for European Parliament and Council Directive on the sale of consumer goods and associated guarantees, Brussels 18 June 1996, COM(95) 520 final, 96/0161 (COD).

64 See Art. 3.4 Amended Proposal for a European Parliament and Council Directive on the sale of consumer goods and associated guarantees, Brussels 31 March 1998, COM(1998) 217 final, 96/0161 (COD).

65 See Explanatory Memorandum ODSD Proposal, 2: Legal Basis, Subsidiarity and Proportionality, p. 6: '20 Member States have followed this approach, while other Member States have either offered the consumers a free choice of remedies, or have taken over the hierarchy of remedies but have also provided for another remedy'.

66 See for Belgium: Art. 1649*quinquies* Civil Code (CC), and for Germany: §§323, 437–441 BGB.

67 See for France: Art. L217-13 Code de Consommation: 'Les dispositions de la présente section ne privent pas l'acheteur du droit d'exercer l'action résultant des vices

follow the approach of the Consumer Sales Directive, favoring repair and replacement over termination and price reduction.[68] However, not all Member States chose to follow this approach and some have introduced a more favorable 'hierarchy' of remedies.[69]

12 *Priority of repair and replacement in Belgium.* The Belgian legislator has quite literally implemented the hierarchy of remedies of the Consumer Sales Directive in its Civil Code (Article 1649*quinquies* CC) (see also *supra*, para. 1). The consumer can only request price reduction or termination if repair and replacement are impossible or cannot be done within a reasonable period of time or without significant inconvenience to the consumer. The courts are applying this provision faithfully by favoring repair and replacement over price reduction and termination. In some cases, the hierarchy has been confirmed in situations where the consumer has respected this hierarchy.[70] However, in other cases the consumers have not respected the hierarchy of remedies and have erroneously chosen price reduction or the rescission/termination of the contract while they should have opted for repair or replacement. This was the situation in the following cases.

The Court of Appeal of Ghent decided a case about a second-hand car on 27 May 2009.[71] A car broke down because of a defect in the timing belt. The consumer had his car repaired by a garage which was not the garage

rédhibitoires telle qu'elle résulte des articles 1641 à 1649 du code civil ou toute autre action de nature contractuelle ou extracontractuelle qui lui est reconnue par la loi'.

68 Explanatory Memorandum ODSD Proposal, p. 6: '20 Member States have followed this approach [the hierarchy of remedies], while other Member States have either offered the consumers a free choice of remedies, or have taken over the hierarchy of remedies but have also provided for another remedy, for instance a right to reject non-conforming goods within a short deadline'.

69 Milieu Ltd. and Europe Economics, 'Impact assessment of proposed substantial EP amendments extending the scope of the Commission proposal on online sales of goods to offline sales', presented at the EP IMCO Committee Meeting, 8 June 2017, p. 53 (Croatia, Hungary, Greece, Lithuania, Portugal, and Slovenia have opted for a free choice of remedies).

70 Liège 28 May 2009, *JLMB* 2011, 447; Liège 25 March 2011, *DCCR* 2012, 83, note M. Dupont, *DAOR* 2011, 505, note, *JLMB* 2012, 221, *RDTI* 2012, 67, note J. Henrotte (rescission/termination is awarded); Antwerp 29 April 2013, *RW* 2014–15, 1067 (price reduction and damages are awarded); Rb. Brussels 7 May 2009, *JT* 2009, 737, *RRD* 2009, 362, note Y. Ninane. Cf.: Rb. Antwerp 11 April 2008, *RW* 2010–11, 115, note (the consumer may, however, not choose termination, and only price reduction, because he has acted in a way irreconcilable with termination: he did not offer to hand back the car to the seller).

71 Ghent 27 May 2009, *NjW* 2010, 200, note R. Steennot, *RW* 2010–11, 540, note S. Marysse, *TGR-TWVR* 2009, 300.

from which he had purchased the car. He claimed a price reduction because of the cost of the repair. The court made it clear that the consumer's right to choose between the remedies was not arbitrary: he had to respect the hierarchy of remedies. Remedies such as free repair and free replacement (which are qualified as 'repair in kind') enjoyed preference. The consumer could ask for price reduction or termination of the contract only if repair or replacement by the seller was impossible or could not be done within a reasonable time or without significant inconvenience to the consumer. In this case the seller had reacted in a timely fashion and proposed to repair the car. The consumer had not given the seller a chance to repair. This all resulted in the rejection of the price reduction remedy asked by the consumer.[72]

The second case that has to be mentioned is the case regarding a couch, illustrated in the introduction to this book, of the Court of Appeal of Ghent of 20 October 2010.[73] In that case, the consumers wanted to rescind (terminate) the contract, but according to the judge – similarly to the case from 2009 discussed in the previous paragraph – the consumers ought to have asked for the primary remedies of repair and replacement (Article 1649 *quinquies*, §3 CC).

Another insight is given by a case of the Court of First Instance of Tongeren of 14 June 2010,[74] regarding a defective mobile home. The consumer had arranged on his own initiative for a third party to repair this defect. He wanted to recover the cost of this repair, as damages, from the seller. The judge stressed in this case that there was a clear hierarchy of remedies which had to be respected by the consumer, giving precedence to performance in kind (specific performance) by replacement or repair of the goods. The consumer can only ask for price reduction or rescission (termination) of the contract as secondary step. By going to a third party to repair the mobile home; without even putting the seller in default

72 This decision has been criticized in so far as the consumer had been deprived all damages; the consumer had merely infringed his duty to mitigate damages: Marysse, Steven, 'De Wet Consumentenkoop: enkele beschouwingen' (note under Gent 27 May 2009), *RW* (2010), p. 547; Steennot, Reinhard, 'Garantietermijn tweedehandsgoederen' (note under Gent 27 May 2009), *NjW* (2010), p. 204. See also: Jansen, Sanne, 'Hiërarchie in de remedies bij consumentenkoop: bescherming van consumenten en verkopers?' (note under Gent 20 October 2010), *DCCR* (2012), p. 144; Stijns, Sophie, and Swaenepoel, Elke, 'Consumentenkoop' in Tilleman, Bernard, and Terryn, Evelyne (eds.), *Beginselen van Belgisch Privaatrecht* (Brussels: die Keure, 2011), p. 1318.

73 Ghent 20 October 2010, *DCCR* 2012, 124, note S. Jansen.

74 Rb. Tongeren, 14 June 2010, *T. Vred.* 2012, 298, note C. Delforge (see also for the same case: *T. Vred.* Bree 2 October 2008).

(see *infra*, para. 139), the consumer had deprived the seller of the possibility to repair the good and to fulfill its obligations under the law. The judge also pointed out that, as a consequence, the conditions of application of the secondary price reduction remedy[75] were not fulfilled. The consequences were harsh[76] for the consumer: his claim in damages was rejected.

Another case also involved a second-hand car. The Court of Appeal of Mons decided this case on 22 December 2016.[77] Here the judge stressed that there was a hierarchy between the remedies and that the consumer had to ask first for repair in kind before asking to rescind (terminate) the contract. This decision confirmed that the consumer did not have a discretionary power to choose the remedy he wanted and that a judge had to verify if the conditions of application of the subsidiary remedies were met. Because of this, the court rejected the consumer's claim for rescission (the consumer had in the meantime already resold the car to someone else). It was clear from the facts that the replacement of a part of the vehicle would have brought relief and solved the problem. The garage (i.e. the seller) had also showed its willingness to repair the car. So, instead of rescinding the contract, the buyer should have asked for a repair.

The consumer who chooses a wrong remedy often loses the case all together. As has been discussed, this has been criticized by Belgian doctrine.[78] It is unfair that the consumer will e.g. be deprived of all damages if he chooses price reduction when he should have asked for repair or replacement; the consumer has merely infringed his duty to mitigate damages. His damages could e.g. be reduced to compensate the seller for his losses. Another author defends the idea that the judge should suggest the correct remedies to the consumer and still give him the possibility to choose for repair and replacement.[79] When taking into account the *Duarte* case of the CJEU[80] and recent jurisprudence of the Belgian Court of

---

75 However, the qualification as a judicial 'replacement' (which is a form of performance in kind) would perhaps be more appropriate: Delforge, Catherine, 'Garantie des biens de consommation: primauté de l'exécution en nature par le vendeur' (note under Bree 2 October 2008, Tongeren 14 June 2010), *T. Vred.* (2012), p. 305.

76 See also for this conclusion: Delforge, Catherine, 'Garantie des biens de consommation: primauté de l'exécution en nature par le vendeur' (note under Bree 2 October 2008, Tongeren 14 June 2010), *T. Vred.* (2012), p. 304.

77 Mons 22 December 2016, *DCCR* 2017, note S. Vandemaele, and *TBBR* 2017, note S. Jansen.

78 See *supra*, footnote 72.

79 Vandemaele, Sanne, 'Hiërarchie tussen de remedies bindt zowel de eindverkoper als de consument: focus op herstel en vervanging is en blijft essentieel', *DCCR* 2017, n° 7.

80 CJEU Judgement of 3 October 2012, *Soledad Duarte Hueros v. Autociba SA, Automóviles Citroën España SA*, C-32/12, ECLI:EU:C:2013:637.

Cassation,[81] this might indeed be a solution in most situations. However, it has to be noted that the *Duarte* case does not require an automatic obligation on the national judge to propose the correct remedy(ies). In the *Duarte* case, the CJEU decided indeed that national law is precluded insofar that it

> does not allow the national court hearing the dispute to grant of its own motion an appropriate reduction in the price of goods which are the subject of a contract of sale in the case where a consumer who is entitled to such a reduction brings proceedings which are limited to seeking only rescission of that contract and such rescission cannot be granted because the lack of conformity in those goods is minor, even though that consumer is not entitled to refine his initial application *or to bring a fresh action* to that end.[82]

So the European Court does not oblige the national court in every situation to grant of its own motion the correct remedy or to let the consumer refine his initial application. It is also sufficient if the consumer is allowed to bring a fresh action to this end. Under Belgian law, the Court of Cassation would require the judge to raise of his own motion the legal grounds of the dispute, at least if they result from the facts directly invoked by the claimant and the defendant (without, of course, breaching the *ultra petita* prohibition,[83] which the judge can counter by using his right to ask questions and to allow the applicant to refine his application).[84] However, in the unlikely case when the remedies of repair and replacement do not result from the facts directly invoked by the claimant and the defendant, the judge will not be obliged to do this, and a possibility for a fresh action by the consumer will be considered in accordance with EU law. This last approach might

81 See e.g. Cass. 14 April 2005, *Arr. Cass.* 2005, 868, concl. P. De Koster, *JT* 2005, 659, note J. Van Compernolle, err. *JT* 2005, 796, *JLMB* 2005, 856, note G. De Leval, *Pas.* 2005, I, 862, concl. P. De Koster, *RABG* 2005, 1663, note R. Verbeke, *Soc. Kron.* 2008, 497 and *P&B* 2005, 300, concl. O.M., note.

82 Emphasis added.

83 See for a consumer sales case in which the *ultra petita* prohibition was breached: Cass. 23 January 2015, *RW* 2016–17, 503, note S. Jansen (a judge who rejects the termination of the contract – which was asked principally by the consumers – because this choice did not respect the hierarchy of remedies of Art. 1649*quinquies* CC and who grants of his own motion a price reduction equal to the whole price, instead of a price reduction of a smaller amount as was asked by the consumer in the alternative, breaches the *ultra petita* prohibition).

84 See e.g. Cass. 14 April 2005, *Arr. Cass.* 2005, 868, concl. P. De Koster, *JT* 2005, 659, note J. Van Compernolle, err. *JT* 2005, 796, *JLMB* 2005, 856, note G. De Leval, *Pas.* 2005, I, 862, concl. P. De Koster, *RABG* 2005, 1663, note R. Verbeke, *Soc. Kron.* 2008, 497 and *P&B* 2005, 300, concl. O.M., note.

also not be a solution if the consumer has already relied upon a remedy – such as price reduction or termination – which the consumer has invoked erroneously by having a third party repair the goods or by reselling the goods.

The current state of affairs is that it is often the consumer who loses out. Delforge puts it quite correctly: the irony is that rules that were intended to protect consumers, can indeed turn against them.[85] This means that consumers in Belgium must be well informed in order to enforce their rights.

13 *French (case) law*. In the French Code de Consommation, the hierarchy of remedies is implemented in Articles L217-9 and L217-10 (old Arts L211-9 and L211-10). The consumer can only choose price reduction or termination if repair and replacement are impossible or if they cannot be executed within a month after the complaints of the consumer or without significant inconvenience for the consumer. Because these rules clarify the 'reasonable time within which the seller has to repair or to replace', it is more likely that price reduction and termination can easily be invoked by the consumer. At least it will be more clear or certain for the consumer – compared to the Belgian rules – when price reduction or termination can be invoked in that regard. There is also another difference compared to the Belgian implementation of the Consumer Sales Directive. Article L217-13 *Code de Consommation* introduces an even more 'consumer-friendly' regime: it allows the consumer to invoke the action resulting from hidden defects (in Arts 1641–1649 *Code civil*) and *all other contractual or extra-contractual action* recognized by law. Of course, this opens perspectives for a consumer who wants to ask for remedies which are not the ones proposed by the strict hierarchy of remedies in Articles L217-8 and L217-9 *Code de Consommation*.

In some cases, the hierarchy is confirmed by the judges while the consumer respects this hierarchy.[86] What happens if a consumer erroneously invokes price reduction or termination of the contract?

---

[85] Delforge, Catherine, 'Garantie des biens de consommation: primauté de l'exécution en nature par le vendeur' (note under Bree 2 October 2008, Tongeren 14 June 2010), *T. Vred.* (2012), p. 306. See also Delforge, Catherine, and Ninane, Yannick, 'La garantie de conformité des biens de consommation, Chronique de jurisprudence (2005–2015)' in Wéry, Patrick (ed.), *Théorie générale des obligations et contrats spéciaux* (Brussels: Larcier, 2016), p. 404, n° 80.

[86] Cour d'appel Douai 8 March 2010, n° 09/02507, *inédit*, www.lexisnexis.com; Cour d'appel Douai 31 May 2010, n° 09/03522, JurisData 2010-014018; Cour d'appel

Well, the consumer can ask, in the alternative, for another remedy (a general contractual action), which is allowed under French law.

This is clearly shown in a case decided by the Court of Appeal of Caen on 8 December 2016.[87] A couple bought a second-hand car from a professional seller which was affected by multiple defects. In principal, the consumers asked for the termination (rescission) of the contract. In the alternative they asked, based on Article 1147 *Code civil*, a sum of money corresponding to the costs to repair the car and a sum of money for the loss of use. In the first instance and on appeal the action for termination was rejected, because the consumer had not respected the hierarchy of remedies prescribed by Article L217-10. The conditions of application for termination were thus not fulfilled because repair of the car was still possible. But the court granted on appeal the sum of money for repair and the loss of use.

However, if the consumer forgets this, and does not ask for remedies under common contract law, he can end up in a similar situation as described under Belgian law.

In a case decided on 24 October 2016 by the Court of Appeal of Colmart, the consumers only requested termination of the sales contract for a secured entrance door.[88] The consumers did not demonstrate that repair or replacement was impossible: they did not complain to the seller. Consequently, the consumers could not demonstrate that repair or replacement would not be feasible within a month or not without significant inconvenience for the consumer. Because of these reasons, the claim for termination (and additional damages) was rejected by the Court of Appeal.

Also, in a case decided on 26 April 2016 by the Court of Appeal of Aix-en-Provence the consumer's choice for termination (principally) and price reduction (alternatively) was rejected.[89] The case was about a

Douai 31 May 2010, n° 09/05514, *inédit*, www.lexisnexis.com; Cour d'appel Rennes 20 September 2012, n° 396, 10/05996, *inédit*, www.lexisnexis.com; Cour d'appel Paris 27 November 2014, n° 13/01912, JurisData 2014-030406; Cour d'appel Caen 22 January 2015, n° 13/02554, JurisData 2015-001149; Cour d'appel Aix-en-Provence 12 March 2015, n° 2015/155, JurisData 2015-005021; Cour d'appel Versailles 9 June 2015, n° 14/02052, *inédit*, www.lexisnexis.com; Cour d'appel Lyon 24 September 2015, n° 13/06068, JurisData 2015-021441; Cour d'appel Paris 8 October 2015, n° 13/11820, JurisData 2015-023882; Cour d'appel Paris 8 July 2016, n° 15/04619, *inédit*, www.lexisnexis.com. Cf.: Cour d'appel Poitiers 10 June 2016, n° 15/01159, JurisData 2016-018287 (the seller did not want to repair the car: the consumers requested a refund of the price of the car, but they were only granted a price reduction).

87 Cour d'appel de Caen 8 December 2016, n° 15/01485, www.dalloz.fr.

88 Cour d'appel Colmart 24 October 2016, n° 16/0771, 15/04722, JurisData 2016-022096.

89 Cour d'appel Aix-en-Provence 26 April 2016, n° 15/03912, *inédit*, www.lexisnexis.com.

kitchen with some small non-conformities. The remedy of termination was rejected because the non-conformities were only minor (see also *infra*, para. 16). Price reduction was refused because the non-conformities could be fixed by some small adjustments and because the consumer had never complained to the seller. Article L211-10 (now L217-10) *Code de Consommation* prescribes that a price reduction can only be granted if repair or replacement are impossible.

In another case, a consumer complained that the color of the kitchen cabinet doors did not match the color of the sides of the cabinets. The Court of Appeal of Paris decided on 13 April 2012[90] that the consumer could not claim the termination/rescission of the contract because he had not respected, among others, the rule in Article L211-10 *Code de Consommation* (now L217-10), favoring repair and replacement over termination. The seller proposed replacing the kitchen cabinets in such a way that they would match the color of the doors, which the consumer unjustly refused.

14 *Dutch (case) law.* The Dutch legislator has also maintained the hierarchy of remedies proposed by the Consumer Sales Directive in its Articles 7:21–22 Civil Code (CC). However, the legislator has softened some subtle aspects of this hierarchy. Article 7:21 CC states that a consumer can ask for delivery of the missing goods, or repair or replacement of the goods. Later, it states that if the seller cannot repair within a reasonable time after the consumer has asked the seller to do so, the consumer has the power to ask a third person to repair and to recover the costs from the seller.[91] Article 7:22, para 1 CC provides for the right of termination/rescission and price reduction. Those remedies are only available if repair and replacement are impossible or cannot be requested from the seller, or if the seller cannot provide for repair or replacement within a reasonable time or without significant inconvenience for the consumer. Nevertheless, similarly to its French counterpart, Article 7:22, para 4 CC prescribes that the consumer is allowed to invoke, alongside to his rights in Articles 7:20, 21, and 22 para 1, all his other rights and actions.[92]

---

90 Cour d'appel Paris 13 April 2012, n° 09/18440, JurisData 2012-007693.

91 See e.g. Rechtbank Rotterdam 22 January 2008, n° 829679 (ECLI:NL:RBROT:2008:BC4859).

92 See e.g.: Rechtbank Zwolle-Lelystad 16 May 2012, n° 18329/HZ ZA 11-358, *rechtspraak.nl* (ECLI:NL:RBZLY:2012:BW8222) (Art. 7:22 para 1 CC does not prohibit the right of the consumer to invoke termination under Art. 6:265 *et seq.* CC).

How does this hierarchy of remedies play out in the Dutch case law? Some consumers respect the established hierarchy of remedies.[93] What happens if a consumer erroneously invokes price reduction or termination of the contract?

Also, in the Netherlands, judges do not hesitate to enforce the hierarchy of remedies. The Court of First Instance of Rotterdam decided on 13 May 2016 that a claim for termination/rescission of the sales contract of a sofa had to be rejected.[94] The consumer terminated the contract during the repair phase and did not respond to a message of the seller attempting to fix a date for the delivery of the repaired sofa. The court rejected the termination claim of the consumer with reference to Article 7:22 CC and to the hierarchy of remedies.

In a case before the Court of Arnhem of 20 March 2012, where a consumer did not give his garage (the seller) the opportunity to repair the motor of a Volkswagen Beetle, the judge rejected his claim to terminate the contract.[95] The possibility to terminate the contract only existed when repair or replacement were impossible, could not be requested from the seller, or could not be done within a reasonable time or without significant inconvenience for the consumer.

Also, in a case before the Court of First Instance of Arnhem of 27 November 2009, the claim for termination/rescission of the contract by the consumer was rejected.[96] In this case some pieces of delivered furniture showed some imperfections and blemishes. Because the independent consultant's report determined that the imperfections could be repaired,

---

93 Gerechtshof Amsterdam 1 March 2007, n° 1818/05 (ECLI:NL:GHAMS:2007:BA9978); Rechtbank 's-Gravenhage 11 November 2009, n° 329751 – HA ZA 09-410, *rechtspraak.nl*, *NJF* 2010, 55 (ECLI:NL:RBSGR:2009:BK5204); Rechtbank Dordrecht 18 March 2010, n° 240769 CV EXPL 788/08, *rechtspraak.nl* (ECLI:NL:RBDOR:2010:BM0772); Rechtbank Haarlem 15 February 2012, n° 182745 – HA ZA 11-769, *rechtspraak.nl* (ECLI:NL:RBHAA:2012:BV8727); Rechtbank Limburg 4 December 2013, n° 2175464 CV EXPL 13-5925, *rechtspraak.nl*, *Prg.* 2014/42 (ECLI:NL:RBLIM:2013:9404); Rechtbank Oost-Brabant 26 June 2014, n° 2796388, *rechtspraak.nl*, *TvC* 2014, 289, note M.B.M. Loos, *Prg.* 2014/208 (ECLI:NL:RBOBR:2014:3396); Gerechtshof Arnhem-Leeuwarden 25 November 2014, n° 200.128.340, *rechtspraak.nl*, *RCR* 2015/39 (ECLI:NL:GHARL:2014:9065); Gerechtshof Arnhem-Leeuwarden 17 May 2016, n° 200.118.541/01, *Prg.* 2016/180 (ECLI:NL:GHARL:2016:3808).

94 Rechtbank Rotterdam 13 May 2016, n° 4336461 CV EXPL 15-33620, *Prg.* 2016/178 (ECLI:NL:RBROT:2016:3579).

95 Gerechtshof Arnhem 22 March 2012, n° 200.084.819/01, *rechtspraak.nl* (ECLI:NL: GHARN:2012:BV9647).

96 Rechtbank Arnhem 27 November 2009, n° 613122 CV EXPL 09-3350, *rechtspraak.nl*, *RCR* 2010, 10, *Prg.* 2010, 10 (ECLI:NL:RBARN:2009:BK4878).

the consumer had prematurely invoked the termination of the contract. However, since the consumer had asked in the alternative to repair the defects, the latter claim was awarded to the consumer.

15 *German (case) law*. In 2002, the German legislator chose to radically integrate the consumer sales remedies in the general sales provisions. This 'Schuldrechtsmodernisierung' in 2002 followed the Consumer Sales Directive in that it confirms the hierarchy of remedies. §437 Bürgerliches Gesetzbuch 'BGB' gives an overview of the remedies. The buyer/consumer may ask for cure, termination, or price reduction. However, the remedies of termination and price reduction are clearly considered 'secondary remedies'. The primacy of specific performance in sales contracts is confirmed by subjecting termination to a *Nachfrist* ('period of grace') requirement (§§440, 323, and 326(5) BGB).[97] The *Nachfrist* requirement is, moreover, also applicable to the *Minderung* ('reduction') remedy if the legal or material defect of the good can be repaired or the good can be delivered without any defects (§§441 juncto 323(1) BGB).[98] This also implies a hierarchy between the *Minderung* remedy and performance of the contract: specific performance has a privileged position in comparison to the *Minderung*.[99] The seller actually has a 'Recht zur zweiten Andienung' or a second chance before the buyer can invoke termination or price reduction (right to cure). The *Nachfrist* (and giving a right to cure) is not required in certain situations: e.g. (1) if the seller has refused to carry out both kinds of cure under §439(3) (§440 BGB); (2) if the kind of cure that the buyer is entitled to receive has failed or cannot reasonably be expected of him (§440 BGB); (3) if the seller does not render performance by a date specified in the contract or within a period specified in the contract

---

[97] See for detail, Weller, Marc-Philippe, *Die Vertragstreue: Vertragsbindung, Naturalerfüllungsgrundsatz, Leistungstreue* (Tübingen: Mohr Siebeck, 2009), at p. 493.

[98] This requirement can be inferred by the wording '*statt zurückzutreten*' in §441(1) BGB: in '*Einführung*' by Claus-Wilhelm Canaris in Canaris, Claus-Wilhelm, *Schuldrechtsmodernisierung 2002* (Munich: Beck, 2002), XXVI. See also BGH, *Urteil* vom 23.02.2005, *BB* 2005, 909, *WM* 2005, 945; BGH, *Urteil* vom 21.12.2005, *WM* 2006, 1355, n° 18; OLG Hamm, *Urteil* vom 27.08.2008, n° 11 U 143/05, *BeckRS* 2010, 01835.

[99] Büdenbender, Ulrich, '§441' in Dauner-Lieb, Barbara, et al. (eds.), *Schuldrecht* (Bonn: Deutscher Anwalt Verlag, 2002), p. 596, n° 4; Kötz, Hein, *Vertragsrecht* (Tübingen: Mohr Siebeck, 2012), n° 957 *et seq.*; Looschelders, Dirk, *Schuldrecht, Besonderer Teil* (Munich: Vahlen, 2011), n° 82; Matusche-Beckmann, A., '§441' in Martinek, M., *von Staudingers Kommentar zum BGB* (Berlijn: Sellier – de Gruyter, 2013), n° 3; Fikentscher, Wolfgang, and Heinemann, Andreas, *Schuldrecht* (Berlijn: De Gruyter, 2006), n° 870; Westermann, H.P., '§441' in Krüger, W., and H.P. Westermann, *Münchener Kommentar BGB* (Munich: Beck, 2012), n° 1; Zimmermann, Reinhard, *The New German Law of Obligations* (Oxford: Oxford University Press, 2004), pp. 104–06.

and the buyer made clear that time is of the essence by notice prior to the conclusion of the contract (§323(2)2. BGB).

However, the so-called '*Fristsetzung*' before one can reduce the price or terminate the contract, is a major concern of German doctrine about consumer sales law.[100] The Consumer Sales Directive only requires that repair and replacement should be done within a reasonable time (Article 3 CSD). The obligatory *Fristsetzung* possibly goes too far, encroaching on the minimum consumer protection level that has been set by the Directive.[101] This means that this strand in German doctrine and jurisprudence does not require the consumer to set (notify) the seller of a reasonable period to cure the non-conformity, but cure must happen within a reasonable time before the consumer can invoke termination or price reduction. This does not fundamentally change the hierarchy of remedies, but makes it somewhat weaker and more consumer-friendly.

How does this hierarchy of remedies play out in German case law? Often the consumer respects the hierarchy of remedies set forth in the legislation.[102] But what happens if the consumer did not give the seller the opportunity to cure within a reasonable time (when following the strand

---

100 Gärtner, Anette, *Die Umsetzung der Verbrauchsgüterkaufrichtlinie in Deutschland und Grossbritannien* (Frankfurt am Main: Peter Lang, 2006), pp. 101–02; Herrestal, Carsten, 'Die Grenzen der richtlinienkonformen Rechtsfortbildung im Kaufrecht', *WM* (2007), p. 1360; Hoffmann, Jan, 'Verbrauchsgüterkaufrechtsrichtlinie und Schuldrechtsmodernisierungsgesetz', *ZRP* (2001), V.3.

101 A *Fristsetzung* is not required if a consumer wants to terminate the contract and refers to Art. 3 of the Directive: AG Köln, *Urteil* vom 28.01.2010, 137 C 436/09, *NJOZ* 2011, 148 ('*Auch Unterabs. 3 von Art. 3 III verlangt nicht, dass der Verbraucher vor Vertragsauflösung eine Frist zur Nachbesserung oder Ersatzlieferung gesetzt haben muss. Er fordert lediglich, dass beides - ersichtlich, wenn es denn verlangt wird - binnen einer angemessenen Frist erfolgen muss*'); LG Meiningen, *Urteil* vom 06.12.2012, 1 O 201/12, *BeckRS* 2015, 02613 (ECLI:DE:LGMEINI:2012:1206.1O201.12.0A: '*für den vorliegenden Fall bedeutet dies, dass §323 Abs. 1 BGB dahingehend richtlinienkonform auszulegen ist, dass der Käufer vor Vertragsrücktritt lediglich eine angemessene Nacherfüllungsfrist abzuwarten hat, ohne dass er diese selbst setzen muss*'). Cf.: a very lenient way of approaching the *Fristsetzung*: BGH, *Urteil* vom 13.07.2016, Az. VIII ZR 49/15, *OpenJur* 2016, 9351 ('*Nach der Rechtsprechung des Senats genügt es im Hinblick auf den Wortlaut der §323 Abs. 1, §281 Abs. 1 BGB sowie den Sinn und Zweck der Fristsetzung zur Nacherfüllung, wenn der Gläubiger durch das Verlangen nach sofortiger, unverzüglicher oder umgehender Leistung oder durch vergleichbare Formulierungen deutlich macht, dass dem Schuldner für die Erfüllung nur ein begrenzter (bestimmbarer) Zeitraum zur Verfügung steht. Der Angabe eines bestimmten Zeitraums oder eines bestimmten (End-)Termins bedarf es nicht*').

102 See e.g. BGH, *Urteil* vom 26.10.2016, VIII ZR 240/15, *NJW* 2017, 153; LG Lüneburg, *Urteil* vom 02.06.2016, 4 O 3/16, *BeckRS* 2016, 17486; LG Arnsberg, *Urteil* vom 24.03.2017, 2 O 254/16, *BeckRS* 2017, 106864.

that does not require a *Fristsetzung*) or by a *Fristsetzung*? What if the consumer fails to respect the hierarchy of remedies under German law?[103]

In a case before the Court (OLG) of Düsseldorf of 24 October 2005, a buyer[104] lost his right to terminate the contract because he did not give the seller the opportunity to fix the quite unique car he delivered with defects.[105] The buyer forgot to give the seller a *Nachfrist*, which prevented him (among others) to terminate the contract.

The *Bundesgerichtshof* ('BGH') decided in a case on 23 February 2005 that a buyer[106] who fixed a defect of a motor vehicle without *Fristsetzung* to allow the seller to cure, could not recover the cost of the repair from the seller.[107] The remedy to reduce the price and damages instead of performance are subject to a *Nachfrist* which gives the seller the opportunity to perform (§437 *et seq.* BGB and esp. §439 BGB).

Returning to the Volkswagen case which was discussed in Chapter 1 (*supra*, para. 1), the question is whether or not a consumer can terminate the contract due to a defect in the Volkswagen software. Especially in Germany, many cases of this kind have arisen. It will depend on the circumstances or the leniency of the judge whether such a claim for termination will be successful and whether a certain *Fristsetzung* is required or considered sufficient.[108] In e.g. a case of 25 April 2017 before the Court (LG) of

---

103 See in a B2B case: OLG Köln, *Urteil* vom 09.09.2003, 10 0 113/02, 19 u 80/03, *BeckRS* 2004, 01038 (rejection of termination because the buyer did not give the seller a *Nachfrist* to repair).

104 Who is qualified as 'a hunter' (i.e. the buyer, the driver of the car); however, later in the decision the judge refers to 'consumer protection'.

105 OLG Düsseldorf, *Urteil* vom 24.10.2004, I-1 U 84/05, *SVR* 2006, Heft 9, 330, *OpenJur* 2011, 41252.

106 It is unclear whether this relates to a consumer or a professional buyer.

107 BGH *Urteil* vom 23.02.2005, n° VIII ZR 100/04, *BGHZ* 162, 219–230.

108 See for *successful* claims for termination e.g.: LG Lüneburg, *Urteil* vom 2.6.2016, 4 O 3/16, *BeckRS* 2016, 17486; LG Krefeld, *Urteil* vom 14.09.2016, 2 O 83/16, *Juris*; LG Essen, *Urteil* vom 16.09.2016, 16 O 165/16, *Juris* (ECLI:DE:LGE:2016:0916. 16O165.16.00); LG Hamburg, *Urteil* vom 16.11.2016, 301 O 96/16, *Justiz-Portal*; LG Bückeburg, *Urteil* vom 11.01.2017, 2 O 39/16, *BeckRS* 2017, 102958 (ECLI:DE: LGBUECK:2017:0111.2O39.16.0A); LG Kleve, *Urteil* vom 31.03.2017, 3 O 252/16, *BeckRS* 2017, 106026 (ECLI:DE:LGKLE:2017:0331.3O252.16.0A).
See for other *unsuccessful* claims for termination e.g. LG Regensburg, *Urteil* vom 15.06.2016, 3 O 2161/15, *Juris*; LG Düsseldorf, *Urteil* vom 23.08.2016, 6 O 413/15, *MMR* 2017, 198, *BeckRS* 2016, 15047; LG Münster, *Urteil* vom 04.10.2016 2 O 1/16, *BeckRS* 2016, 112062 (ECLI:DE:LGMS:2016:1004.2O1.16.0A); LG Traunstein, *Endurteil* vom 10.10.2016, 3 O 709/16, *BeckRS* 2016, 117540 (ECLI:DE:LGTRAUN: 2016:1010.3O709.16.0A; the buyer must wait a bit longer for repair); LG Ansbach, *Urteil* vom 31.10.2016, 2 O 226/16, *Juris*; LG Stuttgart, *Urteil* vom 02.11.2016, 18 O 21/16, *Juris*; LG Ellwangen, *Urteil* vom 14.11.2016, 5 O 2/16, *Juris*.

Braunschweig a buyer was not successful in claiming termination.[109] In this case, a buyer of a VW Passat wanted to recover the price of his car by terminating his sales contract. The NOx-value thresholds that are required by the EU Regulation n° 715/2007 were only reached in test conditions and not in real-life street traffic. The buyer was informed that his car needed a software update and that the seller would organize this by putting the buyer into contact with an authorized garage. The buyer gave the seller notice and a period of one week to fix the car. The seller replied that he did not have the means to repair the car, but that he would negotiate repair in an authorized garage. The buyer finally terminated the sales contract. The court did not grant the claim of termination by the buyer. The buyer did not set, according to the court, a reasonable or appropriate period of time ('*angemessene Frist*'). The court decided, first, that a period of time of one week is unreasonably short. Moreover, there were no exceptions available to the *Fristsetzung*. *Fristsetzung* was necessary because the car was not affected with an irreparable defect (§326 para. 5 BGB). Also, §323 para. 2, n° 3 BGB did not excuse the buyer from the *Fristsetzung*, because there was not a situation of intentional fraud/deception. In addition, a *Fristsetzung* was necessary due to §440 para. 1 BGB, because repair would not necessarily cause the buyer significant inconvenience. Often, judges do not allow termination in these circumstances;[110] however, judges are not always so harsh upon the buyers and sometimes allow a termination even in very similar circumstances.[111] In one case, the judge even made it clear that consumers are not obliged to provide the seller with a *Fristsetzung*.[112] Moreover, it has to be noted that in this period of time the Volkswagen dealers were still encouraging consumers to go to recognized garages to get a software update, which did not leave the consumer totally empty handed. Anyhow, is clear that jurisprudence is quite divided and that there is legal uncertainty with regard to this matter.

Relationship between the secondary remedies of price reduction and 16
termination. It is clear that the CSD prescribes a hierarchy of remedies,

See also for an oversight of case law: Krämer, Hannes, 'VW "Dieselgate" – eine juristisch saubere Sache?', *SVR* (2017), p. 56 *et seq.*

109 LG Braunschweig, *Urteil* vom 25.04.2017, 11 O 4/17, *Juris*.

110 See also Ring, Gerhard, 'Absgas-Manipulationssoftware und Gewährleistungsrechte der Käufer', *NJW* (2016), p. 3121 *et seq.* See also Sievers, Alexander, 'Rechtsprechungsübersicht zur Abgasthematik (EA 189)', *DAR* (2016), pp. 543–544.

111 See footnote 108.

112 LG Köln, *Urteil* vom 02.03.2017, 2 O 317/16, *BeckRS* 2017, 103462 (ECLI:DE:LGK:2017:0302.2O317.16.0A).

preferring repair/replacement over the secondary remedies of price reduction and termination. But what about the relationship between the secondary remedies: price reduction and termination? The consumer can only call upon the remedy of termination if the lack of conformity is not minor.[113] This is not the case for the remedy of price reduction, which can be called upon independently of the fact whether or not the non-conformity is minor. This means that a price reduction is more readily available as a remedy, compared to termination of the contract.

17 *And what about damages?* One of the most important remedies under US common law and the UCC is the remedy of damages (see *infra*, section 2). Surprisingly, the Consumer Sales Directive does not devote any attention to this remedy.[114] Perhaps this can be explained by the fact that it expressly deals with the remedy of price reduction, which is regarded by many authors as a substitute for damages. The proportionate character of price reduction and its applicability in case of breach of contract *and* in case of *force majeure* are, already, two elements showing that both remedies are not alike. Of course, this Directive is only a 'minimum harmonization' instrument (see also *infra*, para. 11), which implies that States can introduce more favorable regimes for consumers, and thus implying a damages regime. The Directive also proposes in recital 12 that the seller may always offer the consumer by way of settlement, any available remedy (such as damages), which the consumer can accept or reject.

1.2. PRIORITY OF REPAIR AND REPLACEMENT UNDER THE PROPOSAL FOR A CONSUMER RIGHTS DIRECTIVE

18 *Full harmonization instead of minimum harmonization.* This Proposal opts for a different approach compared to the Consumer Sales Directive.[115]

---

113 See Art. 3(6) CSD and Art. 26.3 final sentence, old Consumer Rights Directive Proposal.

114 See, however, recital 6 of the CSD: 'it is therefore appropriate to approximate national legislation governing the sale of consumer goods in this respect, without however impinging on provisions and principles of national law relating to contractual and non-contractual liability' and Art. 8 CSD: 'The rights resulting from this Directive shall be exercised without prejudice to other rights which the consumer may invoke under the national rules governing contractual or non-contractual liability'.

115 Proposal for a Directive of the EU Parliament and of the Council on consumer rights, Brussels, 8 October 2008, COM(2008) 614 final, 2008/0196 (COD).

(Note that it originally contained consumer sales provisions on remedies but these never reached the finish line.) It embraces a 'full harmonization' method, which means that EU Member States cannot maintain or adopt provisions that diverge from the ones in the Directive. Consequently, the hierarchy of remedies that was laid down in the Proposal would be binding upon the Member States. However, as mentioned, the proposed rules on remedies have never been adopted.

Priority of repair and replacement and introduction of a choice by 19
the trader. Identical to the Consumer Sales Directive, the Proposal for a Consumer Rights Directive reiterates the hierarchy between the different remedies for the consumer.[116] Repair and replacement enjoy the highest place in the hierarchy. The secondary remedies are price reduction and termination. However, the regulation in the Proposal also *differs* from the Consumer Sales Directive because the Proposal indicates that the *trader* (and not the consumer) may choose between the remedies of repair or replacement[117] and the *trader* has to *prove* that the primary remedies are unlawful, impossible, or would cause *himself* a disproportionate effort, when he wants to invoke the secondary remedies.[118] In comparison, Article 3.3 of the Consumer Sales Directive indicates that the *consumer* may choose between the remedy of repair or replacement, and that his choice is only restricted if the remedy chosen is impossible to complete or if the remedy is disproportional.

That the Proposal foresees that it is the *trader* who may initially choose for repair or replacement, and the addition that the trader has to prove the disproportionate effort, may seem surprising at first sight. However, the practical applicability of the *consumer's* choice for one of the remedies encounters some problems, *because* of the hierarchy of remedies (see introductory example, *supra*, para. 1). The consumer is not always best placed to evaluate which remedy is disproportional or impossible for the trader or which one will cause himself (the consumer) significant inconvenience. The hierarchy of remedies makes it difficult for the consumer to choose the 'appropriate' and 'legitimate' remedy. It might

---

[116] See Art. 26.3 of the Consumer Rights Directive Proposal. Loos, Marco B.M., 'Consumer Sales Law in the Proposal for a Consumer Rights Directive', *ERPL* (2010), p. 37.

[117] See Art. 26.2 of the Consumer Rights Directive Proposal of 2008.

[118] Twigg-Flesner, Christian, and Meltcafle, D., 'The Proposed Consumer Rights Directive – Less Haste More Thought?', *ERCL* (2009), p. 386; Whittaker, Simon, 'Unfair Contract Terms and Consumer Guarantees: The Proposal for a Directive on Consumer Rights and the Significance of "Full Harmonisation"', *ERCL* (2009), p. 242.

be possible that under national law, the consumer is then 'punished' for choosing the wrong or an 'inappropriate' remedy, taking into account the hierarchy of the remedies provided for in the Directive. The Proposal tries to counter this inconvenience imposed by the Directive by giving the choice of the remedy and allocating the burden of proof to the trader. However, another solution would have been to clarify that the (wrongful) choice of the consumer of a remedy cannot backfire on the consumer (e.g. in a judicial procedure controlling the legitimacy of the invoked remedy). Indeed, when the consumer has chosen an inappropriate remedy, a judge must be able to decide to impose the rightful remedy, without depriving the consumer of a remedy (see also *supra*, para. 10).

20 *No hierarchy in specific situations?* However, the new Proposal seems to reconnect[119] with the Consumer Sales Directive and even to broaden the rights of the consumer in Article 26.4, stating that the consumer can choose between the four remedies if (1) the trader has implicitly/explicitly refused to remedy; if (2) the trader has failed to remedy the lack of conformity within a reasonable time or (3) without significant inconvenience to the consumer;[120] and if (4) the same defect has reappeared more than once within a short period of time. The Proposal goes further in providing the choice to the *consumer* between the four remedies (without any hierarchy) in these four situations and provides two extra grounds to invoke the four remedies – namely, if the trader has refused to remedy and if there is a recurrent defect in a short period of time.[121]

21 *Relation between the secondary remedies: price reduction and termination.* Similarly to the Consumer Sales Directive (see *supra*, para. 16), the Proposal provides in Article 26.3 that the consumer may

[119] See also: Twigg-Flesner, Christian, and Meltcafle, D., 'The Proposed Consumer Rights Directive – Less Haste More Thought?', *ERCL* (2009), p. 386.

[120] Art. 26.5 of the Proposal clarifies that the assessment of the significant inconvenience for the consumer and the reasonable time needed for the trader to remedy the lack of conformity, takes into account the nature of the goods or the purpose for which the consumer acquired the goods.

[121] Whittaker is not convinced that this 'broadens the rights of the consumer': the four situations only relate to circumstances where the trader can only blame himself: Whittaker, Simon, 'Unfair Contract Terms and Consumer Guarantees: The Proposal for a Directive on Consumer Rights and the Significance of "Full Harmonisation"', *ERCL* (2009), p. 242; Loos is also critical of the extra grounds and rightly proposes another ground that should have been incorporated in this list that allows the buyer/consumer to choose between the four remedies: a breach of confidence between buyer and seller (e.g. when the delivered good is dangerous): Loos, Marco B.M., 'Consumer Sales Law in the Proposal for a Consumer Rights Directive', *ERPL* (2010), pp. 40–41.

only terminate the contract if the lack of conformity is not minor; however, this is not required for the right to price reduction. Price reduction is thus more readily available than termination.

1.3. PRIORITY OF SPECIFIC PERFORMANCE UNDER THE CONSUMER RIGHTS DIRECTIVE

Slimmed-down version. As previously mentioned (see *supra*, para. 18), the Proposal for a Consumer Rights Directive was slimmed down. The consumer sales provisions on remedies never reached the finish line. Nevertheless, some consumer sales remedies provisions survived in the final Consumer Rights Directive (CRD).[122] 22

Late delivery. Article 18.2 CRD foresees remedies in the case of failure to deliver the goods *at the time* agreed upon in the contract. In contrast, the Consumer Sales Directive merely foresees remedies in case of non-conformity of the goods with the contract, which is not necessarily the same as late delivery. This Directive answers the question of what the consumer can ask for in the case of late delivery. 23

Right to cure and the priority of specific performance. According to Article 18.2 CRD, the consumer must first 'call upon the seller' to deliver and give the seller an additional period to deliver. This actually means that the seller has a so-called 'right to cure'. He is given additional time to perform the contract; which implies that he is given a second chance. A right to cure of the seller can be interpreted as a system that gives preference to performance of the contract, because the consumer can only ask for other remedies after this period of time has elapsed. 24

Indeed, Article 18.2 CRD foresees that the consumer can invoke termination of the contract if the trader fails to deliver the goods within the additional period of time. However, the seller will not be given a right to cure if he has refused to deliver the goods or if delivery at a certain moment is essential for the consumer. In the last case the circumstances of the conclusion of the contract will be taken into account, and also whether

[122] Directive 2011/83/EU of the EU Parliament and the Council of 25 October 2011 on consumer rights amending Council Directive 93/13/EEC and Directive 1999/44/EC of the EU Parliament and of the Council and repealing Council Directive 85/577/EEC and Directive 97/7/EC of the EU Parliament and of the Council, OJ L 304, 22 November 2011, pp. 64–88.

or not the consumer has informed the trader, prior to the conclusion of the contract, of the importance of the date of delivery.

Finally, Article 18.4 CRD prescribes that 'in addition to termination of the contract', as prescribed by the Directive, 'the consumer may have recourse to other remedies provided for by national law'. This means that he can ask e.g. for additional damages.

1.4. WITHDRAWN PROPOSAL ON A COMMON EUROPEAN SALES LAW WHICH WOULD HAVE PROVIDED A FLAT HIERARCHY OF REMEDIES IN B2C CONTRACTS

25 *Influential withdrawn proposal.* In October 2011, the EU Commission finally decided upon an approach towards the harmonization of European contract law and chose to introduce a so-called '28th regime'. The proposal to introduce a 'Common European Sales Law (CESL)'[123] rested on the foundation that its regime was a voluntary and consumer-friendly 'opt-in' system, applicable in B2B and B2C cross-border contracts.[124] Consumers would recognize it by the symbolic 'blue button' that they would have to click on if a web shop opted into this regime. Parties had to choose to take part in this system, and this was why the CESL was acceptable for many actors; but this also constituted the biggest weakness of the instrument. What if nobody would opt-in? After many amendments, made by the EU Parliament, that tried to incorporate the (doctrinal) critiques on the CESL, the proposal was finally withdrawn by the Commission. The new approach would be much more e-commerce focused. Notwithstanding the fact that the Commission has withdrawn this proposal, the CESL is still very influential in doctrine and will certainly be a model for many legislators for their future contract law.[125] This alone justifies an examination of its remedial system.

26 *Remedial system.* The CESL devotes different sections to the remedies depending on whether the buyer or the seller is the aggrieved party and whether it is a sales contract or a services contract. In this book,

---

123 See: Proposal for a Regulation of the European Parliament and of the Council on a Common European Sales Law, Brussels 11 October 2011, COM(2011) 635 final, 2011/0284 (COD), http://eur-lex.europa.eu/LexUriServ/LexUriServ.do?uri=COM:2011:0635:FIN:en:PDF.

124 See, e.g., Arts. 3–5 Regulation of the CESL-proposal.

125 Schulze, Reiner, and Zoll, Fryderyk, *European Contract Law* (Munich: Beck, 2016), p. V.

which focuses on the consumer's remedies in case of a breach of a sales contract, only the buyer's remedies in the Proposal will be discussed.[126] Article 106.1 CESL gives an overview of all buyer's remedies, which are: requiring performance (including specific performance, repair, or replacement); withholding performance; termination of the contract; price reduction; and damages.

Right to cure[127]. Very importantly, Article 106.2 CESL then differentiates immediately between buyers who are *traders* and buyers who are *consumers*. In the first case (B2B), all buyer's remedies (except for withholding performance) are subject to the *right to cure* by the seller under Article 109 CESL (and notification and examination duties, see *infra*, para. 119), where this does not apply when the buyer is a consumer (B2C).[128] So the hierarchy of remedies is clearly different according to whether the 27

126 See, for the seller's remedies: Chapter 13 CESL, Arts. 131–139. See, for the remedies in services contracts: Arts. 155–157 CESL.

127 For more detail, see Kruisinga, Sonja A., 'The Seller's Right to Cure in the CISG and the Common European Sales Law' in Keirse, Anne L.M., and Loos, Marco B.M. (eds.), *Alternative Ways to Ius Commune* (Cambridge: Intersentia, 2012), pp. 157–167 (the author concludes that the seller's right to cure in the CESL is much stronger compared to the CISG). See also Schulze, Reiner, and Zoll, Fryderyk, *European Contract Law* (Munich: Beck, 2016), p. 229.

128 Notice that there was critique regarding the fact that there is no right to cure in consumer contracts under the CESL: Schulze, Reiner, and Zoll, Fryderyk, *European Contract Law* (Munich: Beck, 2016), p. 241, footnote 62. The EU Parliament has tried to incorporate this critique in its amendments (see amendment 192) allowing a right to cure in B2C contracts if it concerns 'goods or digital content which are manufactured, produced or modified according to the consumer's specifications or which are clearly personalized'. Criticizing the distinction between B2B and B2C contracts in respect of the right to cure; other differentiations might be more reasonable: Zoll, Fryderyk, 'Article 109' in Schulze, Reiner (ed.), *Common European Sales Law (CESL)* (Munich: Beck, 2012), p. 497. Critical of the very high level of consumer protection: Zöchling-Jud, Brigitta, 'Rechtsbehelfe des Käufers im Entwurf eines Gemeinsamen Europäischen Kaufrechts' in Schmidt-Kessel, Martin (ed.), *Ein einheitliches europäisches Kaufrecht?* (Munich: Sellier, 2012), p. 345 (see also more recently: Zöchling-Jud, Brigitta, 'Art. 106 GEK-E' in Schmidt-Kessel, Martin (ed.), *Der Entwurf für ein Gemeinsames Europäisches Kaufrecht* (Munich: Sellier, 2014), p. 558). Criticism of the fact that there is no right to cure in consumer sales contract if it concerns very specific goods, specially made or personalized for the buyer in Wendehorst, Christiane, 'Rücktritt ("Beeindigung") im Entwurf für ein Gemeinsames Europäisches Kaufrecht' in Schmidt-Kessel, Martin (ed.), *Ein einheitliches europäisches Kaufrecht?* (Munich: Sellier, 2012), p. 381. See also, Feltkamp, Regine, and Vanbossele, Frederic, 'Remedies Under the Optional Common European Sales Law – A Good Alternative for Belgian Sales Law?' in Claeys, Ignace, and Feltkamp, Regine (eds.), *The Draft Common European Sales Law: Towards an Alternative Sales Law?* (Antwerp: Intersentia, 2013), n° 34.

buyer is a trader or a consumer.[129] On the one hand, the hierarchy is quite clear when the buyer is a trader: by introducing the right to cure, the pre-eminence of (specific) performance is confirmed.[130] The debtor has a so-called '*Zweite Chance*' (i.e. a second chance). He cannot, however, remain passive: he has to exercise/invoke his right to cure.[131] Article 109.4 CESL[132] makes clear that the buyer in that situation may *refuse* an offer to cure if: (1) it cannot be done without 'significant inconvenience'; (2) if the buyer has 'reason to believe that the seller's future performance cannot be relied on'; or (3) if the delay in the performance 'would amount to a fundamental non-performance'. On the other hand, if the buyer is a *consumer*, there is *a 'flat' hierarchy* of remedies due to the lack of a seller's right to cure: there is no single 'preferred' remedy.[133] Each remedy can be applied if its

---

[129] Zöchling-Jud, Brigitta, 'Rechtsbehelfe des Käufers im Entwurf eines Gemeinsamen Europäischen Kaufrechts' in Schmidt-Kessel, Martin (ed.), *Ein einheitliches europäisches Kaufrecht?* (Munich: Sellier, 2012), pp. 328 and 343 *et seq*.

[130] Kruisinga, Sonja A., 'The Seller's Right to Cure in the CISG and the Common European Sales Law' in Keirse, Anne L.M., and Loos, Marco B.M. (eds.), *Alternative Ways to Ius Commune* (Cambridge: Intersentia, 2012), p. 159 ('Allowing the seller a right to cure any lack of conformity is in line with the principle of maintaining the contract').

[131] This is different in comparison with the hierarchy of remedies that has been spelled out in the CSD, in which price reduction and termination, as secondary remedies, are only possible in certain situations: Zöchling-Jud, Brigitta, 'Rechtsbehelfe des Käufers im Entwurf eines Gemeinsamen Europäischen Kaufrechts' in Schmidt-Kessel, Martin (ed.), *Ein einheitliches europäisches Kaufrecht?* (Munich: Sellier, 2012), p. 344 (see also more recently: Zöchling-Jud, Brigitta, 'Art. 109 GEK-E' in Schmidt-Kessel, Martin (ed.), *Der Entwurf für ein Gemeinsames Europäisches Kaufrecht* (Munich: Sellier, 2014), p. 572).

[132] The right to cure is provided for in the situations of an early tendered performance and in case performance is not in conformity with the contract: Art. 109 CESL '1. A seller who has tendered performance early and who has been notified that the performance is not in conformity with the contract may make a new and conforming tender if that can be done within the time allowed for performance. 2. In cases not covered by paragraph 1 a seller who has tendered a performance which is not in conformity with the contract may, without undue delay on being notified of the lack of conformity, offer to cure it at its own expense'.

[133] Schulze, Reiner, and Zoll, Fryderyk, *European Contract Law* (Munich: Beck, 2016), p. 251 ('There is no hierarchy of remedies in B-C contracts under the CESL'). See also Schopper, Alexander, 'Verpflichtungen und Abhilfen der Parteien eines Kaufvertrages oder eines Vertrages über die Bereit-stellung digitaler Inhalte (Teil IV CESL-Entwurf)' in Wendehorst, Christiane, and Zöchling-Jud, Brigitta (eds.), *Am Vorabend eines Gemeinsamen Europäischen Kaufrechts* (Vienna: Manzsche Verlags- und Universitätsbuchhandlung, 2012), p. 128; Straetmans, Gert, and Meys, Shana, 'The New Proposals for Directives Concerning Digital Content and Online/ Distance Sales' in Claeys, Ignace, and Evelyne Terryn (eds.), *Digital Content & Distance Sales* (Cambridge: Intersentia, 2017), pp. 334 and 350, Zöchling-Jud, Brigitta, 'Rechtsbehelfe des Käufers im Entwurf eines Gemeinsamen Europäischen Kaufrechts' in Schmidt-Kessel, Martin (ed.), *Ein einheitliches europäisches Kaufrecht?*

individual conditions of application are fulfilled. This actually leads to a higher level of consumer protection[134] in the CESL, compared to the Consumer Sales Directive subordinating price reduction and termination to repair and replacement (see *supra*, para. 10).[135]

28 *Specific performance as remedy*. Furthermore, specific performance is conceived as a 'remedy' for the buyer[136] in Article 110 CESL. Consequently, specific performance is conceived by the drafters as one of the remedies and not as a *right* (such as is the case in e.g. German law).[137] Commentators interpret this as being part of the solution of the drafters trying to reflect the different legal traditions in Europe with regard to specific performance (common and civil law perspectives).[138] Nevertheless, the way in which

---

(Munich: Sellier, 2012), p. 345; Zöchling-Jud, Brigitta, 'Art. 106 GEK-E' in Schmidt-Kessel, Martin (ed.), *Der Entwurf für ein Gemeinsames Europäisches Kaufrecht* (Munich: Sellier, 2014), p. 558. The authors warn that one always has to take into account the 'complex interplay of definitions and the conditions that have to be fulfilled for one or the other remedy': Feltkamp, Regine, and Vanbossele, Frederic, 'Remedies Under the Optional Common European Sales Law – A Good Alternative for Belgian Sales Law?' in Claeys, Ignace, and Feltkamp, Regine (eds.), *The Draft Common European Sales Law: Towards an Alternative Sales Law?* (Antwerp: Intersentia, 2013), n° 12, 32, and 34.

134 For a critique of the total absence of a right to cure in consumer contracts and free choice of consumers between the different remedies, see footnote 128.

135 Schopper, Alexander, 'Verpflichtungen und Abhilfen der Parteien eines Kaufvertrages oder eines Vertrages über die Bereit-stellung digitaler Inhalte (Teil IV CESL-Entwurf)' in Wendehorst, Christiane, and Zöchling-Jud, Brigitta (eds.), *Am Vorabend eines Gemeinsamen Europäischen Kaufrechts* (Vienna: Manzsche Verlags- und Universitätsbuchhandlung, 2012), p. 128 (but critical of this from a law and economics perspective, p. 129).

136 This also includes remedying a defect in the performance free of charge (Art. 110.2 CESL). If the buyer is a consumer, he can choose between repair and replacement, except if the chosen remedy is unlawful or impossible or if – compared to the other option – its costs would be disproportionate to the seller (Art. 111 CESL). See, regarding this relative disproportionality: Schulze, Reiner, and Zoll, Fryderyk, *European Contract Law* (Munich: Beck, 2016), pp. 247–48.

137 Schulze, Reiner, and Zoll, Fryderyk, *European Contract Law* (Munich: Beck, 2016), p. 244. See also: Grädler, Thomas, and Köchel, Manuel, 'Das kaufrechtliche Abhilfenrecht nach dem Kommissionsentwurf für ein Gemeinsames Europäisches Kaufrecht' in Schmidt-Kessel, Martin (ed.), *Ein einheitliches europäisches Kaufrecht?* (Munich: Sellier, 2012), p. 353; Zöchling-Jud, Brigitta, 'Rechtsbehelfe des Käufers im Entwurf eines Gemeinsamen Europäischen Kaufrechts' in Schmidt-Kessel, Martin (ed.), *Ein einheitliches europäisches Kaufrecht?* (Munich: Sellier, 2012), p. 332; Zöchling-Jud, Brigitta, 'Art. 110 GEK-E' in Schmidt-Kessel, Martin (ed.), *Der Entwurf für ein Gemeinsames Europäisches Kaufrecht* (Munich: Sellier, 2014), p. 574; Zoll, Fryderyk, 'Article 106' in Schulze, Reiner (ed.), *Common European Sales Law (CESL)* (Munich: Beck, 2012), p. 491 and Zoll, Fryderyk, 'Article 110' in Schulze, Reiner (ed.), *Common European Sales Law (CESL)* (Munich: Beck, 2012), p. 504.

138 Schulze, Reiner, and Zoll, Fryderyk, *European Contract Law* (Munich: Beck, 2016), pp. 247–248; Zoll, Fryderyk, 'Article 110' in Schulze, Reiner (ed.), *Common European*

Article 110 CESL is constructed – specific performance as the rule unless certain exceptions are applicable – shows that specific performance is considered important under the CESL.[139] Specific performance is only precluded if performance would be (1) impossible or unlawful[140] or (2) if 'the burden or expense of performance would be disproportionate to the benefit that the buyer would obtain'.[141] Due the fact that the seller often has a right to cure (in B2B contracts, see *supra*, para. 27), it can be said that it is also a right for the breaching party.[142] Although specific performance is indeed just 'one' of the remedies listed in Article 106 CESL, this demonstrates the intention of the drafters to stress the importance of the performance of the contract.

29 *Termination restricted.* Moving on to the remedy of termination, as discussed earlier, its application is restricted by the seller's right to cure in B2B contracts. Moreover, it is – in principle – subject to the requirement that the seller's *non-performance* is *fundamental*[143] (Article 114.1 CESL). For B2C contracts, this requirement has been framed differently *in case of a lack of conformity*: a consumer can terminate the contract, 'unless the lack of conformity is *insignificant*' (emphasis added). It is uncertain what the difference between these two requirements is, because contrary to a 'fundamental non-performance', a 'significant non-conformity' has not been defined.[144] However, it seems obvious that a 'fundamental

Sales Law (CESL) (Munich: Beck, 2012), p. 504. Cf. the CESL follows the common law approach: Schopper, Alexander, 'Verpflichtungen und Abhilfen der Parteien eines Kaufvertrages oder eines Vertrages über die Bereit-stellung digitaler Inhalte (Teil IV CESL-Entwurf)' in Wendehorst, Christiane, and Zöchling-Jud, Brigitta (eds.), *Am Vorabend eines Gemeinsamen Europäischen Kaufrechts* (Vienna: Manzsche Verlags- und Universitätsbuchhandlung, 2012), p. 127; Zöchling-Jud, Brigitta, 'Rechtsbehelfe des Käufers im Entwurf eines Gemeinsamen Europäischen Kaufrechts' in Schmidt-Kessel, Martin (ed.), *Ein einheitliches europäisches Kaufrecht?* (Munich: Sellier, 2012), p. 332; Zöchling-Jud, Brigitta, 'Art. 110 GEK-E' in Schmidt-Kessel, Martin (ed.), *Der Entwurf für ein Gemeinsames Europäisches Kaufrecht* (Munich: Sellier, 2014), p. 574.

139 Zoll, Fryderyk, 'Article 110' in Schulze, Reiner (ed.), *Common European Sales Law (CESL)* (Munich: Beck, 2012), p. 504 ('The right to require performance is seen as a principle').

140 About impossibility and illegality, see Schulze, Reiner, and Zoll, Fryderyk, *European Contract Law* (Munich: Beck, 2016), p. 247.

141 Art. 110.3 CESL. See, e.g. Schulze, Reiner, and Zoll, Fryderyk, *European Contract Law* (Munich: Beck, 2016), pp. 247–48.

142 See, for the same reasoning: ibid., p. 229.

143 For the meaning of a 'fundamental non-performance', see Art. 87(2) CESL.

144 See also Schopper, Alexander, 'Verpflichtungen und Abhilfen der Parteien eines Kaufvertrages oder eines Vertrages über die Bereit-stellung digitaler Inhalte (Teil IV CESL-Entwurf)' in Wendehorst, Christiane, and Zöchling-Jud, Brigitta (eds.), *Am Vorabend eines Gemeinsamen Europäischen Kaufrechts* (Vienna: Manzsche Verlags- und Universitätsbuchhandlung, 2012), pp. 134–35 (critical); Schulze, Reiner, and

non-performance' is stricter than a 'significant non-conformity'.[145] In combination with the right to cure in B2B contracts (see *supra*, para. 27),[146] this means that termination is considered the 'ultimate' remedy in B2B contracts, while in B2C contracts termination is more often considered at the same level compared to the other remedies.[147] Moreover, Article 115 CESL prescribes a second way of terminating a contract: if there is *a delay* in delivery, which is not fundamental in itself, the buyer can notify the seller and fix an additional period of time of reasonable length (i.e. a *Nachfrist*). If the seller does not perform within this period of time, the buyer may terminate the contract. This second[148] way of terminating the contract requires, of course, a period in which the seller can still cure, confirming the importance of performance of the contract.[149]

Zoll, Fryderyk, *European Contract Law* (Munich: Beck, 2016), p. 255; Zöchling-Jud, Brigitta, 'Rechtsbehelfe des Käufers im Entwurf eines Gemeinsamen Europäischen Kaufrechts' in Schmidt-Kessel, Martin (ed.), *Ein einheitliches europäisches Kaufrecht?* (Munich: Sellier, 2012), p. 341 (critical). See also Feltkamp, Regine, and Vanbossele, Frederic, 'Remedies Under the Optional Common European Sales Law – A Good Alternative for Belgian Sales Law?' in Claeys, Ignace, and Feltkamp, Regine (eds.), *The Draft Common European Sales Law: Towards an Alternative Sales Law?* (Antwerp: Intersentia, 2013), n° 45; Wendehorst, Christiane, 'Rücktritt ("Beeindigung") im Entwurf für ein Gemeinsames Europäisches Kaufrecht' in Schmidt-Kessel, Martin (ed.), *Ein einheitliches europäisches Kaufrecht?* (Munich: Sellier, 2012), p. 377 (compare this with the requirement that the non-conformity has to be 'minor' in case of termination (rescission) under the CSD; see also Wendehorst, Christiane, 'Art. 114 GEK-E' in Schmidt-Kessel, Martin (ed.), *Der Entwurf für ein Gemeinsames Europäisches Kaufrecht* (Munich: Sellier, 2014), pp. 590–91).

145 Schopper, Alexander, 'Verpflichtungen und Abhilfen der Parteien eines Kaufvertrages oder eines Vertrages über die Bereit-stellung digitaler Inhalte (Teil IV CESL-Entwurf)' in Wendehorst, Christiane, and Zöchling-Jud, Brigitta (eds.), *Am Vorabend eines Gemeinsamen Europäischen Kaufrechts* (Vienna: Manzsche Verlags- und Universitätsbuchhandlung, 2012), p. 134; Schulze, Reiner, and Zoll, Fryderyk, *European Contract Law* (Munich: Beck, 2016), pp. 257–258; Wendehorst, Christiane, 'Art. 114 GEK-E' in Schmidt-Kessel, Martin (ed.), *Der Entwurf für ein Gemeinsames Europäisches Kaufrecht* (Munich: Sellier, 2014), p. 590; Zoll, Fryderyk, 'Article 114' in Schulze, Reiner (ed.), *Common European Sales Law (CESL)* (Munich: Beck, 2012), pp. 518–19.

146 Art. 114.1 *juncto* 109.2 CESL. See also Schopper, Alexander, 'Verpflichtungen und Abhilfen der Parteien eines Kaufvertrages oder eines Vertrages über die Bereit-stellung digitaler Inhalte (Teil IV CESL-Entwurf)' in Wendehorst, Christiane, and Zöchling-Jud, Brigitta (eds.), *Am Vorabend eines Gemeinsamen Europäischen Kaufrechts* (Vienna: Manzsche Verlags- und Universitätsbuchhandlung, 2012), p. 133.

147 Zoll, Fryderyk, 'Article 114' in Schulze, Reiner (ed.), *Common European Sales Law (CESL)* (Munich: Beck, 2012), p. 517.

148 The CESL also foresees termination for anticipated non-performance and inadequate assurance of performance.

149 Zoll, Fryderyk, 'Article 115' in Schulze, Reiner (ed.), *Common European Sales Law (CESL)* (Munich: Beck, 2012), p. 518.

30 *Price reduction*. As discussed earlier, price reduction will be – in principle – subject to the seller's right to cure if the buyer is a trader.[150] This is not the case if the buyer is a consumer. Another requirement, following from the wording of Article 120 CESL, is that the buyer has to '*accept*' the *nonconforming* goods. However, price reduction can be applied in case of a 'non-fundamental' and an 'insignificant' nonconforming performance by the seller.[151] This is in contrast to the remedy of termination, which can only be invoked if the non-performance is 'fundamental'[152] or – in B2C contracts – does not amount to an insignificant lack of conformity (see *supra*, para. 29).[153]

1.5. PRIORITY OF REPAIR AND REPLACEMENT UNDER THE COMMISSION PROPOSALS

31 *After withdrawing the CESL*. After withdrawing the CESL, on 9 December 2015 the Commission issued two new proposals for a directive focused on digital contracts in B2C-relations. One proposed directive covers contracts for online and other distance sales of goods[154] and the other proposed directive covers contracts for the supply of digital content.[155] Since this

---

150 See for detail (and nuances of this requirement): Jansen, Sanne, *Prijsvermindering: remedie tot bijsturing van contracten* (Antwerp: Intersentia, 2015), n° 424. See also: Schmidt-Kessel, Martin, 'Art. 120 GEK-E' in Schmidt-Kessel, Martin (ed.), *Der Entwurf für ein Gemeinsames Europäisches Kaufrecht* (Munich: Sellier, 2014), pp. 606–07.

151 See also Grädler, Thomas, and Köchel, Manuel, 'Das kaufrechtliche Abhilfenrecht nach dem Kommissionsentwurf für ein Gemeinsames Europäisches Kaufrecht' in Schmidt-Kessel, Martin (ed.), *Ein einheitliches europäisches Kaufrecht?* (Munich: Sellier, 2012), pp. 357–58; Schmidt-Kessel, Martin, 'Art. 120 GEK-E' in Schmidt-Kessel, Martin (ed.), *Der Entwurf für ein Gemeinsames Europäisches Kaufrecht* (Munich: Sellier, 2014), n° 13, p. 603; Schulze, Reiner, and Zoll, Fryderyk, *European Contract Law* (Munich: Beck, 2016), p. 262.

152 See Art. 87.2 CESL for a definition of a fundamental non-performance.

153 See Art. 114 CESL. See also Dang Vu, Tâm, 'Remedies in the European Harmonisation Projects: Enforced Performance, Termination and Damages' in Keirse, Anne L.M., and Loos, Marco B.M. (eds.), *Alternative Ways to Ius Commune* (Cambridge: Intersentia, 2012), p. 148.

154 Proposal for a Directive of the European Parliament and of the Council on certain aspects concerning contracts for the online and other distance sales of goods, Brussels 9 December 2015, COM(2015) 635 final, 2015/0288(COD), http://eur-lex.europa.eu/legal-content/EN/TXT/PDF/?uri=CELEX:52015PC0635&from=EN. See also http://www.europarl.europa.eu/oeil/popups/ficheprocedure.do?reference=2015/0288%28COD%29&l=en.

155 Proposal for a Directive of the European Parliament and of the Council on certain aspects concerning contracts for the supply of digital content, Brussels

book focuses on consumer sales contracts and the remedies available to buyers, only the first proposal will be discussed here (hereafter: the 'ODSD proposal').

Recently, the EU Parliament has issued amendments to also include offline sales contracts in the proposal, which would make the current Consumer Sales Directive superfluous (see also *supra*, para. 2). This would counter the critiques that the introduction of a separate directive for online sales contracts would lead to more fragmentation.[156] Of course, this would mean the introduction of a new system for both online and offline sales contracts. Since the proposal aims for full harmonization, this extension would have even more impact on the hierarchy of remedies (see also *infra*, para. 35). On 31 October 2017, the Commission issued a new proposal for a directive, taking into account the critiques about a separate online and offline regime of consumer sales.[157] With regard to the hierarchy of remedies, nothing important changes in comparison with the 2015 ODSD Proposal. Nevertheless, where relevant reference will be made to the newest Commission proposal ('the 2017 Proposal'). For the sake of completeness, it has to be noted that on 22 February 2018, the IMCO committee adopted its report on the proposal (see also *supra*, para. 2). It proposes substantial amendments to the latest Commission proposal.

The IMCO amendments can be briefly summarized as follows.[158] The Directive would again become a minimum harmonization directive. However, many articles would remain under a maximum harmonization regime. This is the case, for example, for the hierarchy of remedies under Article 9 confirming the priority of repair and replacement. Nevertheless,

9 December 2015, COM(2015) 634 final, 2015/0287(COD), http://eur-lex.europa.eu/legal-content/EN/TXT/PDF/?uri=CELEX:52015PC0634&from=EN.

156 EU Parliament Committee on the Internal Market and Consumer Protection, Draft Report on the Proposal for a Directive of the European Parliament and of the Council on certain aspects concerning contracts for the online and other distance sales of goods, 18 November 2016, www.europarl.europa.eu/sides/getDoc.do?pubRef=-//EP//NONSGML+COMPARL+PE-593.817+03+DOC+PDF+V0//EN&language=EN. See also: Milieu Ltd. and Europe Economics, Impact assessment of proposed substantial EP amendments extending the scope of the Commission proposal on online sales of goods to offline sales, presented at the EP IMCO Committee Meeting, 8 June 2017.

157 See also footnote 21: amended Proposal for a Directive of the European Parliament and of the Council on certain aspects concerning contracts for the online and other distance sales of goods, amending Regulation (EC) No 2006/2004 of the European Parliament and of the Council and Directive 2009/22/EC of the European Parliament and of the Council and repealing Directive 1999/44/EC of the European Parliament and of the Council, COM(2017) 637 final.

158 See for detail, http://www.europarl.europa.eu/sides/getDoc.do?type=REPORT&mode=XML&reference=A8-2018-0043&language=EN.

amended Article 3(3) would have a lot of impact on the hierarchy of remedies: 'Notwithstanding paragraph 2, Member States may maintain or introduce, in their national laws, provisions on remedies for "hidden defects" or on a short-term right to reject to ensure a higher level of consumer protection. In the case of Article 8(2a), Member States may maintain more stringent provisions in their national law that are already in force at the date of entry into force of this Directive.' This means that Member States are allowed to maintain or introduce rules on remedies for hidden defects and to maintain or introduce provisions on the consumer's short-term right to reject the goods when non-conforming. This would turn the strict hierarchy of remedies upside down; since the right to terminate could then take precedence over the absolute priority of repair and replacement. The absolute priority of repair and replacement also seems to be weakened by, for example, the rules that price reduction and termination can be invoked if the lack of conformity is of such a serious nature as to justify the immediate price reduction or termination of the contract and if a lack of conformity appears despite the trader's attempt to bring the goods into conformity.

Hereafter, the IMCO amendments will not be discussed further. Instead, an overview of the rules in the 2015 ODSD Proposal and the 2017 Proposal will be provided.

32 *Priority of repair and replacement in the remedial system under the proposed directive.* Article 9 ODSD Proposal (also Article 9 of the 2017 Proposal) enumerates and organizes the consumer's remedies in the case of a lack of conformity with the contract. Article 9 does not follow the CESL approach – which provides for a free choice for the consumer – and reconnects with the Consumer Sales Directive, introducing a hierarchy of remedies,[159] subordinating price reduction and termination to repair and replacement.[160] According to Article 9.3, a consumer only has the

---

159 See also, for the term 'hierarchy of remedies' in this respect: Claeys, Ignace, and Vancoillie, Jonas, 'Remedies, Modification of Digital Content and Right to Terminate Long-Term Digital Content Contracts' in Claeys, Ignace, and Terryn, Evelyne (eds.), *Digital Content & Distance Sales* (Cambridge: Intersentia, 2017), p. 178; Loos, Marco B.M., 'Not Good But Certainly Content: The Proposals For European Harmonisation of Online and Distance Selling of Goods and the Supply of Digital Content' in Claeys, Ignace, and Terryn, Evelyne (eds.), *Digital Content & Distance Sales* (Cambridge: Intersentia, 2017), p. 25; Straetmans, Gert, and Meys, Shana, 'The New Proposals for Directives Concerning Digital Content and Online/Distance Sales' in Claeys, Ignace, and Terryn, Evelyne (eds.), *Digital Content & Distance Sales* (Cambridge: Intersentia, 2017), p. 328.

160 See, regarding the discussion whether or not a free choice between the remedies should be allowed: Explanatory Memorandum ODSD Proposal, Results of ex-post evaluations, stakeholder consultations and impact assessment, p. 9.

right to price reduction or to termination if: (1) repair or replacement would be impossible or unlawful; (2) the seller has not completed repair or replacement within a reasonable time; (3) repair or replacement would cause significant inconvenience to the consumer; or (4)[161] the seller has declared (or it is clear from the circumstances) that he will not bring the goods in conformity within a reasonable time.[162]

This means that the remedies of repair/replacement are the primary remedies and price reduction/termination are secondary remedies, which is also the case under the current Consumer Sales Directive. This means that the seller has actually a 'right to cure', which is thought to balance the consumer's and the seller's interests.[163]

Repair and replacement. Repair and replacement are the primary remedies. The consumer may choose freely between those two remedies (see Article 11 ODSD/2017 Proposal about the consumer's choice), unless his choice is impossible, unlawful, or would impose disproportionate costs to the seller, compared to the other option.[164] In assessing this, one has to take into account every circumstance, and more specifically: (1) the value of the goods if there was no lack of conformity; (2) the significance of the lack of conformity; and (3) whether the other remedy can be completed without significant inconvenience to the consumer. 33

Termination and price reduction. As indicated above, termination and price reduction are considered 'secondary remedies'. However, termination is – contrary to the Consumer Sales Directive – not restricted to a non-minor lack of conformity (see *supra*, para. 16).[165] This is also 34

---

161 The list of situations in which a consumer is entitled to price reduction/termination differs from the one in the CSD (Art. 3.5), by adding a (fourth) possibility 'the seller has declared, or it is equally clear from the circumstances that the seller will not bring the goods in conformity with the contract within a reasonable time' and expressly enumerates the possibility when 'repair or replacement are impossible or unlawful' instead of 'if the consumer is entitled to neither repair or replacement'. All in all, in the present author's opinion, both lists, notwithstanding their differences of wording, have the same aim.

162 See also Claeys, Ignace, and Vancoillie, Jonas, 'Remedies, Modification of Digital Content and Right to Terminate Long-Term Digital Content Contracts' in Claeys, Ignace, and Terryn, Evelyne (eds.), *Digital Content & Distance Sales* (Cambridge: Intersentia, 2017), pp. 186–87.

163 See also ibid., p. 178.

164 The ODSD Proposal and the 2017 Proposal make clear that the proportionality test is only applicable between the two primary remedies, and not between the primary and the secondary remedies. This is the codification of the Weber/Putz-cases of the CJEU (see also footnote 56).

165 See for detail, Smits, Jan, 'The new proposal for harmonised rules for the online sales of tangible goods: conformity, lack of conformity and remedies, Policy Dept C

clearly stated by recital 29 of the preamble of the ODSD/2017 Proposal. This increases consumer protection.[166] Even the CESL required a 'significant' lack of conformity in Article 114.2 CESL (see *supra*, para. 29). Articles 12.2 and 12.3 ODSD/2017 Proposal provide for termination with regard to the contract as a whole or in relation to some of the goods (i.e. partial termination). The only restriction to (partial) termination is the primacy of repair and replacement. If, however, one of the conditions of Article 9 ODSD/2017 Proposal is fulfilled (see *supra*, para. 32), the consumer may terminate the contract. Also, price reduction is only restricted by the primacy of repair and replacement and can be applied by the consumer if one of the conditions of Article 9 is fulfilled. This means that there is no hierarchy between termination and price reduction and that the consumer may choose one of the two remedies.

35 *Full harmonization*. Contrary to the Consumer Sales Directive, which provided for minimum harmonization (allowing Member States to implement more consumer-friendly rules), the ODSD Proposal and the 2017 Proposal provide for full harmonization.[167] This means that Member States would not be able to derogate from this hierarchy of remedies and will have to respect the priority of repair and replacement.[168] This will inevitably decrease the existing level of consumer protection in some Member States (i.e. Member States that have introduced a more favorable choice of remedies for the consumers, see *supra*, para. 11).[169] Moreover, the 2017 Proposal which is to be applied equally to online *and offline* sales contracts, will have an even bigger impact on the hierarchy of remedies.

---

in-depth analysis, PE 536.492', http://www.epgencms.europarl.europa.eu/cmsdata/upload/3f55190a-e9dc-43f0-a977-b7ee0e824485/pe_536.492_en_print.pdf (2016), p. 13.

166 Loos, Marco B.M., 'Not Good But Certainly Content: The Proposals For European Harmonisation of Online and Distance Selling of Goods and the Supply of Digital Content' in Claeys, Ignace, and Terryn, Evelyne (eds.), *Digital Content & Distance Sales* (Cambridge: Intersentia, 2017), p. 23.

167 Art. 3 ODSD Proposal/2017 Proposal.

168 See Explanatory Memorandum ODSD Proposal, 1. Context of the Proposal, p. 3 (see also the 2017 Proposal).

169 Loos, Marco B.M., 'Not Good But Certainly Content: The Proposals For European Harmonisation of Online and Distance Selling of Goods and the Supply of Digital Content' in Claeys, Ignace, and Terryn, Evelyne (eds.), *Digital Content & Distance Sales* (Cambridge: Intersentia, 2017), p. 25; Smits, Jan, 'The new proposal for harmonised rules for the online sales of tangible goods: conformity, lack of conformity and remedies, Policy Dept C in-depth analysis, PE 536.492', http://www.epgencms.europarl.europa.eu/cmsdata/upload/3f55190a-e9dc-43f0-a977-b7ee0e824485/pe_536.492_en_print.pdf (2016), pp. 11 and 16.

Indeed, it will imply an even higher decrease in the existing level of consumer protection in some Member States.[170]

1.6. CONCLUSION ON THE PRIORITY OF REPAIR AND REPLACEMENT

Only one exception to the priority of repair and replacement. When comparing the Consumer Sales Directive, the Consumer Rights Directive (Proposal), the CESL, and the ODSD/2017 Proposal, we can only identify one exception to the rule that specific performance (under the form of repair and replacement by the seller, or the right to cure) is the primary remedy. It is only in the CESL, in B2C contracts, that a consumer will not have to give priority to specific performance. Nevertheless, in the case of the Consumer Sales Directive it has to be stressed that this is only an instrument of minimum harmonization, allowing Member States to introduce a more favorable hierarchy of remedies for consumers (allowing e.g. a free choice between the remedies). 36

The priority of those performance-oriented remedies (specific performance, repair, replacement, and the right to cure) can be explained by the leading principle *pacta sunt servanda*.[171] This principle protects the performance interest of the promise: obligations are binding upon those who have promised them. It is said to be in line with the idea of corrective justice:[172] if a non-performance disturbs the balance between the contractual parties, the law must correct it by giving the injured party an entitlement to performance.[173] Mak also defends the priority of performance-oriented remedies because 'they give a party exactly the performance that he bargained for, instead of damages, which can merely be an approximation of the loss suffered as a result of a defective

170 See also Milieu Ltd. and Europe Economics, Impact assessment of proposed substantial EP amendments extending the scope of the Commission proposal on online sales of goods to offline sales, presented at the EP IMCO Committee Meeting, 8 June 2017, p. 51 *et seq.*

171 Mak, Vanessa, *Performance-oriented Remedies in European Sale of Goods Law* (Oxford: Hart Publishing, 2009), pp. 8 and 48 *et seq.*

172 Weinrib, Ernest J., 'Corrective Justice in a Nutshell', *The University of Toronto Law Journal* (2002), p. 354 ('Among these rights are […] the right to contractual performance in accordance with the mutually consensual exercises of the parties' purposiveness'). See also Weinrib, Ernest J., *Corrective Justice* (Oxford: Oxford University Press, 2012), 368p.

173 Mak, Vanessa, *Performance-oriented Remedies in European Sale of Goods Law* (Oxford: Hart Publishing, 2009), p. 9.

performance'.[174] Moreover, she argues that damages are typically under-compensatory e.g. not protecting the sentimental value of the performance (see also *infra*, para. 53).[175] She also points out that performance-oriented remedies do not necessarily infringe upon the debtor's individual liberty, because he has agreed in the first place to be bound by a contract which can be specifically performed.[176]

Another important aspect is that the priority of specific performance is not absolute.[177] If this were always the case, the other remedies would never be applicable. Repair or replacement are ruled out in case of impossibility or unlawfulness. The application of repair and replacement is also restricted if the seller has not completed repair or replacement within reasonable time or if those remedies would cause significant inconvenience to the consumer; or if it seems that the seller will not bring the goods in conformity within a reasonable time. This implies that, even though repair and replacement are the preferred remedies, an unfettered right to specific performance does not exist in the EU consumer sales acquis.[178]

37 *Termination often restricted by the seriousness of the breach.* The Consumer Sales Directive and the Consumer Rights Directive Proposal both provide that the consumer may only terminate the contract if the lack of conformity is not minor. Even the CESL requires a 'significant' lack of conformity. Nevertheless, the most recent instruments, the ODSD/2017 Proposal – which also allow for partial termination – do not restrict termination to a significant or non-minor lack of conformity.

2. COMMON LAW APPROACH

2.1. GENERAL

38 *No comprehensive set of consumer sales remedies.* The comparison between the EU consumer sales remedial system with the US system

174 Ibid., p. 61.
175 Ibid., pp. 61–3.
176 Ibid., p. 64 *et seq.*
177 See also ibid., p. 9.
178 The limitation of the performance-oriented remedies (in case of impossibility, or (which is not the case in the EU consumer *acquis* in the relation with the secondary remedies) disproportionality) is economically efficient by keeping transaction costs low: ibid., p. 69 *et seq.*

immediately encounters an important difficulty. The EU remedial system is harmonized at the level of consumer sales law. Although there is a body of statutory federal and state law protecting consumer interests in certain areas,[179] there is no comprehensive and separate regulation available with regard to the consumer remedies in case of breach of a sales contract in the US. Therefore, first, the hierarchy of the contractual remedies will be briefly discussed in general common law; next, this will be compared with the remedies for breach under UCC Article 2, applicable to B2B and B2C sales contracts (with some extenuations for consumer sales contracts). Finally, the federal 'Magnuson-Moss Warranty Act'[180] of 1975 will be taken into account, which prescribes minimum requirements of (non-obligatory) warranties when consumer goods are involved. In some situations this Act will provide an alternative set of remedies as compared to the remedies prescribed in UCC Article 2.

2.2. COMMON CONTRACT LAW

2.2.1. *Priority of Damages*

2.2.1.1. Irreparable Injury Rule, Adequacy, Discretion, and Equitable Defenses

Clear hierarchy[181] *giving a privileged position to damages due to the irreparable injury rule.* As mentioned in Chapter 1, the remedy of 'damages' seems to enjoy a privileged position in common law systems 39

179 For federal law, see e.g., Fair Credit Billing Act; Bankruptcy Abuse Prevention and Consumer Protection Act of 2005; Consumer Leasing Act; Fair Packaging and Labeling Act; Home Ownership and Equity Protection Act; Motor Vehicle Information and Cost Savings Act; Restore Online Shopper's Confidence Act, https://www.ftc.gov/enforcement/statutes. See for state law e.g., California Civil Code §§1750 *et seq.* (the 'California Consumers Legal Remedies Act'), the Uniform Deceptive Trade Practices Act (e.g. Illinois or Delaware).

180 See 15 U.S.C. §§2301 *et seq.*

181 Also mentioning a hierarchy between the remedies: Freitheit, Jessica, 'The Breakdown of Hierarchy: Damages at Law versus Damages in Equity', 27 *Man. L.J.* (1999–00), pp. 186–88; Wright, David, 'Discretion with Common Law Remedies', 23 *Adel. L. Rev.* (2002), pp. 243–75 (does not support the current hierarchy of remedies: 'The reluctance of the judiciary to introduce equitable doctrines and remedies into the commercial setting is based on a false belief that the common law is certain and without discretion').

compared to specific performance.[182] The predilection for damages is allegedly rooted in the history of common law and has also been more recently defended on the basis of economic and commercial considerations (see also *infra*, paras. 51 and 53). The rule for choosing among the remedies is the so-called 'irreparable injury rule'. This is also true for contractual remedies.[183] This means that damages are the rule and specific remedies the exception. Only if an 'injury' cannot be adequately[184] repaired by damages, one can call upon the specific remedies (i.e. the 'adequacy test'). In other words, the equitable remedies (i.e. the specific remedies) are not available if legal remedies (such as damages and termination) will adequately repair the breach of contract.[185] Damages are typically not considered adequate in cases in which it is difficult or uncertain to calculate the exact amount of the compensation, e.g. in case of heirlooms, land, and unique goods (see also *infra*, UCC Article 2, paras. 63–64).[186]

40 *Discretionary power of the judge*. The irreparable injury rule, which implies that specific remedies are only granted when damages are inadequate, gives rise to a so-called 'discretionary power' of the judge to grant them.[187] This means that specific performance is not a right to one of

---

[182] See for the US e.g.: Corbin, Arthur Linton, et al., *Corbin on Contracts* (New Providence, San Francisco: Matthew Bender & Co., Inc., 2016), §63.1; Farnsworth, E. Allan, 'Legal Remedies for Breach of Contract', 70 *Colum. L. Rev.* (1970), p. 1156; Hillman, Robert A., *Principles of Contract Law* (St. Paul: West Academic, 2014), p. 207; Perillo, Joseph M., *Contracts* (St. Paul: West Academic, 2014), §16.1; Shoben, Elaine W., 'Of Carts and Horses: Organizing Remedies for the Classroom', 57 *St. Louis U. L.J.* (2012–13), p. 596. See, for more detail on Anglo-Australian Common Law: Musgrave, Thomas D., 'Comparative Contractual Remedies', *U.W. Austl. L. Rev.* (2008–09), pp. 300–72. See, regarding the English-Canadian Common Law: Miller, Lucinda, 'Specific Performance in the Common and Civil Law: Some Lessons for Harmonisation' in Giliker, Paula (ed.), *Re-examining Contract and Unjust Enrichment* (Leiden: Martinus Nijhoff Publishers, 2007), pp. 281–310.

[183] This rule extends beyond contract law, regulating also the hierarchy of remedies in, for example, tort law.

[184] See, regarding this 'adequacy': Corbin, Arthur Linton, et al., *Corbin on Contracts* (New Providence, San Francisco: Matthew Bender & Co., Inc., 2016), §63.7 and .19.

[185] See, for definitions of the 'irreparable injury rule': Laycock, Douglas, 'The Death of the Irreparable Injury Rule', 103 *Harv. L. Rev.* 3 (1990), p. 689.

[186] Fischer, James M., *Remedies* (New Providence, San Francisco: Matthew Bender & Co., Inc., 2014), §21.2.3 and §21.2.8; Murray, John E., *Murray on Contracts* (Durham: Carolina Academic Press, 2011), §128, [B1-2].

[187] See extensively on the discretionary power of the court: Corbin, Arthur Linton, et al., *Corbin on Contracts* (New Providence, San Francisco: Matthew Bender & Co., Inc., 2016), §63.1. See also Ferriell, Jeff, *Understanding Contracts* (New Providence, San Francisco: Matthew Bender & Co., Inc., 2009), p. 869; Fischer, James M., *Remedies*

the parties, but the subject of discretion.[188] Nevertheless, the court is not completely free and cannot exercise its power arbitrarily.[189]

Special defenses against specific remedies (equitable defenses). 41
Closely related to the discretionary power of the judge when deciding upon equitable remedies, such as specific performance, are the special defenses that can be raised against those remedies.[190] When comparing legal and equitable remedies, it has to be noted that more defenses can be raised against applying a specific remedy than against a legal remedy.[191] This means that some defenses are common to both specific and legal remedies (such as inadequacy of consideration) and that some defenses are unique to specific remedies. These are the so-called 'equitable defenses'.[192] Specific enforcement may not e.g. entail disproportionate hardship to the debtor, involve high costs to supervise,[193] or imply prohibitory involuntary service[194] (see also *infra*, 2nd restatement of contract law, para. 44). This also means that courts have more discretion with regard to specific

(New Providence, San Francisco: Matthew Bender & Co., Inc., 2014), §23; Perillo, Joseph M., *Contracts* (St. Paul: West Academic, 2014), §16.7. See also for Australia (esp. with relation to common law remedies): Wright, David, 'Discretion with Common Law Remedies', 23 *Adel. L. Rev.* (2002), pp. 243–75.

188 *Willard v. Tayloe*, 75 U.S. 557, 19 L. Ed. 501 (1870).

189 *Seymour v. Delancy*, 3 Cow. 445 (N.Y. 1824); *Willard v. Tayloe*, 75 U.S. 557, 19 L. Ed. 501 (1870); *Da Silva v. Musso*, 428 N.E.2d 382, 53 N.Y.2d 543 (1981); *Rockland Exposition, Inc. v. Alliance of Auto. Serv. Providers of N.J.*, 2009 U.S. Dist. LEXIS 39931 (S.D.N.Y. 2009).

190 See Dobbs, Dan B., *Law of Remedies* (St. Paul: West Academic, 1993), §12.1(1).

191 In support of broader equitable defenses based on a normative approach, see Yorio, Edward, 'A Defense of Equitable Defenses', 51 *Ohio St. L. J.* (1990), pp. 1201–241. *Contra*: Schwartz, Alan, 'The Case for Specific Performance', *Yale L.J.* (1979), pp. 298–305. See, for an early study of a small sample of cases: Frank, John P., and Endicott, John, 'Defenses in Equity and "Legal Rights"', 14 *La. L. Rev.* (1954), pp. 380–90 (a defeat due to a defense in equity is most likely to be final, which means that no remedy in law is assigned). See also on this: Dobbs, Dan B., *Law of Remedies* (St. Paul: West Academic, 1993), §12.8(5); Fischer, James M., *Remedies* (New Providence, San Francisco: Matthew Bender & Co., Inc., 2014), §20.3.2.

192 On these equitable defenses, see e.g., Corbin, Arthur Linton, et al., *Corbin on Contracts* (New Providence, San Francisco: Matthew Bender & Co., Inc., 2016), §63.1; Ferriell, Jeff, *Understanding Contracts* (New Providence, San Francisco: Matthew Bender & Co., Inc., 2009), pp. 870–74 (without calling it equitable defenses); Knapp, Charles L., *Commercial Damages: A Guide to Remedies in Business Litigation* (New York: Matthew Bender & Co., Inc., 2016), n° 12.09.

193 Often invoked in cases of construction contracts.

194 Based on the 13th amendment to the Constitution of the United States. Often invoked in cases of personal service contracts. See e.g., *American Broadcasting Companies v. Warner Wolf*, 52 N.Y.2d 394 (1981).

relief compared to damages (see also *supra*, para. 40).[195] This influences the position of specific remedies in the hierarchy, and explains their secondary role.

42 *Historical background.* The priority of damages can be explained from a historical perspective.[196] It is important to know that there was a sharp division between the common law courts and the equitable jurisdictions of Chancery in England. In common law, the primary remedy for breach of contract was (and still is) an award of damages.[197] Under the Court of Chancery, a parallel system developed and could provide for equitable relief. Equity provided for two extra remedies: specific performance and a prohibitory or mandatory injunction[198] (specific remedies). However, plaintiffs could only resort to the Court of Chancery – and to the equitable remedies – if the award under common law did not adequately remedy the breach of contract. This means that the remedy of damages was considered the 'normal' remedy and specific remedies the 'exceptional' ones.[199]

---

195 Corbin, Arthur Linton, et al., *Corbin on Contracts* (New Providence, San Francisco: Matthew Bender & Co., Inc., 2016), §63.1.

196 See Berryman, Jeff, 'The Specific Performance Damage Continuum: An Historical Perspective', 17 *Ottawa L. Rev.* (1985), pp. 295–323; Corbin, Arthur Linton, et al., *Corbin on Contracts* (New Providence, San Francisco: Matthew Bender & Co., Inc., 2016), §63.1; Farnsworth, E. Allan, 'Legal Remedies for Breach of Contract', 70 *Colum. L. Rev.* (1970), p. 1151 *et seq.*; Farnsworth, E. Allan, *Farnsworth on Contracts* (New York: Kluwer, 2004), pp. 161–67; Miller, Lucinda, 'Specific Performance in the Common and Civil Law: Some Lessons for Harmonisation' in Giliker, Paula (ed.), *Re-examining Contract and Unjust Enrichment* (Leiden: Martinus Nijhoff Publishers, 2007), p. 291; Murray, John E., *Murray on Contracts* (Durham: Carolina Academic Press, 2011), §128 [A]; Musgrave, Thomas D., 'Comparative Contractual Remedies', *U.W. Austl. L. Rev.* (2008–09), p. 319 *et seq.* (very detailed); Szladits, Charles, 'The Concept of Specific Performance in Civil Law', 4 *Am. J. Comp. L.* (1955), pp. 209–12. See also: Simpson, Alfred W.B., *A History of the Common Law of Contract. The Rise of the Action of Assumpsit* (Oxford: Clarendon Press, 1987), pp. 595–98.

197 The *actio assumpsit* developed during the 16th century, giving relief by way of damages: Szladits, Charles, 'The Concept of Specific Performance in Civil Law', 4 *Am. J. Comp. L.* (1955), p. 209.

198 A prohibitory injunction is an order to the defendant to refrain from doing what he has promised not to do and a mandatory injunction is an order for the defendant to undo what he has done in breach of the contract. See for this definition: Musgrave, Thomas D., 'Comparative Contractual Remedies', *U.W. Austl. L. Rev.* (2008–09), pp. 323–24.

199 See e.g., the resistance of Coke against specific performance (which would be always unjust according to him): Langbein, John H., et al., *History of the Common Law. The Development of Anglo-American Legal Institutions* (New York: Kluwer, 2009), p. 331.

In other words, specific remedies were only granted when damages were considered inadequate, which implied a discretionary power of the judge to grant them. This is how the irreparable injury rule came into existence.

Influence today. Even though both courts fused in the nineteenth century,[200] the irreparable injury rule was so established that courts in all common law jurisdictions are still heavily influenced by this rule. Apart from the clear hierarchy between damages and specific performance, other differences also remain. If a defendant has been compelled to specific performance, he is under the threat of imprisonment for contempt, which is not the case for damages.[201] Furthermore, the remedy of damages, as a common law remedy, still gives rise to a right to a jury trial, which is not always the case for equitable remedies (such as specific performance), at least in federal courts and in most state courts.[202] 43

---

200 See, for the US (starting with Texas in 1845 and New York in 1848 and later on the Federal Rules of Civil Procedure, (1938)): Emmerglick, Leonard J., 'A Century of the New Equity' in Re, Edward D. (ed.), *Selected Essays on Equity* (New York: Oceana, 1955), pp. 53–4; Glenn, Garrard, and Redden, Kenneth R., 'Equity: a Visit to the Founding Fathers' in Re, Edward D. (ed.), *Selected Essays on Equity* (New York: Oceana, 1955), pp. 15–6; Langbein, John H., et al., *History of the Common Law. The Development of Anglo-American Legal Institutions* (New York: Kluwer, 2009), pp. 377–403. See for the UK: Supreme Court of Judicature Act 1873 (36 & 37 Vict. c. 66) and the Supreme Court of Judicature Act 1875 (38 & 39 Vict. c. 77); Miller, Lucinda, 'Specific Performance in the Common and Civil Law: Some Lessons for Harmonisation' in Giliker, Paula (ed.), *Re-examining Contract and Unjust Enrichment* (Leiden: Martinus Nijhoff Publishers, 2007), p. 291.

201 See e.g., Ferriell, Jeff, *Understanding Contracts* (New Providence, San Francisco: Matthew Bender & Co., Inc., 2009), p. 856. See also Dobbs, Dan B., *Law of Remedies* (St. Paul: West Academic, 1993), §2.8.

202 See the 7th Amendment of the US Constitution: 'In suits at common law, where the value in controversy shall exceed twenty dollars, the right of trial by jury shall be preserved, and no fact tried by a jury, shall be otherwise reexamined in any court of the United States, than according to the rules of the common law'. See also Federal Rules of Civil Procedure F.R.C.P. 38(a). See also *Dairy Queen v. Wood*, 369 U.S. 469 82 S.Ct. 894, 8 L.Ed.2d 44 (1962) ('Where both legal and equitable issues are presented in a single case, any legal issues for which a trial by jury is timely and properly demanded must be submitted to a jury.'). See Dobbs, Dan B., *Law of Remedies* (St. Paul: West Academic, 1993), §2.6(2) (also on state exemptions) and Authenticated U.S. Government Information, 'Seventh Amendment', https://www.gpo.gov/fdsys/pkg/GPO-CONAN-REV-2014/pdf/GPO-CONAN-REV-2014-10-8.pdf (2014), pp. 1684–86. See also for California: *Walton v. Walton*, 31 Cal. App. 4th 277 (1995). See also, for more detail on other States: Pound Civil Justice Institute, 2011 Forum for State Appellate Court Judges, 'The Jury Trial Implosion: The Decline of Trial by Jury and Its Significance for Appellate Courts': http://www.poundinstitute.org/sites/default/files/docs/2011%20judges%20forum/2011%20Forum%20State%20Jury%20Trial%20Provisions.pdf.

The previous paragraph made clear that historical factors were very influential in confining specific performance (or other equitable remedies) to special cases. Indeed, the fact that the Court of Chancery only granted specific relief to remedy the deficiencies in the common law system led to the development of the adequacy test. It also explains why equitable relief is discretionary. The Chancellor had to act according to his conscience and could take into account moral considerations.[203] Another reason to prefer damages over specific performance is merely practical. It can be, in some circumstances, difficult to oblige the promisor to fulfill his promise or to supervise whether the promisor is correctly performing his obligation.[204]

Dobbs argues that some of the previously cited aspects – the discretionary power of the judge, contempt of court sanctions, and the non-existence of a jury trial – which he calls 'equity's dangerous powers', also explain the secondary rank of specific remedies.[205]

44 *2nd restatement of contract law.* Finally, it has to be noted that the 2nd restatement of contract law of 1981[206] explicitly treats the relation between damages and specific remedies such as specific performance and injunction.[207] §359 clearly states that specific performance or injunctions are subject to the irreparable injury rule: 'Specific performance or an injunction will not be ordered if damages would be adequate to protect the expectation interest of the injured party'.[208] Moreover, §357 and §359 stress the importance of the discretion of the courts in their decision to grant a specific remedy. Nevertheless, the comments of §359 acknowledge that there is a tendency to liberalize the granting of equitable relief, a tendency that has been encouraged by the adoption of the UCC (see *infra*, para. 63). The comments end wisely with the following words: 'the modern approach

---

203 Farnsworth, E. Allan, *Farnsworth on Contracts* (New York: Kluwer, 2004), p. 165.

204 Ibid., pp. 165–66.

205 Dobbs, Dan B., *Law of Remedies* (St. Paul: West Academic, 1993), p. 205.

206 2nd restatement of contract law of 1981 by the American Law Institute (restatements are only persuasive authorities, not binding authorities; however the contract restatements are highly influential in courts).

207 See for the interpretation of the 1st and the 2nd restatement of contract law with regard to the irreparable injury-rule: Linzer, Peter, 'On the Amorality of Contract Remedies – Efficiency, Equity, and the Second *Restatement*', *Colum. L. Rev.* (1981), p. 120 *et seq*.

208 See also: Introductory note to Chapter 16, 2nd restatement of contract law, p. 100 ('and specific performance has not been granted where compensation in damages is an adequate substitute for the injured party').

is to compare remedies to determine which is more effective in serving the ends of justice'.

On the one hand, §360 enlists different (non-limitative) factors affecting the adequacy of damages: (1) the difficulty of proving damages; (2) the difficulty of procuring suitable substitute performance when receiving damages; (3) the difficulties in collecting an award of damages. On the other hand, §§364 *et seq.* treat the circumstances in which specific relief cannot be granted: in situation where it would (1) be unfair because of a mistake, unreasonable hardship or gross inadequacy; or (2) be contrary to public policy; or (3) be a disproportionate burden for the court to supervise[209] or enforce; or (4) imply performance of a promise to render personal service.

Decisive factors in deciding which remedy should be applied. Different 45
factors that might influence the adequacy test and tilt it in favor of one or the other type of remedies (remedies in law or in equity) have been discussed earlier. It might be helpful to sum up those factors, as shown in Table 1.

Table 1. Decisive factors in deciding which remedy should be applied

Money damages	Specific performance/injunction
+ (pro)	+ (pro)
– Many substitutes available. – When specific performance is difficult to administer or to supervise[210] (often found in the case of construction contracts).	– Few substitutes available, uniqueness, such as heirlooms or works of art (see also *infra*, discussing art. 2 UCC).[211]

(continued)

[209] In a civil law system these 'monitoring' difficulties are solved by the mechanism of the '*astreinte*' ('*dwangsom*') which is an order to perform under the threat of the payment of a certain sum of money per day, month, or year's delay in performance. See also Mak, Vanessa, *Performance-oriented Remedies in European Sale of Goods Law* (Oxford: Hart Publishing, 2009), p. 104.

[210] Farnsworth, E. Allan, *Farnsworth on Contracts* (New York: Kluwer, 2004), pp. 184–85, §12.7 (although more modern jurisprudence is less reluctant to use specific performance, specifying that the difficulty of enforcement is often exaggerated: *Grayson-Robinson Stores Inc. v. Iris Constr. Corp.*, 8 N.Y.2d 133, 168 N.E.2d 377 (1960). See also Dobbs, Dan B., *Law of Remedies* (St. Paul: West Academic, 1993), §12.8(3); Ferriell, Jeff, *Understanding Contracts* (New Providence, San Francisco: Matthew Bender & Co., Inc., 2009), pp. 865–66 (with regard to service contracts); Fischer, James M., *Remedies* (New Providence, San Francisco: Matthew Bender & Co., Inc., 2014), §24.

[211] Farnsworth, E. Allan, *Farnsworth on Contracts* (New York: Kluwer, 2004), pp. 175–76, §12.6; Perillo, Joseph M., *Contracts* (St. Paul: West Academic, 2014), §16.3.

Table 1 *continued*

Money damages	Specific performance/injunction
- Contract involves personal services.[212] - Indefinite contracts entailing too much uncertainty allow the scope of the performance to be determined.[215] - Specific performance entailing e.g. disproportionate hardship to the debtor (and 'unfairness').[216] - Specific performance is against public policy.[218] - Inability to specifically perform: impossibility.[219]	- No risk of over- or under-compensation.[213] - Contracts involving land.[214] - Insolvency of the promisor (under some circumstances, does not treat the other creditors unequally).[217] - Damages are difficult to prove.

Source: Compiled by the author.

46 *Landmark cases on the irreparable injury rule.* Some frequently cited cases seem indeed to prefer damages above specific remedies:[220]

The *Sadat v. American Motors Corp.* case is a very striking case, which ties into the heart of the consumer sales domain (for the Magnuson-Moss

---

212 Taking into account the 13th Amendment to the Constitution prohibiting involuntary servitude. See also: Dobbs, Dan B., *Law of Remedies* (St. Paul: West Academic, 1993), §12.8(3); Farnsworth, E. Allan, *Farnsworth on Contracts* (New York: Kluwer, 2004), pp. 185–86, §12.7; Perillo, Joseph M., *Contracts* (St. Paul: West Academic, 2014), §16.5. See nuanced (distinguishing between unique and non-unique services and personal services (specific performance of the latter is prohibited, but an injunction might be a solution)) Ferriell, Jeff, *Understanding Contracts* (New Providence, San Francisco: Matthew Bender & Co., Inc., 2009), p. 865.

213 Farnsworth, E. Allan, *Farnsworth on Contracts* (New York: Kluwer, 2004), pp. 174–75, §12.6.

214 Ibid., pp. 176–77, §12.6; Ferriell, Jeff, *Understanding Contracts* (New Providence, San Francisco: Matthew Bender & Co., Inc., 2009), pp. 860–62; Perillo, Joseph M., *Contracts* (St. Paul: West Academic, 2014), §16.2.

215 Dobbs, Dan B., *Law of Remedies* (St. Paul: West Academic, 1993), §12.8(3); Farnsworth, E. Allan, *Farnsworth on Contracts* (New York: Kluwer, 2004), pp. 181–82, §12.7. *Cf.* also Fischer, James M., *Remedies* (New Providence, San Francisco: Matthew Bender & Co., Inc., 2014), §171.

216 Dobbs, Dan B., *Law of Remedies* (St. Paul: West Academic, 1993), §12.8(4).

217 Farnsworth, E. Allan, *Farnsworth on Contracts* (New York: Kluwer, 2004), pp. 179–80, §12.6; Perillo, Joseph M., *Contracts* (St. Paul: West Academic, 2014), §16.4.

218 Farnsworth, E. Allan, *Farnsworth on Contracts* (New York: Kluwer, 2004), pp. 188–89, §12.7.

219 See e.g. Fischer, James M., *Remedies* (New Providence, San Francisco: Matthew Bender & Co., Inc., 2014), §172.

220 See e.g. also *Wiles v. Wiles*, 134 W. Va. 81, 58 S.E. 2nd 601 (1950) (dismissing an injunction against the sale of goods and the trespass of land of the plaintiff by the defendant, based on the irreparable injury rule); *Northern Indiana Public Service Co. v. Carbon County Coal Co.*, 799 F.2d 265 (7th Cir. 1986) (see for a law and economics reasoning by judge Posner).

Warranty Act, see *infra*, paras. 73–74).[221] The dealer of the defendant failed seven times in repairing the car of the plaintiff, which was fully warranted. The plaintiff sued for an injunction to deliver a new car based on §§104(a)(4) *juncto* 110(d) Magnuson-Moss Warranty Act. But the court dismissed it because the plaintiff failed to *allege* that there was irreparable harm and that damages were an inadequate remedy. The court first clarified that §104(a)(4) merely gave rise to an election between a refund or a replacement and not to injunctive relief. Subsequently, the court held that a complaint for injunctive relief could not be based upon §110(d)(1) – providing for both legal and equitable relief – of the Magnuson-Moss Warranty Act if the plaintiff did not demonstrate the traditional irreparable injury rule and an inadequate remedy at law.[222]

Another case is *City Center One Associates v. Teacher Insurance & Annuity Association*.[223] This case is about a contract to borrow money. The court had to decide whether the lender was entitled to specific performance requiring the other party to borrow the agreed amount. It should also be noted that the lender's interest did not exist solely of interest on the loan but also in an expected return that included a share of the profits in the real estate that would be acquired with the said loans. The court began its reasoning by stating that specified specific performance was only an appropriate remedy where legal remedies are inadequate. A legal remedy is deemed to be inadequate in two situations: (1) where the benefit for which specific performance was sought was unique; or (2) where relief in the form of damages was not capable of estimation. The court noted that these conditions were not present, considering that the only harm which the lender suffered was solely pecuniary and fully compensable in damages. Therefore, the court dismissed the action for specific performance. Nevertheless, it has to be noted that the envisaged share of profits by the lender is to be considered difficult to estimate, which makes a damage award inadequate.[224] This case clearly shows the 'the common law reluctance to order specific performance'.[225]

---

221 *Sadat v. American Motors Corp.*, 104 Ill. 2nd 105, 470 N.E. 2nd 997 (1984).

222 Not in agreement: Laycock, Douglas, 'The Death of the Irreparable Injury Rule', 103 *Harv. L. Rev.* 3 (1990), p. 725 (he criticizes this case because it would *de facto* repeal the statute, which was especially conceived to protect consumers against the ineffectiveness of contractual damage remedies).

223 *City Center One Associates v. Teacher Insurance & Annuity Association*, 656 F. Supp. 658 (D. Utah 1987).

224 Laycock, Douglas, 'The Death of the Irreparable Injury Rule', 103 *Harv. L. Rev.* 3 (1990), p. 724.

225 See *City Center One Associates v. Teacher Insurance & Annuity Association*, 656 F. Supp. 658 (1987), U.S. Dist. LEXIS 2627 at 662.

In other cases, the hurdle of the irreparable injury rule and the inadequacy rule was overcome.

In *Walgreen Co. v. Sara Creek Property Co.*,[226] Walgreen asked for an injunction to prevent Sara Creek letting an important premise in a mall to another pharmacy. Walgreen operated a pharmacy in the same mall and rented these premises from Sara Creek. In the lease contract there was a clause stating that Sara Creek promised not lease a premise in the mall to someone else who wanted to operate a pharmacy. After many years one of the most important tenants of Sara Creek had to close its store in the mall and Sara Creek intended to lease this spot to a 'deep discount' pharmacy chain (Phar-Mor). (Walgreen was just a discount chain.) Walgreen sued for breach of contract and wanted to stop Sara Creek from leasing the premises to Phar-Mor by asking for an injunction. Judge Posner, after a lengthy law and economics assessment (see also *infra*, para. 53), concluded that the first judge did not exceed his bounds of reasonable judgement in concluding that specific performance was the appropriate remedy. He could assess that the costs of damages would be higher than the costs of an injunction. Posner considered that: 'the determination of Walgreen's damages would have been costly in forensic resources and inescapably inaccurate', justifying the view that damages ought to be considered inadequate in this case.

2.2.1.2. Critique on the Irreparable Injury Rule

47 *Chafee's criticism of the barrier between law and equity.* In 1995, Chafee had already expressed his wish that the fusion of law and equity should be more 'thorough' than it was at that time. He considered the barrier between equity and common law remedies more and more as a fiction.[227]

---

226 *Walgreen Co. v. Sara Creek Property Co.*, 966 F.2d 273 (7th Cir. 1992).

227 Chafee, Zechariah, 'Foreword' in Re, Edward D. (ed.), *Selected Essays on Equity* (New York: Oceana, 1955), iv ('How absurd for us to go on until the year 2000 obliging judges and lawyers to climb over a barrier which was put up by historical accident in 14th century England and built higher by the eagerness of three extinct courts to keep as much business as possible in their own hands, so that these hands might be full of fees!'). See also Dawson, John P., 'Specific Performance in France and Germany', 57 *Mich. L. Rev.* (1959), pp. 532 and 538 (criticizes the restrictions upon specific performance in US law specifically in the area of promises to 'give' ('as to any physical object that can be found and is reachable by direct execution')); Van Hecke, M.T., 'Changing Emphases in Specific Performance', 40 *N.C.L. Rev.* (1961–62), pp. 1–22 (with special attention to the sale of corporate stocks, the sale of a business, output and requirement contracts, personal services and contracts for building and construction); Wright, Charles Alan, 'The Law of Remedies as a Social Institution', 18 *U. Det. L.J.* (1955), pp. 377–78 and 382.

Linzer inferred from case law in 1981 that courts were increasingly eager to apply equitable remedies such as specific performance in contracts.[228]

Laycock's 'death of the irreparable injury rule'. In the early 1990s, Laycock vigorously defended the invalidity of the irreparable injury rule, which is the consequence of the barrier between law and equity.[229] He surveyed more than 1,400 cases and concluded that the irreparable injury rule 'almost never affects the results of cases'. He stated that the plaintiff often got the remedy he requested. If the court did not honor the plaintiff's choice, there was almost always another explanation for the rejection than the irreparable injury rule. Therefore, he proposed abolition of the irreparable injury rule and suggested a statute by Congress as most promising solution.[230] The main idea is that there would be *no preset hierarchy of remedies*, such as the irreparable injury rule implies. He hoped that the abolishment of the irreparable injury rule would mean that there would be 'continued judicial development of the real reasons for remedial choices under the rubric of appropriateness'.[231] 48

Doctrinal reactions upon Laycock's views. The first reactions to Laycock's book were mixed. Many applauded the fact that Laycock made clear that the irreparable injury rule could not explain all current case law.[232] However, some authors were not that enthusiastic.[233] Shreve's reaction to Laycock's book points out that by declaring 'the death' of the irreparable injury rule Laycock is misleading his readers.[234] He agrees with 49

228 Linzer, Peter, 'On the Amorality of Contract Remedies – Efficiency, Equity, and the Second *Restatement*', *Colum. L. Rev.* (1981), p. 126 *et seq.*

229 Laycock, Douglas, 'The Death of the Irreparable Injury Rule', 103 *Harv. L. Rev.* 3 (1990), pp. 687–771; Laycock, Douglas, *The Death of the Irreparable Injury Rule* (New York: Oxford University Press, 1991), 356p.

230 He proposes the following statute: 'The existence of another adequate remedy does not preclude a final judgement of injunction, specific performance, or other equitable relief, in cases where such relief is appropriate'.

231 Laycock, Douglas, 'The Death of the Irreparable Injury Rule', 103 *Harv. L. Rev.* 3 (1990), p. 771.

232 See e.g. Knapp, Charles L., *Commercial Damages: A Guide to Remedies in Business Litigation* (New York: Matthew Bender & Co., Inc., 2016), p. 12.02, after footnote 81 (defends the idea of a rebuttable presumption of a right to specific performance).

233 Comp. Rendleman, Doug, 'Irreparability Irreparably Damaged', 90 *Mich. L. Rev.* (1991–92), pp. 1642–71 (agrees with Laycock's main theme that the irreparability rule has become obsolete; but vigorously criticizes the fact that he does not emphasize the important difference between personal orders (with a unique concentration of power) and compensation).

234 Shreve, Gene R., 'Book Review. The Premature Burial of the Irreparable Injury Rule', 70 *Tex. L. Rev.* (1992), pp. 1063–72.

the fact that the plaintiff should be the 'judge' of the remedy he chooses and of the adequacy of damage remedy and that often rules other than the irreparable injury rule explain a denial of the judge to respect the plaintiff's choice of an equitable remedy. But he also stresses that even Laycock has to admit that the irreparable injury rule is very alive in cases for preliminary relief and that damages are indeed – as stated in Laycock's attempt of a restatement – more appropriate in cases if permanent specific relief (1) causes disproportional hardship on the defendant; (2) causes a disproportional harm to innocent third parties; and (3) if the relief would be disproportionally impractical for a court to implement or supervise. Rather than being a book that announces the actual dead of the irreparable injury rule, Shreve is of the opinion that the book makes progress towards the goal of clarifying the organization of remedies.[235] Nonetheless, most authors believe that Laycock made an important point and are of the opinion that equitable exceptionalism has to be rejected.[236]

2.2.1.3. Arguments Pro and Contra the Irreparable Injury Rule

50 *Pro: the general purpose of remedies in common law is not compulsion but redress.* The preference of damages over specific performance can firstly be explained by the general purpose that remedies serve in common contract law. EU consumer law and civil law systems have often designed contractual remedies in such a way as to compel the promisor to perform the contract (*pacta sunt servanda*). In contrast, the whole idea of contract remedies under common law is merely to encourage promisees to rely on the promises of a promisor instead of compelling the promisor to perform.[237] This has even been explicitly articulated in the introduction to contract remedies in the 2nd restatement of contract law.[238] This is a

---

235 Ibid., p. 1072.

236 See e.g.: Anenson, T. Leigh, 'Treating Equity Like Law: A Post-Merger Justification of Unclean Hands', 45 *Am. Bus. L.J.* (2008), p. 509; Laycock, Douglas, 'The Triumph of Equity', 56 *Law & Contemp. Probs.* (1993), p. 53 *et seq.*; Roberts, Caprice L., 'The Restitution Revival and the Ghosts of Equity', 68 *Wash. & Lee L. Rev.* (2011), p. 1060.

237 Holmes, Oliver W., 'The Path of the Law', *Harv. L. Rev.* (1897), p. 462. See also Farnsworth, E. Allan, 'Legal Remedies for Breach of Contract', 70 *Colum. L. Rev.* (1970), p. 1147; Farnsworth, E. Allan, *Farnsworth on Contracts* (New York: Kluwer, 2004), pp. 148–56.

238 Introductory note to Chapter 16, 2nd restatement of contract law, p. 100 ('The traditional goal of the law of contract remedies has not been compulsion of the promisor to perform his promise but compensation of the promise for the loss resulting from breach' [...] 'and specific performance has not been granted where compensation in damages is an adequate substitute for the injured party'). See also Farnsworth, E. Allan, *Farnsworth on Contracts* (New York: Kluwer, 2004), pp. 148–56.

system not aiming at compulsion, but merely at redress (which is assured by protecting the expectation interests of the injured party). The system celebrates the freedom to make contracts but also to break them. This means that the damages remedy – aiming to compensate in the first place the expectation interests of the injured party – is considered to fulfill the general purpose of the remedial system.[239] Hence, specific performance often seems to be 'a bridge too far', and not absolutely necessary to obtain the general purpose of the remedies. These considerations can thus explain the subordinate place of specific performance compared to damages in the US system.[240]

Pro: commercial considerations and economic design. Authors point to 51
an important historical element that can explain the irreparable injury rule. Because access to courts was often limited to the wealthiest people of society, the courts often had to deal with commercial parties. In this commercial context of litigation, contract law developed in a way that the priority of damages was confirmed.[241] However, one author correctly points out that this assumption cannot always be extrapolated to the consumer law context.[242]

According to Farnsworth, the priority of damages can also be explained by the free enterprise economy.[243] In contrast to communist countries, which have a planned economy, a free enterprise economy will always ensure that substitutes are freely available. This explains the preference for damages (a substitutional remedy) above specific relief, whereas in communist countries[244] promisees have a vital interest in specific

239 Holmes, Oliver W., 'The Path of the Law', *Harv. L. Rev.* (1897), p. 462 ('The duty to keep a contract at common law means a prediction that you must pay damages if you do not keep it, – and nothing else. [...] But such a mode of looking at the matter stinks in the nostrils of those who thing it advantageous to get as much ethics into the law as they can').

240 See also Farnsworth, E. Allan, *Farnsworth on Contracts* (New York: Kluwer, 2004), p. 159 (this general purpose of remedies under common contract law is underpinned and supported by the law and economics analysis, taking into account the theory of efficient breach: 'Since the goal is compensation and not compulsion, the promisor who could have performed, but chose not to for financial reasons, should not be dealt with harshly'); Holmes, Oliver W., 'The Path of the Law', *Harv. L. Rev.* (1897), p. 462.

241 Miller, Lucinda, 'Specific Performance in the Common and Civil Law: Some Lessons for Harmonisation' in Giliker, Paula (ed.), *Re-examining Contract and Unjust Enrichment* (Leiden: Martinus Nijhoff Publishers, 2007), p. 291 *in fine.*

242 Ibid., p. 292.

243 Farnsworth, E. Allan, 'Legal Remedies for Breach of Contract', 70 *Colum. L. Rev.* (1970), pp. 1151, 1155 and 1216.

244 See Grossfeld, Bernhard, 'Money Sanctions for Breach of Contract in a Communist Economy', *Yale L.J.* (1963), p. 1331.

performance because substitutes will not always be readily available. However, to systematically align civil law systems – often favoring specific performance – with communist economies seems a bridge too far.

52 *Pro and contra: moral approach, considering fairness and justice.* The influence of 'morality' – which is the main justification[245] for favoring specific performance in civil law countries – is being recognized as an important argument to prefer either *damages* or *specific performance.*[246]

Moral arguments have, for example, been invoked in favor of damages. Taibleson defends the rational underpinning of the preference for damages over specific performance. He first establishes that damages are more lenient than specific performance and that people prefer to have more lenient penalties, such as damages, imposed on them. Secondly, he asserts that contract breachers are imperfect decision makers and must be treated in a *fair* way.[247] From this follows that judges are inclined to prefer damages over specific performance because it is *fairer* towards contract breachers.[248] In sum, he invokes a moral argument – fairness – to prefer one remedy over the other.

On the other hand, over the years many authors have invoked moral arguments in favor of specific performance.[249] They argue that if someone

245 See e.g. Herman, Shael, 'Specific Performance: A Comparative Analysis', *Edin. L.R.* 7 (2003), pp. 5–26 and 194–217 (referring to the *pacta sunt servanda* principle and morality); Musgrave, Thomas D., 'Comparative Contractual Remedies', *U.W. Austl. L. Rev.* (2008–09), pp. 300–72.

246 See also Introductory Note to Chapter 16, 2nd restatement of contract law, p. 100 ('This traditional response is not without its shortcomings. Its focus on the pecuniary aspects of breach fails to take account of notions of the sanctity of contract and the resulting moral obligation to honor one's promises').

247 See, for the same argument, Yorio, Edward, 'In Defense of Money Damages for Breach of Contract', 82 *Colum. L. Rev.* (1982), pp. 1372–76 (the court balances the interests of the promisee, the promisor and the court, concerned with a fair outcome, not only for the promisee but also for the promisor).

248 Taibleson, B., 'Forgiving Breach: Understanding the Preference for Damages over Specific Performance', 27 *Quinnipiac L. Rev.* (2009), pp. 541–77.

249 Shiffrin, Seana V., 'The Divergence of Contract and Promise', 120 *Harv. L. Rev.* (2007), pp. 722–23 ('If contract law ran parallel to morality, then contract law would – as the norms of promises do – require that promisors keep their promises as opposed merely to paying off their promisees'). *Contra* (invoking morality as the explanation for the compensation of expectation interests (and not specific performance)) Fried, Charles, *Contract as Promise* (Cambridge: Harvard University Press, 1981), p. 17 ('If I make a promise to you, I should do as I promise; and if I fail to keep my promise, it is fair that I should be made to hand over the equivalent of the promised performance'). See also later, (while answering the critique 'that if promise really were at the heart of contract, then a promisor would be held to perform his exact undertaking – perhaps by a decree of specific performance or by the imposition of punitive damages': Fried, Charles,

promises something, the other party has the right to get what he bargained for (the *pacta sunt servanda* rule). Therefore, specific performance is the preferred remedy.

Pro & contra: law and economics. The irreparable injury rule, and the resulting priority of damages, is also defended *and* questioned by utilitarian theories[250] – emerging by the end of the 1970s in the US – using an economic analysis of contract law.[251] The most famous scholars of this 'law and economics' movement were Coase, Director, Posner, Friedman, Calabresi, and Epstein. They were often referred to as the 'Chicago School', despite the fact that, for example, Calabresi was a Yale graduate. 53

The law and economics theory aims to maximize wealth by promoting economically efficient rules. This means that, according to this theory, legal rules ought to be economically efficient to be good and sound law.[252] By choosing for efficiency when analyzing private law, another policy value, (re)distribution is most of the time rejected as an approach towards private law.[253] This theory starts from the so-called *homo oeconomicus*: a rational creature who satisfies his needs in the most efficient way. Notwithstanding the claim of law and economists that their framework is 'value-neutral', objective, and scientific, their choice for efficiency reflects a deep policy choice. When applying the law and economics methods, this is not done in a cultural and political vacuum. Indeed, it can be argued that 'economics

---

'Contract as Promise Thirty Years On', XLV *Suffolk U. L. Rev.* (2012), p. 967 *et seq.*). See also: Gold, Andrew S., 'A Moral Rights Theory of Private Law', 52 *Wm. & Mary L. Rev.* (2011), p. 1925 *et seq.* (p. 1926: 'The key insight is to see that, even in cases in which there is a remedial duty to perform, this does not automatically mean the promisee has a moral right to require performance. The move from moral duties to legitimate coercive responses is context dependent').

250 For both perspectives in US law and economics, see the Dutch author: Visscher, Louis, 'De rangorde van remedies voor wanprestatie: subsidiariteit en proportionaliteit versus efficiëntie', *NTBR* (2007), n° 4.

251 See also, for an author that concludes that 'cover' or 'virtual specific performance' (meaning that the promisee purchases the good/service that was promised on the market and then gets money for it) is the most preferred remedy, and if this is not possible, actual specific performance is to be preferred (except if a special moral, policy or experiential proposition suggests otherwise): Eisenberg, Melvin A., 'Actual and Virtual Specific Performance, the Theory of Efficient Breach, and the Indifference Principle in Contract Law', 93 *Calif. L. Rev.* (2005), pp. 1041–50.

252 The law and economic movement started mainly at the University of Chicago, Yale Law School and Harvard Law School. See extensively, e.g., Cooter, Robert, and Ulen, Thomas, S., *Law and Economics* (Boston: Addison-Wesley, 2016), 555p.

253 See e.g. Cooter, Robert, and Ulen, Thomas, S., *Law and Economics* (Boston: Addison-Wesley, 2016), p. 7; Posner, Richard A., 'Law and Economics is Moral', 24 *Valparaiso U. L. Rev.* (1990), p. 167.

assumes a point of view'.[254] In US jargon, the main political ideology behind this reasoning is called 'libertarianism'.[255] The term 'libertarianism' has to be understood as someone who values his individual liberties as the highest good and wishes to avoid interference from the government.[256] Against this background, economic theory is used to figure out what this minimal state can do to correct market failures in a free market.[257] This 'optimal minimal government' should, as a consequence, only promote rules that are economically efficient and wealth maximizing. However, the so-called 'critical legal studies' movement formulated a critique against this point of view.[258] According to this movement, there is no such a thing as an 'efficient' rule or code in the real world (the dream of law and economics scholars). Moreover, according to the critical legal studies movement, mainstream law and economics underestimate the redistribution of wealth and income through private law.[259] Other critiques have also been raised against the law and economics theory.[260] The theory does not take into account the moral and cultural values of different societies, human flourishing, human rights, value choices, etc. Scholars also questioned the objectivity and scientific value of the law and economics theory. In addition, law and economics scholars have – among themselves – never agreed about the efficiency of the irreparable injury rule.

It has to be noted that the law and economics analysis has not been so well received in continental Europe compared to the US.[261] Sibony and

254 Driesen, David M., and Malloy, Robin Paul, 'Critiques of Law and Economics', *SSRN, Working Paper* (2015), p. 10.

255 See for the US Posner, who called himself a proponent of libertarianism: Posner, Richard A., 'Law and Economics is Moral', 24 *Valparaiso U. L. Rev.* (1990), p. 165.

256 See Merriam-Webster Dictionary: https://www.merriam-webster.com.

257 Posner, Richard A., 'Law and Economics is Moral', 24 *Valparaiso U. L. Rev.* (1990), p. 166.

258 See e.g. Kelman, Mark, 'Consumption Theory, Production Theory, and Ideology in the Coase Theorem', 52 *S. Cal. L. Rev.* (1979), pp. 669–98; Kennedy, Duncan, 'Law-and-Economics from the Perspective of Critical Legal Studies' in Newman, Peter (ed.), *The New Palgrave Dictionary of Economics and the Law* (Macmillan), pp. 464–75.

259 Kennedy, Duncan, 'Law-and-Economics from the Perspective of Critical Legal Studies' in Newman, Peter (ed.), *The New Palgrave Dictionary of Economics and the Law* (Macmillan), p. 472.

260 See, for detailed critiques: Driesen, David M., and Malloy, Robin Paul, 'Critiques of Law and Economics', *SSRN, Working Paper* (2015), pp. 1–20.

261 Sibony, Anne-Lise, and Alemanno, Alberto, 'The Emergence of Behavioural Policy Making: A European Perspective' in Alemanno, Alberto, and Sibony, Anne-Lise (eds.), *Nudge and the Law: A European Perspective* (Oxford: Hart Publishing, 2015), pp. 22–23. See also Purnhagen, Kai, 'Never the Twain Shall Meet? A Critical Perspective on Cultural Limits Between Internal Continental Dogmatism and Consequential US-style Law and Economics Theory', *Munich Risk and Insurance Center Working*

Alemanno describe this European attitude of resistance as being 'not necessarily through opposition but through polite marginalization'. Indeed, doctrinal and comparative approaches of the law dominate the academic landscape in Europe.[262] One of the reasons for this reluctance of EU scholarship to embrace law and economics is traced back to World War II.[263] Economic efficiency seems to encourage dangerous moral relativism. Instead, a legal system construed on values and rights was considered the right way forward in Europe.[264] Another reason was that the early post-war law and economics movement did not receive the same funding as the US movement.[265] Nevertheless, more recently law and economics has received increased attention in the EU.[266] However, law and economics is in Europe often only considered an additional tool, next to historical, behavioral, comparative, and dogmatic approaches to the law.

First, the preference of damages over specific remedies by the irreparable injury rule is often justified by economic arguments. The rule is, according to many law and economics experts, the most efficient (and welfare maximizing).[267] They argue that specific performance leads – except

Paper 14 (2013), pp. 1–28 (see esp. p. 13 *et seq.* about the marketing of law and economics by Henry Manne in the US). See generally about law and economics in a civil law context: Mackaay, Ejan, *Law and Economics for Civil Law Systems* (Cheltenham: Edward Elgar, 2013), 560p.

262 It has to be noted that this statement is, of course, a gross generalization of the EU landscape. In Belgium, more and more legal PhDs are (cautiously) interdisciplinary; modelled to their neighbors in the Netherlands.

263 Purnhagen, Kai, 'Never the Twain Shall Meet? A Critical Perspective on Cultural Limits Between Internal Continental Dogmatism and Consequential US-style Law and Economics Theory', *Munich Risk and Insurance Center Working Paper 14* (2013), p. 16.

264 Notwithstanding the fact that the EU is built upon economic integration (and the creation of an internal market).

265 Purnhagen, Kai, 'Never the Twain Shall Meet? A Critical Perspective on Cultural Limits Between Internal Continental Dogmatism and Consequential US-style Law and Economics Theory', *Munich Risk and Insurance Center Working Paper 14* (2013), p. 22 (see also p. 13 *et seq.* about the marketing of law and economics in the US by Henry Manne).

266 Purnhagen, Kai, 'Never the Twain Shall Meet? A Critical Perspective on Cultural Limits Between Internal Continental Dogmatism and Consequential US-style Law and Economics Theory', *Munich Risk and Insurance Center Working Paper 14* (2013), p. 22 (partly due to the fact that big law firms require their lawyers to have an LLM degree from the US). See e.g. Bouckaert, Boudewijn, and De Geest, Gerrit, *Encyclopedia of Law and Economics*, http://reference.findlaw.com/lawandeconomics/contents.html: Elgar, 2000, 1094p.

267 Kronman, Anthony T., 'Specific Performance', 45 *U. Chi. L. Rev.* (1978), pp. 351–82 (the uniqueness test is economically sound: contract parties will favor money damages in the subject matter of the contract is not unique; contract parties will favor specific

in case of a unique performance – to greater costs when compared to damages. They argue, for example, that the non-breaching party – who is allowed to order specific performance – will negotiate with the breaching party upon the amount (of 'bribe') that the breaching party must pay in order not to perform the contract. The bargaining range of these negotiations is situated between the costs of breach to the non-breaching party and the costs of performance by the breaching party. This situation is explained by the term 'bilateral monopoly', which means that there is only one supplier and one buyer. Both parties have goals that conflict, leading to *costly negotiations* between the parties to agree upon a satisfactory solution. In sum, specific performance would be less economically efficient compared to damages, which would not lead to these costly negotiations. Moreover, those scholars also point at the societal costs of monitoring specific performance by the breaching party.[268]

Nevertheless, authors of the same law and economics movement have also asserted that efficiency is most likely to be achieved by specific performance. Schwartz pleaded in 1979 that specific performance must be freely available, just as damages are.[269] He argues that damages are more likely to *undercompensate* the creditor, which makes specific performance actually even a 'superior method for achieving the compensation goal' which does not increase the transaction costs compared to damages.

---

performance in case of unique goods and services; which means that he is a supporter of the irreparable injury-rule and the adequacy test); Muris, Timothy J., 'The Cost of Freely Granting Specific Performance', 1982 *Duke L.J.* (1982), pp. 1053–69 (prefers the fine-tuning of the uniqueness-test instead of its abandonment); Posner, Richard A., *Economic Analysis of Law* (New York: Kluwer, 2011), pp. 163–64; Yorio, Edward, 'In Defense of Money Damages for Breach of Contract', 82 *Colum. L. Rev.* (1982), pp. 1365–424 (is of the opinion that expanding the possibility for specific performance would almost certainly lead to inefficiency: such as increasing the costs of pre- and post-contractual negotiations, costs in monitoring performance by the breaching party, […] and stresses the flexibility of monetary damages). See also Bishop, William, 'The Choice of Remedy for Breach of Contract', 14 *J. Legal Stud.* (1985), pp. 299–320 (refuting the arguments that Schwartz and Shavell develop (see *infra*)). Cf.: Shavell, Steven, 'Specific Performance Versus Damages for Breach of Contract: An Economic Analysis', 84 *Tex. L. Rev.* (2006), pp. 831–76 (in cases of contracts to produce goods (contracts 'to do') the remedy of damages is to be preferred and in case of contracts to convey property (contracts 'to give') specific performance is to be preferred).

268 In civil law systems, these 'monitoring' difficulties are solved by the mechanism of the '*astreinte*' ('*dwangsom*') which is an order to perform under the threat of the payment of a certain sum of money per day, month, or year delay in performance. See also Mak, Vanessa, *Performance-oriented Remedies in European Sale of Goods Law* (Oxford: Hart publishing, 2009), p. 104.

269 Schwartz, Alan, 'The Case for Specific Performance', *Yale L.J.* (1979), pp. 271–306.

He also points out that damages are not capable of adequately measuring the emotional costs of breach such as anger or frustration.[270] Linzer is of the opinion that the scope of specific performance should be broadened generally and used in cases in which the cost of non-performance is difficult to quantify, such as emotional costs and other idiosyncratic values. According to him, this will lead to 'truer economic efficiency' because it is difficult to take these values into account when granting money damages.[271] Ulen's most important argument is that if specific performance was the 'normal' remedy for breach, parties would conclude more mutually beneficial exchanges of promises and at a lower cost compared to any other remedy.[272]

Both analyses contradict each other: one justifying a wider scope for damages and the other justifying specific performance. Thus, it can be concluded that the law and economics approach fails to give a conclusive justification for the scope of specific performance versus damages.[273]

Pro and contra: empirical and behavioral research. More recently, 54
behavioral scientists have started to become interested in the damages/specific performance dilemma.[274] It has to be noted that the behavioral approach towards the legal science is of a more recent date than the law and economics movement (*supra*, para. 53).[275] Some consider it as an alternative to the law and economics movement, the latter only focusing upon unrealistic rational behavior of humankind. Others consider it as a refinement or an 'enrichment' of the law and economics movement.[276] They consider 'behavioral law and economics' as a mere explanation for anomalies of individual decision-making. It is clear that the term 'behavioral analysis of law' is the common denominator for a multitude of

---

270 ibid., p. 276 (anger and frustration will often occur in the consumer context).

271 Linzer, Peter, 'On the Amorality of Contract Remedies – Efficiency, Equity, and the Second *Restatement*', *Colum. L. Rev.* (1981), pp. 111–39 (also stresses the moral duty to perform one's obligations, see also *supra*, para. 52).

272 Ulen, Thomas, S., 'The Efficiency of Specific Performance: Toward a Unified Theory of Contract Remedies', 83 *Mich. L. Rev.* (1984), pp. 341–403.

273 Mak, Vanessa, *Performance-oriented Remedies in European Sale of Goods Law* (Oxford: Hart Publishing, 2009), p. 67.

274 See for an overview: Eisenberg, Theodore, and Miller, Geoffrey P., 'Damages Versus Specific Performance: Lessons from Commercial Contracts', 12 *J. Empirical Legal Stud.* (2015), pp. 41–2.

275 See, for an important pioneering paper: Jolls, Christine, et al., 'A Behavioral Approach to Law and Economics', *Stan. L. Rev.* (1998), pp. 1471–550.

276 Mackaay, Ejan, *Law and Economics for Civil Law Systems* (Cheltenham: Edward Elgar, 2013), p. 25.

approaches.[277] It includes, for example, empirical sociology and empirical psychology, analyses of beliefs, desires and emotions, and the influences of neurosciences and biology.[278]

In 2005, Listokin wrote an article using an empirical analysis to underpin the preference for one over the other.[279] He is correctly of the opinion that is very difficult to find a theoretical explanation to claim that one remedy is better than the other.[280] Although he admits that the material on which he bases his assessment is limited, he makes a case for specific performance in a particular set of circumstances.

He takes the IBP-Tyson litigation as an example.[281] In this case, Tyson wanted to acquire IBP, but Tyson tried to terminate the agreement by calling upon a material adverse change (MAC) clause in the merger agreement. IBP did not agree and asked the court to specifically perform the merger agreement. After the specific performance was granted by the court, the combined value of the two companies rose, which implies that the merger created a value. This means that in a case where a merger is value-creating, specific performance is empirically the most efficient remedy, and not money damages. Listokin stresses that the results of his research are not conclusive and that in each case empirical research has to be undertaken.

Arbel did not obtain clear answers from his qualitative empirical research published in 2015.[282] He stresses that other factors, not taken into account by the law and economics approach, play an important role: such as a lawyer's bias towards collecting his fees when advising clients to opt for damages or the reluctance of parties to renegotiate. At one point he seems to discourage a free choice between specific performance and damages because it would increase the instrumental use of specific performance: not choosing this remedy could give a sign to the judge that the plaintiff would no longer be interested in the contract, so he might be compelled

---

277 Sibony, Anne-Lise, and Alemanno, Alberto, 'The Emergence of Behavioural Policy Making: A European Perspective' in Alemanno, Alberto, and Sibony, Anne-Lise (eds.), *Nudge and the Law: A European Perspective* (Oxford: Hart Publishing, 2015), pp. 8–10.

278 Elster, Jon, *Explaining Social Behavior. More Nuts and Bolts for the Social Sciences* (Cambridge: Cambridge University Press, 2007), 484p.; Sibony, Anne-Lise, and Alemanno, Alberto, 'The Emergence of Behavioural Policy Making: A European Perspective' in Alemanno, Alberto, and Sibony, Anne-Lise (eds.), *Nudge and the Law: A European Perspective* (Oxford: Hart Publishing, 2015), pp. 9–10.

279 Listokin, Yair, 'The Empirical Case for Specific Performance: Evidence from the IBP-Tyson Litigation', *J. Empirical Stud.* (2005), pp. 469–93.

280 Ibid., pp. 470–71 and 493.

281 *In re IBP S'Holders Litig. v. Tyson Foods, Inc.*, 789 A.2d 14 (Del. Ch. 2001).

282 See later for other qualitative research on this topic: Arbel, Yonathan, A., 'Contract Remedies in Action: Specific Performance', *W. Va. L. Rev.* (2015), pp. 369–410.

to choose specific performance while he is actually more interested in pecuniary damages.[283] Eisenberg and Miller did empirical research as to the frequency with which specific performance clauses had been inserted, taking into account that it is not certain whether such clauses are binding[284] upon a judge.[285] The majority of contracts implemented the default rule (silence was also read as an approval of the irreparable injury rule), therefore endorsing in most cases the subordination of specific performance. Nevertheless, the authors emphasize that one must differentiate between different contract types: e.g., parties often insert specific performance clauses in corporate merger contracts.

None of the previously treated behavioral studies are very convincing. It can be concluded that the behavioral studies have also failed to give a conclusive justification for the scope of specific performance versus damages.

2.2.1.4. Latest Developments of the Irreparable Injury Rule

New equity. The critique on the irreparable injury rule has been quite effective in convincing conventional legal scholarship to abolish the sharp distinction between the remedies in law and equity (*cf. supra*, para. 47 *et seq.*). Also, recent scholarship[286] is still pleading for the abolishment of the difference between actions at law and in equity.[287] However, Bray observes a peculiar and surprising turn in the jurisprudence 55

[283] Ibid., 407–08.

[284] See the Comments of §359 2nd restatement of contract law: '[...] the parties cannot vary by agreement the requirement of inadequacy of damages, although a court may take appropriate notice of facts recited in their contract'.

[285] See Eisenberg, Theodore, and Miller, Geoffrey P., 'Damages Versus Specific Performance: Lessons from Commercial Contracts', 12 *J. Empirical Legal Stud.* (2015), pp. 29–69 (this research cannot be done in the consumer context, because consumers are almost never able to negotiate their contract, and thus unable to express their preferences with regard to remedies).

[286] See e.g. Corbin, Arthur Linton, et al., *Corbin on Contracts* (New Providence, San Francisco: Matthew Bender & Co., Inc., 2016), §63.4. See also Knapp, Charles L., *Commercial Damages: A Guide to Remedies in Business Litigation* (New York: Matthew Bender & Co., Inc., 2016), P.12.01, P 12.02, around footnote 81, and P 14.04.

[287] Or ascertain that contemporary applications of the irreparable injury rule/adequacy test are fairly liberal: Dobbs, Dan B., *Law of Remedies* (St. Paul: West Academic, 1993), p. 197 (although recognizes that the adequacy test is 'very much still the rule'; he is, nevertheless, not a fan of the adequacy test and proposes to directly address the question whether 'their powers of compulsion are warranted' (because equitable remedies involve more compulsion).

of the Supreme Court. Instead of confirming conventional legal scholarship pleading for the abolishment of the irreparable injury rule and the distinction between remedies in law and in equity, it seems to reinforce the line between law and equity remedies.[288] Bray calls these cases the 'new equity' cases. These cases appear in a wide array of areas of substantive law, among others commercial contract law.[289] But one of the most important cases has arisen in the field of patent law: the *eBay v. MercExchange, L.L.C.* case.[290] Indeed, in this case the court developed a 'four-factor test' for granting a permanent injunction, i.e. an equitable remedy:

> According to well-established principles of equity a plaintiff seeking a permanent injunction must satisfy a four-factor test before a court may grant such relief. A plaintiff must demonstrate: (1) that it has suffered an irreparable injury; (2) that remedies available at law, such as monetary damages, are inadequate to compensate for that injury; (3) that, considering the balance of hardships between the plaintiff and defendant, a remedy in equity is warranted; and (4) that the public interest would not be disserved by a permanent injunction. [...] The decision to grant or deny permanent injunctive relief is an act of equitable discretion by the court, reviewable on appeal for abuse of discretion.[291]

This four-factor test is indeed not burying the irreparable injury rule, but in fact restoring it. The US Supreme Court makes at least clear that equitable remedies, such as injunctions, are to be considered 'exceptional'. The term 'exceptional' should not be understood by meaning 'marginal or unusual' but by meaning 'departing from the norm'.[292] Although this 'new equity' jurisprudence of the US Supreme Court has received harsh criticism because of its erroneous and overly-simplified use of historical

---

288 Bray, Samuel L., 'The Supreme Court and the New Equity', 68 *Vand. L. Rev.* 4 (2015), pp. 997–1054. Bray later pleads in an article that equitable remedies and doctrine work together as a system (e.g., equitable remedies require greater managerial powers and raise concerns about cost and abuse which explains the restraint upon them), explaining and underpinning the distinction between equitable and legal remedies: Bray, Samuel L., 'The System of Equitable Remedies', 63 *UCLA L. Rev.* (2016), pp. 530–93.

289 Bray, Samuel L., 'The Supreme Court and the New Equity', 68 *Vand. L. Rev.* 4 (2015), p. 997.

290 *EBay v. MercExchange*, 547 U.S. 388, 391 (2006).

291 Justice Thomas delivering the opinion of the Court: *EBay v. MercExchange*, 547 U.S. 388, 391 (2006).

292 Bray, Samuel L., 'The Supreme Court and the New Equity', 68 *Vand. L. Rev.* 4 (2015), p. 1038.

arguments,[293] these cases might be of importance for the future of the law of remedies.[294]

2.2.2. *Other Factors Influencing the Hierarchy of Remedies*

Beyond the irreparable injury rule. It is not only the irreparable injury rule which influences the ease with which a creditor can invoke a remedy against his debtor; other factors also play an important role. When the damages remedy is examined, it has to be noted that the creditor cannot always recover the amount of money he had envisaged: different interests are protected with a different intensity. Secondly, the position of the termination remedy has to be assessed. 56

Expectation interest vs reliance and restitution interest and nominal damages. The remedy of damages is often called 'the most common type of remedy for breach of contract'. Three different interests can be protected: expectation, reliance, and restitution interest.[295] The general standard[296] for contract damages is that it is supposed to place the creditor in the same position he would have been if the contract had been performed correctly (sometimes also called expectation interest[297]).[298] Only where the expectation interest (performance interest) cannot be recovered, e.g. because of lack of proof or difficulties in calculating reliance interests, 57

---

293 Langbein, John H., 'What ERISA Means by "Equitable": The Supreme Court's Trail of Error in Russel, Mertens and Great-West', 103 *Colum. L. Rev.* (2003), pp. 1321 and 1351 *et seq.*

294 Bray, Samuel L., 'The Supreme Court and the New Equity', 68 *Vand. L. Rev.* 4 (2015), pp. 997–1054.

295 See for a short overview: Dobbs, Dan B., *Law of Remedies* (St. Paul: West Academic, 1993), §12.1; Fischer, James M., *Remedies* (New Providence, San Francisco: Matthew Bender & Co., Inc., 2014), §§6.1–6.3.

296 2nd restatement of contract law, §347.

297 See, regarding the difference between expectation and reliance interests: Fuller, Lon L., and Perdue, William R., 'The Reliance Interest in Contract Damages: 1', *Yale L.J.* (1936), and 'The Reliance Interest in Contract Damages: 2', *Yale L.J.* (1936).

298 2nd restatement of contract law, §344(a). See e.g. Hillman, Robert A., *Principles of Contract Law* (St. Paul: West Academic, 2014), p. 154 *et seq.* See also Ferriell, Jeff, *Understanding Contracts* (New Providence, San Francisco: Matthew Bender & Co., Inc., 2009), p. 709 ('expectation recovery includes elements of both reliance and restitution'); Perillo, Joseph M., *Contracts* (St. Paul: West Academic, 2014), §14.4. (explains the difference between expectation interest and 'the losses caused and gains prevented by the defendant's breach'; the expectation interest in its broadest meaning includes reliance and restitution interests).

can the creditor try to have recovery based on the so-called reliance[299] or restitution interests.[300] Reliance interests allow the creditor to recover the costs made in reliance to the performance of the contract and would put the creditor in the situation he was before concluding the contract.[301] Finally, restitution interests boil down to having 'restored any benefit that someone has conferred on the other party'.[302] If damages cannot be proved, only nominal damages can be awarded (which, in the US, is often rated at one dollar or six cents).[303]

58 *The doctrine of material or total breach and the right to cure.* A two-step approach has to be taken when considering the right to suspend a contract or to treat reciprocal obligations as discharged upon breach by the other party.[304] A *material breach*[305] of a reciprocal contract by the debtor justifies that the creditor suspends his performance (which is a right to self-help, see also *infra*, para. 103). After a certain period of time – in which the debtor has *the right to cure* the non-performance if the non-performance can be cured (see *infra*, this para) – the creditor can treat the contract as discharged, which means that the creditor can exercise his right to self-help by cancelling or terminating the contract.[306] This implies that termination can only be invoked (in absence of a breach of an express promissory condition)[307]

299 2nd restatement of contract law, §349.

300 Perillo, Joseph M., *Contracts* (St. Paul: West Academic, 2014), p. 516.

301 2nd restatement of contract law, §344(b). See e.g. Ferriell, Jeff, *Understanding Contracts* (New Providence, San Francisco: Matthew Bender & Co., Inc., 2009), 706; Perillo, Joseph M., *Contracts* (St. Paul: West Academic, 2014), p. 193.

302 2nd restatement of contract law, §344(c).

303 Perillo, Joseph M., *Contracts* (St. Paul: West Academic, 2014), p. 511 and §14.2.

304 See extensively Farnsworth, E. Allan, *Farnsworth on Contracts* (New York: Kluwer, 2004), §8.15; Murray, John E., *Murray on Contracts* (Durham: Carolina Academic Press, 2011), §108; Perillo, Joseph M., *Contracts* (St. Paul: West Academic, 2014), §11.8.

305 The concept of 'material breach' is the counterpart of the concept 'substantial performance'; which is the object of the famous *Jacob & Youngs, Inc. v. Kent*, 230 N.Y. 239, 129 N.E. 889 (1921) (Cardozo opinion: there was substantial performance). See also *Plante v. Jacobs*, 10 Wis. 2d 567, 103 N.W.2d 296 (1960) ('no mathematical rule relating to the percentage of the price, of cost of completion, or of completeness can be laid down to determine substantial performance of a building contract').

306 See extensively Farnsworth, E. Allan, *Farnsworth on Contracts* (New York: Kluwer, 2004), §§8.15 *et seq.*

307 An express promissory condition precedent requires a perfect performance: Hillman, Robert A., *Principles of Contract Law* (St. Paul: West Academic, 2014), p. 325. See also on the failure of an express condition and its excuse 'forfeiture by cancellation': Tiefer, Charles, 'Forfeiture by Cancellation or Termination', 54 *Mercer L. Rev.* (2003), p. 1031 *et seq.*

if (1) there is a material (total)[308] breach of a reciprocal contract; and often if (2) a certain period of time to cure the breach has passed. If the creditor then chooses to terminate the contract, he treats the *breach as total.*

§241 2nd restatement of contract law enumerates all factors that determine the *'fundamental' or 'material'* character of the *non-performance* such as the likelihood of cure by the debtor, the extent that the creditor will be deprived of the benefit he reasonably expected, and the good faith of the breaching party.[309] There have been complaints about the vagueness and difficulty of defining the term 'material breach', which renders it more difficult for creditors to decide whether they can apply termination or suspension.[310] Courts encourage 'keeping the deal together' if the expectations of the creditor are not seriously disappointed: it is, for example, considered an abuse to invoke a material breach of contract in the case of a minor breach.[311] This vague standard implies that it is up to case law to sort the matter out.[312]

§237 2nd restatement of contract law touches discretely upon the *debtor's right to cure*:[313] 'Except as stated in §240, it is a condition of each

---

308 'A total breach occurs after an uncured material breach; or a breach by nonperformance accompanied or followed by a repudiation; or a breach that substantially impairs the value of the contract to the injured party at the time of the breach': Corbin, Arthur Linton, et al., *Corbin on Contracts* (New Providence, San Francisco: Matthew Bender & Co., Inc., 2016), §68.2.

309 The full list in §241 is: (1) the extent of the harm to the injured party; (2) the adequacy of monetary damages to compensate for the injured party's loss; (3) the ability and willingness of the breaching party to implement a cure; (4) the good faith of the breaching party; and (5) the extent to which the breaching party will suffer a forfeiture if the breach is treated as material.

310 See e.g. Taylor, Celia R., 'Self-help in Contract law: An Exploration and Proposal', 33 *Wake Forest L. Rev.* (1998), p. 863 *et seq.* See also Ferriell, Jeff, *Understanding Contracts* (New Providence, San Francisco: Matthew Bender & Co., Inc., 2009), p. 533.

311 Farnsworth, E. Allan, *Farnsworth on Contracts* (New York: Kluwer, 2004), §8.15.

312 See e.g. regarding a material breach (and substantial performance): *K & G Constr. Co. v. Harris*, 223 Md. 305, 164 A.2d 451 (1960) (failure of performance constitutes substantial performance (i.e. material breach) because of a damaged wall by a subcontractor); *Youell v. Grimes*, 217 F. Supp. 2d 1167, 1174 (D. Kan. 2002) (material breach by the insured by breaching the cooperation clause in the contract). *O.W. Grun Roofing & Constr. Co v. Cope*, 529 S.W.2d 258 (Tex. Civ. App. 1975) (the roofing company failed to substantially perform the contract: taking into account the extent of the nonperformance, the ratio of money value of the tendered performance and the promised performance [...]: 'there is evidence to support the conclusion that plaintiff can secure a roof of uniform coloring only by installing a completely new roof').

313 See also Farnsworth, E. Allan, *Farnsworth on Contracts* (New York: Kluwer, 2004), §8.17.

party's remaining duties to render performances to be exchanged under an exchange of promises that there be no uncured material failure by the other party to render any such performance due at an earlier time'. Also, §241 indicates that one of the factors that has to be taken into account whether or not a breach is material is 'the likelihood that the party failing to perform [...] will cure his failure'. The right to cure means that the breaching party has a second chance to perform his side of the contract (notwithstanding the fact that the injured party is still entitled to remaining damages caused by the initial breach). The fact that the 2nd restatement of contract law introduces this right to cure undoubtedly has an effect on the hierarchy of remedies. The comments to §237 explain that in case of a material failure of performance the injured party may suspend his duties and will be discharged of his duties if it has not been cured before it is too late for the performance (see for this period of time between suspension and discharge: §242). This means that the inclusion of the right to cure in §237 can actually prevent the injured party from discharging and terminating the contract immediately after a material breach of contract.[314] Consequently, even in case of a material failure to perform, the right to terminate the contract is not readily available, which influences the hierarchy of remedies. This means that the right to cure, which might eventually lead to the performance of the contract, is sometimes positioned higher in the hierarchy than termination. This unveils a contradiction in common law. Specific performance is thought to be the 'marginal' remedy in its relation with damages. However, with regard to termination, common law shows a certain affinity to the performance-oriented seller's right to cure.

However, for (consumer) sales contracts – which is the focus of this book – the UCC does not perfectly copy these last rules. Although it does insert a right to cure (see *infra*, para. 69), the 'material' non-performance rules are not reiterated in the Code[315] in case of 'rejection' and, in principle, a 'perfect tender rule' applies (see *infra*, para. 70).[316] However, in case of revocation of acceptance, other rules apply, such as a substantial impairment test (see *infra*, para. 70), which is similar to the material breach test.

---

314 Lawrence, William H., 'Cure After Breach of Contract Under the Restatement (Second) of Contracts: An Analytical Comparison with the Uniform Commercial Code', 70 *Minn. L. Rev.* (1986), p. 721.

315 See, however, on the requirement of a substantial impairment when revoking acceptance, *supra*, para. 70.

316 See also Farnsworth, E. Allan, *Farnsworth on Contracts* (New York: Kluwer, 2004), §8.12.

2.2.3. *Conclusion on the Priority of Damages and Restriction of Termination*

Irreparable injury rule still alive. When comparing damages and specific performance, it has to be concluded that the irreparable injury rule – favoring damages – has suffered losses, without being defeated. The rule has been attenuated by doctrine and case law, but the US Supreme Court refuses to let go. 59

Termination made exceptional. Termination (or cancellation) by discharge of a contract by the creditor is, in principle, only possible if two conditions are fulfilled: there must be a material breach of a reciprocal contract and a period of time to cure the breach must have passed. 60

2.3. UCC ARTICLE 2

Introduction. After this overview of the common contract law remedies, we go one step further and compare them with the buyer's remedies for breach under UCC Article 2. As has been mentioned, US law does not provide for a unified set of consumer sales remedies for the buyer. Therefore, UCC Article 2 will be discussed, which is applicable to B2B and B2C sales contracts (with some extenuations for consumer contracts).[317] The analysis of general common contract law and the 2nd restatement will be useful to interpret some of the rules under UCC Article 2. 61

The UCC is a recommendation for statutory laws drawn up by the initiative of the American Law Institute (ALI) and the National Conference of Commissioners on Uniform State Laws (NCCUSL).[318] It is up to the various States to adopt the UCC. All 50 US States have adopted the UCC, although some States have implemented the UCC somewhat differently.

Simplified scheme for the buyer's remedies in sales contracts. At first sight, the remedial[319] system under the UCC might seem complex to a foreign lawyer. The main difference is between the remedies that can be invoked in situations in which the buyer *has not accepted* the goods (breach of 62

---

317 See e.g. PEB Study Group: Uniform Commercial Code, Article 2 Executive Summary, 46 *The Business Lawyer* (1991), p. 1876.

318 The UCC is the result of a joint project of the NCCUSL and the ALI. The first version was published in 1952.

319 The term 'remedy' is used here for judicial *and* extrajudicial relief (for the buyer) in case of breach of contract. Some US scholars reserve the term 'remedies' for judicial relief: Smiley, Michael S., 'Where Do We Start Professor? An Approach to Starting and Navitaging Article 2 of the Uniform Commercial Code', 40 *Idaho L. Rev.* (2003), p. 148 ('in the context of the UCC, a remedy is something that the court provides').

contract) and in which the goods have been delivered and the buyer *has accepted the goods*. The scheme shown in Table 2 gives a rough overview of the framework of the buyer's remedies under Article 2 UCC.

Table 2. Framework of the buyer's remedies under Article 2 UCC[320]

Goods not delivered and goods not accepted	Goods delivered and accepted
- seller's repudiation[321] - seller wrongfully failed to deliver/does not deliver on time Menu: §2-711 UCC => **Recover so much of the price that has already been paid** 1° Cover **damages**[322] (§2-712 UCC) or 2° **Damages** for non-delivery[323] (§2-713 UCC) => **or alternatively** 3° **Recover** (insolvency)[324] (§2-502 UCC) or 4° **Specific performance**[325] (uniqueness of goods or proper circumstances) or replevin (inability to cover) §2-716 UCC	- breach of warranty **Damages:** §2-714 UCC (direct damages) Incidental damages (§2-715(1) UCC) Consequential damages (§2-715(2) UCC) Cure OK
- seller delivered non-conforming goods which the buyer refused Buyer's **right to rejection** (+ damages, see box 1) §§2-601, 2-602 & 2-612 UCC = perfect tender rule[326] for single delivery contracts (but rule is declining)[327] + RIGHT TO CURE (§2-508 UCC/§2-612(2))	- buyer has accepted the goods but revokes this acceptance later on (only possible in limited situations)[328] Buyer's right **to revoke acceptance** (+ damages, see box 1) §2-608 UCC Substantial impairment required + revocation of acceptance only possible in limited situations (difficult to apply this remedy) RIGHT TO CURE?
Buyer has **successfully revoked acceptance**	

Source: Compiled by the author. See also footnote 320 for additional source material.

---

320 Very useful texts and textbooks to establish this scheme were: Carter, Caroline, et al., *Consumer Warranty Law* (Boston: National Consumer Law Center, 2010), 1136p.; Davis, T., 'UCC Breach of Warranty and Contract Claims: Clarifying the Distinction', 61 *Baylor L. Rev.* (2009), pp. 783–817; Smiley, Michael S., 'Where Do We Start Professor? An Approach to Starting and Navigating Article 2 of the Uniform Commercial Code', 40 *Idaho L. Rev.* (2003), pp. 133–54; White, James J. and Summers, Robert S., *Principles of Sales Law* (St. Paul: Thomson Reuters, 2009), 802p.

321 The seller expresses his will that he will not perform his obligations under the contract.

322 Cover damages of UCC §2-712 means that the buyer may obtain the goods himself and then receives damages for the difference between the cost of the substitute goods and the original contract price (together with any incidental or consequential damages) (see e.g. White, James J. and Summers, Robert S., *Principles of Sales Law* (St. Paul: Thomson Reuters, 2009), p. 331 *et seq.*).

323 UCC §2-713 provides the buyer with the 'contract-market differential' which is the difference between the market price at the time when the buyer learnt of the breach and the contract price (together with any incidental or consequential damages) and less the expenses saved in the consequence of the seller's breach. In other words this is: the market price – contract price – expenses saved as result of seller's

Article 2 UCC gives the buyer different remedies but not all remedies are available in every situation.[329] The acceptance of the goods plays an important role on the availability of the different remedies.

- Acceptance of the goods:
  - If the buyer accepts the non-conforming goods and keeps the goods, the buyer is not able to cancel (terminate) the contract but is entitled to damages.
  - If the buyer accepts the non-conforming goods but then rightfully revokes this acceptance, the buyer can cancel (terminate) the contract and seek for damages.
- Goods are not delivered and/or not accepted:
  - If the seller wrongfully fails to deliver, does not deliver in time or the seller repudiates the contract, the buyer is entitled to recover the price and to seek damages (cover damages or damages for non-delivery) or to seek for specific performance (under some circumstances).

---

breach + incidental and consequential damages (see e.g. White, James J. and Summers, Robert S., *Principles of Sales Law* (St. Paul: Thomson Reuters, 2009), p. 341 *et seq.*).

324 In a case of insolvency, the buyer has a right to recieve the goods identified in the contract and at least partly paid for if the seller becomes insolvent within 10 days after receipt of the first installment (UCC §2-502).

325 Specific performance means that the buyer forces the seller to deliver.

326 The fact that a tender is not in strict compliance with the contract justifies a rejection by the buyer. This rule is present in UCC §2-601 (single-delivery contracts), but another rule, the substantial performance rule (a substantial performance of one of the parties implies that the other party is obliged to perform), is present in UCC §2-612 (installment contracts).

327 Several mitigating factors exist: (1) the contract itself can provide for some leeway and restrain the ability of the buyer to reject goods in case of a minor breach; (2) trade usages may give leeway in determining whether or not the goods are conforming; (3) the seller enjoys a right to cure (see *infra*, para. 69); 4) this rule is only applicable to single-delivery contracts and not to installment contracts; and (5) the buyer may not skip the requirement to give notice of the intend to reject. See also Benfield, Marion W., and Greenfield, Michael M., *Sales: Cases and Materials* (New York: Foundation Press, 2015), p. 322 *et seq.*; Ferriell, Jeff, *Understanding Contracts* (New Providence, San Francisco: Matthew Bender & Co., Inc., 2009), p. 550; Perillo, Joseph M., *Contracts* (St. Paul: West Academic, 2014), p. 402 *et seq.*

328 A buyer can only revoke their acceptance in two situations: (a) on the reasonable assumption that his non-conformity would be cured and it has not been seasonably cured; or (b) without discovery of such non-conformity if his acceptance was reasonably induced either by the difficulty of discovery before acceptance or by the seller's assurances (UCC §2-608).

329 See, for an overview, Benfield, Marion W., and Greenfield, Michael M., *Sales: Cases and Materials* (New York: Foundation Press, 2015), p. 321; Duesenberg, Richard W., et al., *Sales & Bulk Transfers Under the UCC* (New York: Matthew Bender & Co., Inc., 2016), §14.01.

- If the seller delivered non-conforming goods and the buyer rightfully rejected the goods, the buyer can cancel (terminate) the contract and seek for damages.

2.3.1. *Priority of Damages*

63 *Specific performance in the UCC.* From UCC Article 2 it can be derived that specific performance[330] can be requested as an alternative to damages when the seller *fails to deliver or repudiates the contract.* Indeed, UCC §2-711(2)(b) states that a buyer may also obtain specific performance 'in a proper case' if the seller fails to deliver or repudiates. The UCC also includes injunctions as specific remedies because UCC §2-716(2) refers to 'other relief as the court may deem just'.[331] Furthermore, UCC §2-716(1) specifies that 'specific performance may be decreed where the goods are unique or in other proper circumstances'.[332]

This formulation of the right to specific performance makes clear that specific remedies enjoy, similarly to common contract law, a secondary place in the hierarchy of remedies.[333] The drafters of the UCC seem to have taken the relationship between the remedies under common law into account[334] by applying the irreparable injury rule, discussed above (para. 39 *et seq.*). Although UCC §2-716 does not mention that the remedy at law needs to be inadequate to be able to invoke specific performance (or an injunction), the spirit of the irreparable injury rule is reflected by only authorizing specific performance if the goods are 'unique or in other proper circumstances'.[335] While some authors maintain that the Code did

[330] This book will only cover specific performance as described in UCC §2-716(1–2) and not the right to replevin in UCC §2-502 (recover) and UCC §2-716(3). Flechtner makes clear that those rights are also only available in limited circumstances: Flechtner, Harry M., 'Remedies Under the New International Sales Convention: The Perspective from Article 2 of the U.C.C.', *J. L. Commerce* (1988), pp. 60–1.

[331] Schwartz, Alan and Scott, E. Robert, *Sales Law and the Contracting Process* (New York: Foundation Press, 1991), p. 400.

[332] Compare to the old text of the Uniform Sales Act, section 68: 'where the seller has broken a contract to deliver specific or ascertained goods, [...] a court of equity may, if it thinks fit' grant specific performance to the buyer, http://source.gosupra.com/docs/statute/221.

[333] Schwartz, Alan, and Scott, E. Robert, *Sales Law and the Contracting Process* (New York: Foundation Press, 1991), p. 353.

[334] White, James J., and Summers, Robert S., *Principles of Sales Law* (St. Paul: Thomson Reuters, 2009), p. 365.

[335] See also Herman, Shael, 'Specific Performance: A Comparative Analysis', *Edin. L. Rev.* 7 (2003), pp. 17–8.

not change anything about the irreparable injury rule,[336] most correctly point out that the drafters intended to 'liberalize' the irreparable injury rule.[337] Actually, a study committee, considering changes to UCC §2-716, took into account some of the law and economics arguments as pointed out above in favor of specific performance (see *supra*, para. 53). The uniqueness test was thought to be too restrictive, but giving the courts complete discretion to authorize specific remedies would be a bridge too far for the committee. Therefore, it was decided that UCC §2-716(1) would remain how it was.[338]

Unique goods and other proper circumstances. It is thus important to know what the drafters meant by 'unique goods' and by 'other proper circumstances'. Which goods are unique and what can be understood by 'other proper circumstances'?[339] The wider they are interpreted, the more the approach towards specific performance has been liberalized. Most of 64

336 Old law continued: Nordstrom, Robert J., *Law of Sales* (St. Paul: West Academic, 1970), pp. 479–80, §158.

337 Official Comment 1 to UCC §2-716. See very extensively and with unprecedented source material: Greenberg, Harold, 'Specific Performance Under Section 2-716 of the Uniform Commercial Code: "A More Liberal Attitude" in the "Grand Style"', 17 *New Eng. L. Rev.* (1981–82), pp. 321–53. See also: Benfield, Marion W., and Greenfield, Michael M., *Sales: Cases and Materials* (New York: Foundation Press, 2015), p. 381; Cosway, Richard, 'Sales – A Comparison of the Law in Washington and the Uniform Commercial Code', 36 *Wash. L. Rev.* (1961), p. 468; Ferriell, Jeff, *Understanding Contracts* (New Providence, San Francisco: Matthew Bender & Co., Inc., 2009), pp. 862–64; Gilbride, Gerard A., 'The Uniform Commercial Code: Impact on the Law of Contracts', 30 *Brook. L. Rev.* (1964), p. 202; Hawkland, William D., *Sales & Bulk Sales* (Philadelphia: AliAba, 1958), p. 144; Minish, Robert A., 'The Uniform Commercial Code in Minnesota: Articles 2 and 6 – Sales and Bulk Transfers', 50 *Minn. L. Rev.* (1965–66), p. 123; Schmitt, Michael A., and Pasterczyk, M., 'Specific Performance under the Uniform Commercial Code – Will Liberalism Prevail?', 26 *DePaul L. Rev.* (1976), pp. 54–77; Schwartz, Alan, and Scott, E. Robert, *Sales Law and the Contracting Process* (New York: Foundation Press, 1991), pp. 393–400; Van Hecke, M.T., 'Changing Emphases in Specific Performance', 40 *N.C.L. Rev.* (1961–62), pp. 6–7 (careful); White, James J., and Summers, Robert S., *Principles of Sales Law* (St. Paul: Thomson Reuters, 2009), p. 366; Wittenberg, Jeffrey D., and Kaplan, Elizabeth, *Commercial Contracting: Sales Under the UCC* (New York: LJP, 2016), §9.09. See for a similar evolution under the English Sale of Goods Act: Mak, Vanessa, *Performance-oriented Remedies in European Sale of Goods Law* (Oxford: Hart Publishing, 2009), p. 83 *et seq.*

338 PEB Study Group, Uniform Commercial Code Article 2: Preliminary Report 231 (1990).

339 See also extensively Corbin, Arthur Linton, et al., *Corbin on Contracts* (New Providence, San Francisco: Matthew Bender & Co., Inc., 2016), §63.11. See also Nadel, Andrea G., 'Specific performance of sale of goods under UCC §2-716', 26 *A.L.R.4th* 294 (*s.d.*), n° 2a and 3a *et seq.*

the time, authors conclude that case law[340] shows signs of liberalizing the remedy of specific performance.[341]

65 *Trend towards liberalization.* A couple of cases will be discussed to illustrate this trend towards liberalization.[342] One of the most cited cases

---

340 See for cases that illustrate this trend of liberalization: *Sedmak v. Charlies's Chevrolet, Inc.*, 622 S.W.2d 694 (Mo. Ct. App. 1981). See also: *R.L. Kimsey Cotton Co. v. Ferguson*, 233 Ga 962, 214 S.E.2d 360, 16 UCCRS 1223 (1975); *Eastern Air Lines, Inc. v. Gulf Oil Corp.*, 415 F. Supp. 429, 19 UCCRS 721 (S.D. Fla. 1975); *Laclede Gas Co. v. Amoco Oil Co.*, 522 F.2d 33, 17 UCCRS 447 (CA8 Mo 1975); *Copylease Corp. of America v. Memorex Corp.*, 408 F. Supp. 758 (S.D.N.Y. 1976); *Dexter Bishop Co. v. B. Redmond & Son, Inc.*, 58 A.D. 2d 755, 396 N.Y. S.2d 652, 22 UCCRS 406 (1st Dept. 1977); *Cumbest v. Harris*, 363 So. 2d 294 (Miss. 1978); *Stephan's Machine & Tool, Inc. v. D & H Machinery Consultants, Inc.*, 65 Ohio App. 2d 197, 19 Ohio Op. 3d 155, 417 N.E.2d 579 (1979); *United Nuclear Corp. v. Gen. Atomic Co.*, 96 N.M. 155, 629 P.2d 231, 1980–81 CCH Trade Cas. P 63639 (1980); *Chadwell v. English*, 652 P.2d 310, 34 UCCRS 1644 (Okla. App. 1982); *Madariaga v. Morris*, 639 S.W.2d 709 (Tex. App. 12th Dist. 1982); *King Aircraft Sales v. Lane*, 68 Wn. App. 706, 846 P.2d 550, 22 UCCRS 2d 515 (1993).
See for cases that are cited against the liberalization trend: *Hilmor Sales Co. v. Helen Neushaefer Division of Supronics Corp.*, 1969 WL 11054 (N.Y.Sup. 1969); see also: *Weathersby v. Gore*, 556 F.2d 1247, 1977 U.S. App. LEXIS 12176, 22 UCCRS 336 (1977); *Paloukos v. Intermountain Chevrolet Co.*, 99 Idaho 740, 588 P.2d 939, 25 UCCRS 655 (1978).

341 See, e.g., Greenberg, Harold, 'Specific Performance Under Section 2-716 of the Uniform Commercial Code: "A More Liberal Attitude" in the "Grand Style"', 17 *New Eng. L. Rev.* (1981–82), pp. 344–52.

342 See also for other cases: *R.L. Kimsey Cotton Co. v. Ferguson*, 233 Ga 962, 214 S.E.2d 360, 16 UCCRS 1223 (1975) (the cotton involved was unique: 'all and only the cotton' produced by the seller for the crop year 1973); *Eastern Air Lines, Inc. v. Gulf Oil Corp.*, 415 F. Supp. 429, 19 UCCRS 721 (S.D. Fla. 1975) (specific performance granted because if the Gulf ceases to supply fuel to the Air Line Company, the result will be chaos and irreparable damages; the court also refers to the more 'liberal test' under the UCC); *Laclede Gas Co. v. Amoco Oil Co.*, 522 F.2d 33, 17 UCCRS 447 (CA8 Mo 1975) (not referring to the UCC: 'Laclede probably could not find another supplier of propane willing to enter into a long-term contract such as the Amoco agreement'); *Copylease Corp. of America v. Memorex Corp.*, 408 F. Supp. 758 (SD NY 1976) (further testimony is necessary in order to determine whether specific performance is appropriate; refers to the more fundamental refusal of California courts to order specific performance of contracts requiring a continuing series of acts, but considers that if Copylease would not have an '*adequate alternative source of toner*', the product that Memorex should deliver ought to be unique or to be an example of 'other proper circumstances' for the purposes of Cal.U.C.C. §2716); *Dexter Bishop Co. v. B. Redmond & Son, Inc.*, 58 A.D. 2d 755, 396 N.Y. S.2d 652, 22 UCCRS 406 (1st Dept. 1977) (uniqueness of two butter-making machines); *Cumbest v. Harris*, 363 So. 2d 294 (Miss. 1978) (unique value of a stereo system due to scarcity); *Stephan's Machine & Tool, Inc. v. D & H Machinery Consultants, Inc.*, 65 Ohio App. 2d 197, 19 Ohio Op. 3d 155, 417 N.E.2d 579 (1979) (specific performance awarded in case of a unique boring machine); *United Nuclear Corp. v. Gen. Atomic Co.*, 96 N.M. 155, 629 P.2d 231, 1980–81 CCH Trade Cas. P 63639 (1980) ('Thus, specific performance was a proper remedy, even though the goods [nuclear fuel] involved are not 'unique' in the traditional

is *Sedmak v. Charlies's Chevrolet*, a judgement of the Missouri Court of Appeals of 16 June 1981.[343] The plaintiffs (the Sedmaks) contracted with Charlies's Chevrolet to buy a Corvette for USD 15,000. The Corvette was part of a limited number of cars manufactured to commemorate the fact that the Corvette was selected as the 'Pace Car for the Indianapolis 500'.[344] The Sedmaks were of the opinion that Charlie's breached the contract, because after the car arrived at Charlie's premises, the Sedmaks were told they could not purchase the car for USD 15,000, but that they could only bid on the car. The trial court ordered Charlie's to specifically perform the contract. On appeal, Charlie's argued, among others, that the Sedmaks did not show that the legal remedies were inadequate. On appeal, Judge Satz gave the leading opinion and affirmed the judgement of the trial court by holding that the Sedmaks did not have an adequate remedy at law, entitling them to specific performance. The opinion takes into account the limited production of the car: 'The Pace Car [...] was not unique in the traditional legal sense. [...] its "mileage, condition, ownership and appearance" did make it difficult, if not impossible to obtain its replication without considerable expense, delay and inconvenience'. Satz also pointed towards the drafters' intent to 'further a more liberal attitude [...] in connection with the specific performance of contracts of sale'. He furthermore states: 'this discretion is, in fact, quite narrow. When the relevant equitable principles have been met and the contract is fair and plain, "specific performance goes as a matter of right"'.

In another famous case of the same year, *Colorado-Ute Electric Asso. v. Envirotech Corp*, specific performance was granted in a case where there was a breach of implied and express warranties.[345] The plaintiff, a big Colorado electricity generation and transmission cooperative ordered a more effective air pollution control device in order not to breach the new air quality control regulations. Defendant Buell won the bid, and installed the control device. After a few months is was clear that it did not perform effectively. Following unsuccessful negotiations and attempts to remedy the

---

sense of that term'); *Chadwell v. English*, 652 P.2d 310, 34 UCCRS 1644 (Okla. App. 1982) (specific performance can be granted in case of stock option purchase contracts if the stock is scarce and difficult to access); *Madariaga v. Morris*, 639 S.W.2d 709 (Tex. App. 12th Dist. 1982) (about an option to purchase a business which is unique by the goodwill and the hot sauce formula; thereby justifying specific performance as a remedy); *King Aircraft Sales v. Lane*, 68 Wn. App. 706, 846 P.2d 550, 22 UCCRS 2d 515 (1993) (circumstances of the case fall appropriately within the 'other proper circumstances'; entitlement to specific performance due to the rarity of the planes).

343 *Sedmak v. Charlies's Chevrolet, Inc.*, 622 S.W.2d 694 (Mo. Ct. App. 1981).

344 https://en.wikipedia.org/wiki/Indianapolis_500_pace_cars.

345 *Colorado-Ute Electric Asso. v. Envirtech Corp.*, 524 F. Supp. 1152, 33 UCCRS 965 (D. Colo. 1981).

problems, the plaintiff commenced a suit seeking specific performance and damages. The opinion of Carrigan makes clear that the implementation of UCC Article 2 in Colorado prescribes that specific performance is the proper remedy if the goods are unique or in other proper circumstances and stresses that the comments point at a more 'liberal attitude' courts should take towards specific performance: 'Therefore, in view of the irreparable harm Colorado-Ute would suffer if the plant were shut down for air quality violations, coupled with the uniqueness of the equipment and the uncertainty as to future damages, the Court finds that specific performance is the appropriate remedy'.

66 *No liberalization*. On the other side of the spectrum,[346] the *Hilmor Sales Co. v. Helen Neushaefer*-case of 1969 is often cited.[347] In this case the plaintiff ordered a substantial quantity of lipsticks and containers of nail polish. The defendant breached and the plaintiff sued for specific performances stressing that the chattels were unique because they were purchased at close-out prices and were not replaceable at the contract price. Nevertheless, specific performance was not granted. The opinion of Judge Crisona made clear that the plaintiff 'has failed to establish that there is anything unique about these chattels. It appears to the court that plaintiff can be adequately compensated for any breach of the contract herein by an award of money damages. In such a situation, "there should be no specific performance". Finally the plaintiff has failed to demonstrate that it will be irreparably damaged if the injunction which it seeks is not granted'. The language in *Duval & Co. v. Malcom*-case of 1974 is also clear:[348] 'the "other proper circumstances" test is at best vague [...] [and] is plainly unworkable. An authority on sales has criticized the Code's "strange statutory language" on specific performance and says that "courts are free to go on doing what

---

[346] See also, for other cases: *Weathersby v. Gore*, 556 F.2d 1247, 1977 U.S. App. LEXIS 12176, 22 UCCRS 336 (1977) (specific performance is not the appropriate remedy because the plaintiff could have purchased additional cotton on the open market when the defendant informed him that he would not perform; with a reference to the *Duval & Co. v. Malcom*-case, see *infra*); *Paloukos v. Intermountain Chevrolet Co.*, 99 Idaho 740, 588 P.2d 939, 25 UCCRS 655 (1978) ('Although the UCC may have liberalized some of the old common law rules [...] specific performance nevertheless remains an extraordinary remedy [...]'; this pickup truck was not considered that unique to justify specific performance). Comp. *Tower City Grain Co. v. Richman*, 232 N.W.2d 61, 1975 N.D. LEXIS 108, 17 UCCRS 1011 (1975) (there was a manifest abuse of discretion of the trial court to grant specific performance to deliver grain).

[347] *Hilmor Sales Co. v. Helen Neushaefer Division of Supronics Corp.*, 1969 WL 11054 (N.Y.Sup. 1969).

[348] *Duval & Co. v. Malcom*, 233 Ga. 784 (1974).

they did before the Code ..." Nordstrom [...]'. The court concluded: the fact that the cotton prices soared – after the alleged breach of contract by not delivering the cotton – was not in itself adequate to show that the buyer was entitled to specific performance.

White and Summers correctly point to Comment 2 of UCC §2-716 which states that the test 'must be made in terms of the total situation which characterizes the contract. Output and contract requirements involving a particular or peculiarly available source or market present today the typical commercial specific performance situation'.[349] This formulation goes beyond the traditional cases of uniqueness (such as heirlooms and unique works of art). Authors have also tried to explain the meaning of 'other proper circumstances' by referring to (1) the ability of courts to preserve their power to make discretionary decisions regarding specific remedies; (2) the plaintiff's financial position;[350] and (3) cases in which the uniqueness is not characterized by the classical categories (such as heirlooms) but by the economic circumstances, as stated above.[351]

Substitute goods often available. Despite the (intended) liberalization of the 67
irreparable injury rule some authors point out that, in practice, specific performance will not frequently be decreed in sales contracts because substitute goods will often be available.[352] However, notwithstanding the fact that the current – and indeed more liberal – system still seems to favor damages over specific performance, some authors explicitly plead for specific performance and promote the idea that it would have to be applied more often than it is the case now.[353]

2.3.2. Other Factors Influencing the Hierarchy of Remedies

Obstacles to invoking rejection or revocation. Next, the position of the 68
remedy of termination (in the form of rejection and revocation) has to be

---

349 Official Comment 2 to §2-716 UCC. White, James J., and Summers, Robert S., *Principles of Sales Law* (St. Paul: Thomson Reuters, 2009), p. 366. See also Fonseca, Patricia F., and Fonseca, John R., *Williston on Sales* (Eagan: West, 2006), p. 874.

350 *Stephan's Machine & Tool, Inc. v. D & H Machinery Consultants, Inc.*, 65 Ohio App. 2d 197, 417 N.E.2d 579 (1979).

351 See, for these three explanations: White, James J., and Summers, Robert S., *Principles of Sales Law* (St. Paul: Thomson Reuters, 2009), pp. 368–70.

352 Corbin, Arthur Linton, et al., *Corbin on Contracts* (New Providence, San Francisco: Matthew Bender & Co., Inc., 2016), §63.11; Farnsworth, E. Allan, *Farnsworth on Contracts* (New York: Kluwer, 2004), pp. 177–79, §12.6 (specific performance remains the exception).

353 White, James J., and Summers, Robert S., *Principles of Sales Law* (St. Paul: Thomson Reuters, 2009), p. 374.

examined under UCC Article 2. Here too, the so-called 'right to cure' of the seller plays an important role. Moreover, in some circumstances, the buyer will have to prove that there is a substantial impairment of the sales contract. In short, the buyer cannot easily invoke rejection, and especially not revocation of acceptance.

69 *The role of the right to cure in case of rejection (or revocation of acceptance).* As discussed earlier, specific performance is considered secondary in rank compared to damages.[354] Specific performance is then framed as a remedy of the buyer. The same result – performance of the initial contract – can be reached if the seller is willing to cure the non-performance. In the first situation, the seller is forced by the buyer to perform the initial contract. In the second situation, the seller voluntarily performs the initial contract, and restrains the buyer from applying another remedy, such as termination.

UCC §2-508 provides for such a right to cure and restricts the right of the buyer to reject under UCC §§2-601 *et seq.*[355] Before the adoption of the UCC, this rule was unknown in legal doctrine. Nevertheless, it expresses an existing business practice exercised by sellers.[356] UCC §2-508 distinguishes between two situations according to whether or not the time for performance has expired. If the time for performance has not yet expired and the buyer rejects the performance, the seller has a right to cure if he promptly notifies the buyer and cures within the contract time. If time for performance has expired and the buyer rejects the performance, the seller may only exercise his right to cure if he had 'reasonable grounds to believe that the goods would be acceptable'[357]

---

[354] There is, however, *no* right to cure when the buyer has accepted the goods and seeks damages: *Bonebrake v. Cox*, 499 F.2d 951 (8th Cir. 1974); *Boies v. Norton*, 526 S.W.2d 651 (Tex. Civ. App. 1975); *Linscott v. Smith*, 3 Kan. App. 2d 1 (1978); *Dunleavy v. Paris Ceramics USA, Inc.*, 47 Conn. Supp. 565 (2002). See also: Henning, William H., and Lawrence, William H., 'A Unified Rationale for Section 2-607(3)(a)', 46 *San Diego L. Rev.* (2009), p. 575; Hillman, Robert A., 'Keeping the Deal Together After Material Breach – Common Law Mitigation Rules, the UCC, and the Restatement (Second) of Contracts', 47 *U. Colo. L. Rev.* (1976), p. 586 (however, the author argues that cure should be possible in case of revocation of acceptance).

[355] Both the provisions in UCC §2-508 'limit the right of the injured buyer to cancel the contract by rejecting the seller's nonconforming tender': Lawrence, William H., 'Cure After Breach of Contract Under the Restatement (Second) of Contracts: An Analytical Comparison with the Uniform Commercial Code', 70 *Minn. L. Rev.* (1986), p. 718.

[356] White, James J., and Summers, Robert S., *Principles of Sales Law* (St. Paul: Thomson Reuters, 2009), p. 507.

[357] See regarding the interpretation of such 'reasonable grounds': Hillman, Robert A., 'Keeping the Deal Together After Material Breach – Common Law Mitigation Rules, the UCC, and the Restatement (Second) of Contracts', 47 *U. Colo. L. Rev.* (1976), p. 588;

(with or without money allowance), and if he promptly notifies the buyer and exercises his right to cure within a reasonable time. It is clear the seller's right to cure limits the buyer's right to reject (see *infra*, para. 70). This means that the right to cure, which might eventually lead to the performance of the contract, is sometimes considered higher in the hierarchy than termination (in the form of rejection). Here too, a contradiction in common law can be unveiled (see also *supra*, para. 58). Specific performance is thought to be the 'marginal' remedy in its relation with damages. However, at least with regard to rejection, the UCC shows a certain affinity to the performance-oriented seller's right to cure.

Has the seller only one attempt to cure or can he be allowed several attempts to do the job? Must the buyer be patient and wait over and over again for unsuccessful attempts to cure until the seller succeeds? In many cases the seller may try several times to repair. However, one author proposes to restrict it to one attempt, which would force the seller to do an acceptable job first time.[358]

The interesting question arises whether the right to cure can be exercised by repair?[359] It is unclear whether repair is permissible as a means of cure of the seller.[360] Some authors urge the judges to balance, in this regard, two factors: (1) cure by repair can be efficient if the cost of losing the agreed deal would be more costly than the cost of the defect, but (2) cure by repair can also reduce the value of the goods.[361] These authors forget to mention that cure by repair can also increase the value of the goods.

Lawrence, William H., 'Cure After Breach of Contract Under the Restatement (Second) of Contracts: An Analytical Comparison with the Uniform Commercial Code', 70 *Minn. L. Rev.* (1986), p. 720 (taking into account the prior course of dealing, the course of performance or a usage, the surrounding market conditions, see also p. 745 *in fine*); Schwartz, Alan, and Scott, E. Robert, *Sales Law and the Contracting Process* (New York: Foundation Press, 1991), pp. 274–76 (they believe that this rule in UCC §2-508(2) cannot be applied in real life because if a seller would be surprised by a rejection, the rejection must be wrongful because the goods will then conform to the contract; they also believe that there are good reasons to limit the seller's cure opportunities because the buyer can be affected by intangible losses such as lost confidence); Sebert, John A., 'Legal Theory: Rejection, Revocation, and Cure under Article 2 of the UCC: Some Modest Proposals', 84 *Nw. U.L. Rev.* (1990), p. 391.

358 See Phillips, Jerry J., 'Revocation of Acceptance and the Consumer Buyer', 75 *Com. L.J.* (1970), p. 358.

359 Answers this question positively: Phillips, Jerry J., 'Revocation of Acceptance and the Consumer Buyer', 75 *Com. L.J.* (1970), p. 358 (implicitly).

360 Schwartz, Alan, and Scott, E. Robert, *Sales Law and the Contracting Process* (New York: Foundation Press, 1991), pp. 280–83. See also Farnsworth, E. Allan, *Farnsworth on Contracts* (New York: Kluwer, 2004), §8.17.

361 Schwartz, Alan, and Scott, E. Robert, *Sales Law and the Contracting Process* (New York: Foundation Press, 1991), pp. 280–83.

If the seller has a right to cure and if the seller has provided cure under UCC §2-508, the rights of the parties are clear. The buyer then loses his right to reject (or to revoke acceptance, if revocation of acceptance is limited by the right to cure, see *infra*, this para.), but can still try to obtain damages under UCC §2-714 due to the fact that the first tender was nonconforming.[362] A buyer who wrongfully refuses to accept cure after a rejection faces harsh consequences. He is then deprived of all remedies because the breach of contract is 'nullified'.[363]

Finally, the question arises whether or not this limitation is also applicable to the buyer's right to *revoke* acceptance under UCC §2-608. If a buyer has already accepted the goods, he cannot *reject* anymore, but he can *revoke* his acceptance under certain circumstances (see *infra*, para. 70). Can a seller cure after the buyer has *revoked* acceptance?[364] Most courts consider that the seller's right to cure is limited to the buyer's right to reject.[365] Indeed, UCC §2-508 about the right to cure does not refer to 'revocation of acceptance'. Nevertheless, some authors[366] and cases[367] express another point of view, subjecting the buyer's right to revocation

---

362 White, James J., and Summers, Robert S., *Principles of Sales Law* (St. Paul: Thomson Reuters, 2009), p. 509.

363 Ibid., p. 516.

364 See, regarding this (without taking a stance): Schwartz, Alan, and Scott, E. Robert, *Sales Law and the Contracting Process* (New York: Foundation Press, 1991), p. 286.

365 See e.g.: *Jensen v. Seigel Mobile Homes Group*, 105 Idaho 189 (1983); *Gappelberg v. Landrum*, 666 S.W.2d 88, 1984 Tex. LEXIS 322, 27 Tex. Sup. J. 260, 37 U.C.C. Rep. Serv. (Callaghan) 1563 (1984); *Head v. Phillips Camper Sales & Rental, Inc.*, 234 Mich. App. 94 (1998). See also Speidel, Richard E., 'Buyer's Remedies of Rejection and Cancellation under the UCC and the Convention', 6 *J. Contract L.* (1993), p. 134.

366 See for a proponent: Fonseca, Patricia F., and Fonseca, John R., *Williston on Sales* (Eagan: West, 2006), p. 737; Foss, Howard, 'The Seller's Right To Cure When The Buyer Revokes Acceptance: Erase The Line In The Sand', 16 *S. Ill. U. L. J.* (1991–92), pp. 1–37; Hillman, Robert A., 'Keeping the Deal Together After Material Breach – Common Law Mitigation Rules, the UCC, and the Restatement (Second) of Contracts', 47 *U. Colo. L. Rev.* (1976), pp. 586–587; Phillips, Jerry J., 'Revocation of Acceptance and the Consumer Buyer', 75 *Com. L.J.* (1970), p. 358; White, James J., and Summers, Robert S., *Principles of Sales Law* (St. Paul: Thomson Reuters, 2009), pp. 508–09. Cf.: Sebert, John A., 'Legal Theory: Rejection, Revocation, and Cure under Article 2 of the UCC: Some Modest Proposals', 84 *Nw. U.L. Rev.* (1990), p. 426 *et seq.* (proposes, in this regard, a revised Art. 2 UCC, see, for an oversight: p. 392–93); Wittenberg, Jeffrey D., and Kaplan, Elizabeth, *Commercial Contracting: Sales Under the UCC* (New York: LJP, 2016), §5.03, [6] (seems to be slightly in favor because of policy reasons to avoid unnecessary litigation).

367 See, e.g., *Mercury Marine v. Clear River Constr. Co.*, 839 So. 2d 508, 2003 Miss. LEXIS 90, 49 U.C.C. Rep. Serv. 2d (Callaghan) 989 (2003). See also *Wilson v. Scampoli*, 228 A.2d 848, 1967 D.C. App. LEXIS 156, 4 U.C.C. Rep. Serv. (Callaghan) 178 (1967); *Tiger Motor Co. v. McMurty*, 284 Ala. 283 (1969); *Oil Trading Co. v. Amerada Hess Trading Co.*, 1993 US Dist. LEXIS 10801 (S.D.N.Y. 1993).

to the seller's right to cure.[368] In case of acceptance of the nonconforming goods by the buyer in view of recovering *damages* there is, however, no obligation to accept a seller's offer to cure.[369]

Avoidance (termination) option made exceptional. Several factors 70
influence the fact that one cannot easily (avoid or) terminate the contract under UCC Article 2. Two termination options under UCC Article 2 can be distinguished: rejection (before acceptance) and revocation of acceptance (after acceptance). It has to be stressed that both remedies are subject to the requirement that the buyer has (or has not) accepted the good. In case of rejection, this may not have happened, while in case of revocation of acceptance, this must have happened. It should already be noted that revocation is more difficult to invoke compared to rejection (see also *infra*, this para.).

As for the buyer's right to *reject*, we have already seen that UCC §2-508 provides for a *right to cure* by the seller, restricting the right of the buyer to reject under UCC §2-601 *et seq.* (see *supra*, para. 69). Nevertheless, the buyer's right to reject is subject to certain other restrictions.

- The buyer's rejection must, first and foremost, be in good faith.[370]
- Moreover, the buyer must reject within a reasonable time[371] and send a 'seasonable' (i.e. reasonably prompt) notice[372] of rejection (see *infra*, para. 131).[373]

---

368 See also revised UCC Article 2 extending the right to cure to revocation of acceptance, but this is not applicable under consumer contracts: Farnsworth, E. Allan, *Farnsworth on Contracts* (New York: Kluwer, 2004), §8.17. See also PEB Study Group, Uniform Commercial Code Article 2: Preliminary Report 168 (1990) ('The study Group recommends that §§2-608 and 2-508(1) be revised to insure that the seller shall have a right to cure where acceptance is rightfully revoked and the time for performance has not yet expired').

369 Lawrence, William H., 'Cure After Breach of Contract Under the Restatement (Second) of Contracts: An Analytical Comparison with the Uniform Commercial Code', 70 *Minn. L. Rev.* (1986), p. 720; Schwartz, Alan, and Scott, E. Robert, *Sales Law and the Contracting Process* (New York: Foundation Press, 1991), pp. 286–87.

370 UCC §2-103(1)(b) and §1-201(20). Wittenberg, Jeffrey D., and Kaplan, Elizabeth, *Commercial Contracting: Sales Under the UCC* (New York: LJP, 2016), §5.01, [3].

371 UCC §2-602(1).

372 UCC §2-602(1). Flechtner, Harry M., 'Remedies Under the New International Sales Convention: The Perspective from Article 2 of the U.C.C.', *J. L. Commerce* (1988), p. 63; Wittenberg, Jeffrey D. and Kaplan, Elizabeth, *Commercial Contracting: Sales Under the UCC* (New York: LJP, 2016), §5.01, [7a]. See also: Duesenberg, Richard W., et al., *Sales & Bulk Transfers Under the UCC* (New York: Matthew Bender & Co., Inc., 2016), §14.02, [b and d].

373 Note that also in case of damages, the buyer must notify the seller within a reasonable time after he discovers or should have discovered any breach

- It is also required that the buyer who has taken physical possession of the goods, if he rejects them, should hold the goods with 'reasonable care' at the seller's disposition.[374]
- A substantial impairment of the goods is not required in case of single-delivery contracts due to the 'perfect tender rule',[375] nevertheless, such a substantial impairment of the whole contract is required in the case of an installment contract.[376]

As for the buyer's right to *revoke acceptance*, many elements limit the possibility to invoke this remedy, thereby influencing the place that this remedy occupies in the hierarchy. Revocation is much more difficult to invoke, compared to rejection:[377]

- UCC §2-608(1) states that a buyer may revoke under certain circumstances if the non-conformity *'substantially impairs'* the value of the goods to him. This means that the 'perfect tender rule', applicable in case of rejection, is not applicable in case of revocation. The fact that the UCC requires that the non-conformity has to impair substantially the value of goods restricts the use of the remedy of revocation.[378]

UCC §§2-714 and 2-607(3) (however, this is not the same as a 'notice of rejection') and see also: Priest, George L., 'Breach and Remedy for the Tender of Nonconforming Goods Under the Uniform Commercial Code: An Economic Approach', 91 *Harv. L. Rev.* (1978), p. 976.

374 UCC §2-602(2)(b). Duesenberg, Richard W., et al., *Sales & Bulk Transfers Under the UCC* (New York: Matthew Bender & Co., Inc., 2016), §14.02, [c]; Wittenberg, Jeffrey D., and Kaplan, Elizabeth, *Commercial Contracting: Sales Under the UCC* (New York: LJP, 2016), §5.01, [7b].

375 UCC §2-601. Llewellyn defends the argument that consumers should be permitted rescission (termination) for minor defects: Llewellyn, Karl N., 'On Warranty of Quality, and Society: II', *Colum. L. Rev.* (1937), p. 388.

376 UCC §2-612(2); see Flechtner, Harry M., 'Remedies Under the New International Sales Convention: The Perspective from Article 2 of the U.C.C.', *J. L. Commerce* (1988), pp. 72–3: Wittenberg, Jeffrey D., and Kaplan, Elizabeth, *Commercial Contracting: Sales Under the UCC* (New York: LJP, 2016), §5.01, [6].

377 Duesenberg, Richard W., et al., *Sales & Bulk Transfers Under the UCC* (New York: Matthew Bender & Co., Inc., 2016), §14.02 [i]; Phillips, Jerry J., 'Revocation of Acceptance and the Consumer Buyer', 75 *Com. L.J.* (1970), p. 355; Priest, George L., 'Breach and Remedy for the Tender of Nonconforming Goods Under the Uniform Commercial Code: An Economic Approach', 91 *Harv. L. Rev.* (1978), p. 972; Wittenberg, Jeffrey D., and Kaplan, Elizabeth, *Commercial Contracting: Sales Under the UCC* (New York: LJP, 2016), §5.01, [7a] and §5.03, [1].

378 Sebert, John A., 'Legal Theory: Rejection, Revocation, and Cure under Article 2 of the UCC: Some Modest Proposals', 84 *Nw. U.L. Rev.* (1990), p. 399. However, it is challenged whether judges apply this last rule so strictly: Gergen, Mark P., 'A Theory of Self-help Remedies in Contract', 89 *B.U L. Rev.* (2009), p. 1414 ('courts are very protective of buyers' rights').

- The 'substantial impairment test' is to be understood as a subjective one. This means that the value to the buyer has to be impaired.[379] Nevertheless, the test is increasingly understood as a mixed test, containing objective and subjective elements.[380] According to some authors, the substantial impairment test can also be phrased in terms of substantial non-performance or material breach (for details, see also *supra*, paras. 58 and 60).[381] Authors warn not to put a 'dollar value' on this substantial impairment test, because this might be compensated by damages.[382] Instead, one has to show that the impairment has an effect to the reliability of the goods and the credibility of the seller.
- Moreover, the required 'excusing circumstances' described in UCC §2-608(1) also render it more difficult to invoke revocation.[383] This means that the buyer has to establish some excuse for having accepted the goods he now wants to get rid of. Those excusing circumstances are the following: (1) the goods were accepted on the reasonable assumption that the discovered defects would be cured and the seller has failed to cure within a reasonable time; or (2) the buyer's acceptance of goods

379 Schwartz, Alan, and Scott, E. Robert, *Sales Law and the Contracting Process* (New York: Foundation Press, 1991), pp. 299–308. Referring to *Asciolla v. Manter Oldsmobile-Pontiac*, 117 N.H. 85 (1977) (rejecting an objective standard); *Colonial dodge, Inc. v. Miller*, 420 Michigan 452 (1984) (the discovery of the absence of a spare tire upon after delivery of a car, without another spare tire readily available constituted a substantial impairment in value to the buyer because of the special circumstances that he travels a lot for his work). See also *Champion Ford Sales, Inc. v. Levine*, 49 Md. App. 547, 433 A.2d 1218, 32 U.C.C. Rep. Serv. 108 (1981). See also Perillo, Joseph M., *Contracts* (St. Paul: West Academic, 2014), p. 405.

380 Sebert, John A., 'Legal Theory: Rejection, Revocation, and Cure under Article 2 of the UCC: Some Modest Proposals', 84 *Nw. U.L. Rev.* (1990), pp. 399–400; Wittenberg, Jeffrey D., and Kaplan, Elizabeth, *Commercial Contracting: Sales Under the UCC* (New York: LJP, 2016), §5.03, [2a]. See also *Jorgensen v. Pressnall*, 274 Ore. 285 (1976) (referring to a two-step inquiry: subjective and some objective elements, but the test is more subjective than objective). *Accord Web Press Services Corp. v. New London Motors, Inc.*, 203 Conn. 342, 525 A.2d 57, 3 U.C.C. Rep. Serv. 2d 1386 (1987).

381 Ferriell, Jeff, *Understanding Contracts* (New Providence, San Francisco: Matthew Bender & Co., Inc., 2009), pp. 560–61; Perillo, Joseph M., *Contracts* (St. Paul: West Academic, 2014), p. 405.

382 Fonseca, Patricia F., and Fonseca, John R., *Williston on Sales* (Eagan: West, 2006), p. 745.

383 These 'excusing circumstances' are described in §2-608 UCC: '(a) on the reasonable assumption that its non-conformity would be cured and it has not been seasonably cured; or (b) without discovery of such non-conformity if his acceptance was reasonably induced either by the difficulty of discovery before acceptance or by the seller's assurances.' See, regarding these excusing circumstances: Averch, Craig H., et al., *Commercial Law and Practice Guide* (New York: Matthew Bender & Co., Inc., 2016), P 10.03, [d].

with non-discovered defects was reasonably induced either by the difficulty of discovery of a defect before acceptance or by the seller's assurances about the quality of the goods.

- The buyer has to show that the defect existed at the time of delivery of the goods.[384]
- As discussed earlier (see *supra*, para. 69) it is unclear whether or not the buyer's right to revoke acceptance is subject to the seller's right to cure.
- The goods must not have undergone a substantial change in condition that is not caused by their own defects[385] (UCC §2-608(2)).[386] This requirement is justified by the fact that revocation of acceptance mainly unwinds the transaction and implies the return of the goods to the seller.[387]
- The buyer must revoke within a reasonable time and send a notice of revocation in a timely manner under UCC §2-608(2) (see *infra*, para. 132).[388] This notification should be distinguished from the notification under UCC §2-607(3)(a) merely indicating that there is a breach without which the buyer can be barred from any remedy (see *infra*, para. 130).[389]

2.3.3. *Conclusion on the Priority of Damages and Restriction of Termination*

71 *Uniqueness and other proper circumstances.* Similarly to common contract law, UCC Article 2 maintains the priority of damages by requiring 'uniqueness or other proper circumstances' to invoke specific remedies.

---

384 Phillips, Jerry J., 'Revocation of Acceptance and the Consumer Buyer', 75 *Com. L.J.* (1970), p. 356 (this is difficult in case of latent defects; the buyer must then hope for a presumption of defect at the date of delivery if he shows that there is a defect).

385 Flechtner, Harry M., 'Remedies Under the New International Sales Convention: The Perspective from Article 2 of the U.C.C.', *J. L. Commerce* (1988), p. 63; Phillips, Jerry J., 'Revocation of Acceptance and the Consumer Buyer', 75 *Com. L.J.* (1970), p. 357; Sebert, John A., 'Legal Theory: Rejection, Revocation, and Cure under Article 2 of the UCC: Some Modest Proposals', 84 *Nw. U.L. Rev.* (1990), p. 413.

386 See, regarding the influence of the use of the goods by the buyer after revocation: Fonseca, Patricia F., and Fonseca, John R., *Williston on Sales* (Eagan: West, 2006), p. 749 *et seq*.

387 Wittenberg, Jeffrey D., and Kaplan, Elizabeth, *Commercial Contracting: Sales Under the UCC* (New York: LJP, 2016), §5.03, [5].

388 Sebert, John A., 'Legal Theory: Rejection, Revocation, and Cure under Article 2 of the UCC: Some Modest Proposals', 84 *Nw. U.L. Rev.* (1990), pp. 410–12; Flechtner, Harry M., 'Remedies Under the New International Sales Convention: The Perspective from Article 2 of the U.C.C.', *J. L. Commerce* (1988), p. 63.

389 See, regarding this distinction: Wittenberg, Jeffrey D., and Kaplan, Elizabeth, *Commercial Contracting: Sales Under the UCC* (New York: LJP, 2016), §5.03, [4].

Nevertheless, the drafters have attempted to introduce a liberalization of the irreparable injury rule by making specific performance more freely available. However, in practice, specific performance will frequently not be decreed in sales contracts because substitute goods will often be available. Consequently, some authors still plead for the emancipation of specific performance and promote the idea that it would have to be applied more often than is the case now.

Termination made exceptional. Termination of the contract by rejection 72
or revocation of acceptance is difficult to invoke because of the different requirements that have to be fulfilled before it is possible to unwind the contract. A right to cure for the seller hinders the free application of termination by rejection or revocation. Revocation is furthermore hindered by the substantial impairment test and the required excusing circumstances.

2.4. INFLUENCE OF THE MAGNUSON-MOSS WARRANTY ACT

General. The Magnuson-Moss Warranty Act[390] is one of the few 73
federal acts that relates to the contractual remedies of consumer sales contracts.[391] It actually regulates written and implied warranties[392] given to consumers. It is important to note that – contrary to EU consumer sales law – sellers are not obliged to give such a warranty; but if they give a written warranty, it has to meet some minimum requirements in terms of legibility and content.[393] Nevertheless, two implied[394] warranties are always present whether or not the seller includes an express warranty about the goods: the implied warranty of merchantability (i.e. reasonably suitable for ordinary purpose) and of fitness for a particular purpose.

---

390 See also 15 U.S.C.A. (United States Code Annotated) §§2301–2312 (the Magnuson-Moss Warranty Act was enacted in 1975).

391 See also specifically with regard to cars: State Lemon Laws (e.g. for California: CC 1793.22–1793.25 and for New York NY GEN BUS, Chapt. 20, Art. 11-A).

392 And regulates service contracts; which we will not treat here.

393 See e.g. §104 or 15 U.S.C.A. §2304. See also Carter, Carolyn L., et al., *Consumer Warranty Law* (Boston: National Consumer Law Center, 2010), p. 35; Schwartz, Alan, and Scott, E. Robert, *Sales Law and the Contracting Process* (New York: Foundation Press, 1991), p. 273.

394 Other implied warranty guarantees can arise (e.g. due to trade usages) but this is not so common in consumer sales cases: Carter, Carolyn L., et al., *Consumer Warranty Law* (Boston: National Consumer Law Center, 2010), p. 173.

Moreover, the Magnuson-Moss Warranty Act limits the possibility to 'disclaim'[395] such implied warranties.[396]

74 *The (hierarchy) of remedies.* In case of a breach of a *written* warranty or an *implied* warranty, the Act provides for an action of damages, other legal and equitable relief, and attorney fees (if the consumer wins the case): §110(d) or 15 U.S.C.A. §2310(d).[397] With regard to damages, the courts should take into account state law, which is often governed by the UCC (see *supra*, paras. 61 *et seq.*).[398] Most authors agree that the consumer can also sue for revocation of acceptance or rejection as an action at law.[399] The Act foresees that the consumer can sue for equitable relief (such as specific performance). The question arises whether the relationship between damages and equitable relief is subject to the irreparable injury rule. Consumer law authors are inclined to say that consumers who are seeking specific performance must meet the classical requirements for equitable relief.[400] This means that the consumer wishing to invoke equitable relief, must meet the 'irreparable injury rule' test, which means the absence of an adequate remedy at law (see *supra*, para. 39 *et seq.*).[401]

It is also important to note that, with regard to the remedy of revocation of acceptance, the Act loosens under some circumstances the requirements put forward by the UCC (which is often the applicable state law) (see *supra*, para. 70).[402]

Furthermore, if a seller decides to give a *written* warranty, this written warranty has to meet some minimum requirements in terms of content.

---

395 Disclaim in the meaning of 'exonerate'.

396 See §108 or 15 U.S.C.A. §2308.

397 See also 15 U.S.C.A. §2310 about restrictions to claims (e.g. that no claim shall be cognizable in a suit brought under para (1)(B) of the subsection if the amount in controversy of any individual claim is less than the sum or value of USD 25).

398 Carter, Carolyn L., et al., *Consumer Warranty Law* (Boston: National Consumer Law Center, 2010), p. 98.

399 Ibid., pp. 101 and 343 *et seq.*

400 Ibid., p. 101. See also *Sadat v. American Motors Corp.*, 104 Ill. 2nd 105, 470 N.E. 2nd 997 (1984) (see *supra*, para. 46).

401 See also about injunctive relief: *Sadat v. American Motors Corp.*, 104 Ill. 2d 105 (1984) ('While we conclude that the plain language of the Magnuson-Moss Warranty Act extends the full range of equitable remedies to private litigants in appropriate situations, we do not find that the Act's general grant of equitable relief evinces congressional intent to dispense with the traditional equitable pleading requirements').

402 See, e.g., §104(a)(4) (15 U.S.C.A. §2304(a)(4)): refund or replacement available for certain warranties and circumstances not requiring e.g. that the defect is a substantial impairment: Carter, Carolyn L., et al., *Consumer Warranty Law* (Boston: National Consumer Law Center, 2010), p. 102.

§104(a)(1)[403] prescribes a kind of 'right to cure' for the sellers (the seller 'must as a minimum remedy such a consumer product') within a reasonable time and without any charge as a minimum requirement in case of a failure to conform the written warranty, or in case of a defect or malfunction. This 'right to cure' is a remedy that actually implies specific performance by the seller. Moreover, §104(a)(4)[404] prescribes a choice of the consumer between a refund or a replacement without charge (this last remedy can be considered specific performance) if the product that is affected by a defect of a malfunction cannot be remedied by a reasonable number of attempts by the warrantor.[405]

These statutory references to a 'right to cure' and 'replacement' imply an enhanced role for specific performance, compared to the UCC and general contract law. Moreover, the right to revoke acceptance is sometimes loosened. Taking this into account, it must be concluded that the hierarchy of remedies between damages, specific performance, and termination of the contract is somewhat relaxed with regard to consumer contracts, especially when a written warranty is given to the consumer.

2.5. CONCLUSION ON THE PRIORITY OF DAMAGES

Irreparable injury rule still alive. When comparing damages and specific performance, it must be concluded that the irreparable injury rule – favoring damages – has suffered severe losses under common contract law, but without being defeated. Under the UCC, the irreparable injury rule – requiring the uniqueness of goods before specific performance can be invoked – was intended to be liberalized. However, this liberalization did not cause its extinction, partly due to the fact that substitute goods are often available. For written guarantees, the Magnuson-Moss Warranty Act currently offers a performance-oriented remedy of replacement. However, any other specific remedy and cases that do not imply such a written warranty will have to obey the irreparable injury rule under this Act. 75

Termination made exceptional. Termination is regarded as an invasive tool. Therefore it has not been made easy to invoke it. Termination (or cancellation) by discharge of a contract by the creditor is, under 76

[403] Also 15 U.S.C.A. §2304(a)(1).
[404] Also 15 U.S.C.A. §2304(a)(4).
[405] See also *Sadat v. American Motors Corp.*, 104 Ill. 2nd 105, 470 N.E. 2nd 997 (1984) (this does not imply injunctive relief: see *supra*, para. 46).

common contract law, in principle only possible if two conditions are fulfilled: there must be a material breach of a reciprocal contract, and a period of time to cure the breach must have passed. Also, under the UCC it is not easy to invoke the remedies of rejection or revocation, for example, because of the requirement to give the seller a right to cure (rejection) and the requirement that there must be a substantial impairment due to the defect (revocation of acceptance).

77 *Influence of the right to cure.* Nonetheless, the last word has not yet been said about the 'hierarchy' of the remedies in common law. The fact that the seller has in some circumstances a right to cure before the termination of the contract may be invoked definitely has an impact on the organization of the remedies. Indeed, this implies that the right to cure, which might eventually lead to the performance of the contract, is sometimes higher in the hierarchy compared to termination. This unveils a contradiction in the current common law. Specific performance is thought to be the 'marginal' remedy in relation to damages. However, with regard to termination, common law shows a certain affinity to the performance-oriented seller's right to cure.

3. COMPARATIVE ANALYSIS: IN FAVOR OF A FREE CONSUMER CHOICE

3.1. CONTRASTING SYSTEMS?

78 *So different, yet so alike.* The remedial common law system is often contrasted with civil European law systems. The first system favors damages over specific performance and the second sticks with the promised contract,[406] favoring specific performance. When comparing the US and the EU consumer sales law remedies, the same picture emerges. At first sight, both systems' starting points are radically different and even reflect a divergent philosophy on contract law. Nevertheless, the exceptions to these basic rules in both systems are sometimes so important that it cannot be denied that both systems are converging.[407]

[406] Of course, the preference for specific performance is not present to the same extend in civil law countries.

[407] See also Haas, Daniel, et al., 'Introduction' in Smits, Jan, et al. (eds.), *Specific Performance in Contract Law: National and Other Perspectives* (Antwerp: Intersentia, 2008), p. 2 ('the practical difference between the civil law and the common law is not as great as the diverging principles suggest').

The main difference is that the consumer's burden of proof (if damages or specific performance are preferred as a remedy) will differ according to which system is applicable.

So different .... As a starting point it has to be admitted that (consumer) 79
sales remedies are structured in a different way when comparing the US and the EU system.

The Consumer Sales Directive, the Consumer Rights Directive (Proposal), and the ODSD/2017 Proposal all favor specific performance (often under the form of repair and replacement or a right to cure). Only under the (revoked) CESL, in B2C contracts, would the consumer not have to give priority to specific performance: hence there is a 'flat hierarchy' of remedies. Sometimes, the damages remedy is not even regulated at all (e.g. under the current Consumer Sales Directive). This is also an indicator that the damages remedy is not favored compared to specific performance. Common US contract law, UCC Article 2 and the Magnuson-Moss Warranty Act all assume the priority of damages to a higher or lesser degree.

As already mentioned, this difference in approach might be partially explained by Whitman's consumerism versus producerism paradox (see *supra*, para. 2 *in fine*).[408] According to this theory, the US is more consumer-oriented while the EU is more producer-oriented. Whitman's article has suggested that the different approach towards hierarchy of remedies in the US and the EU can be explained by the consumerism/producerism paradox. It argues that the European attachment to performance of the contract (specific performance/performance in kind by repair and replacement) and the 'right to cure' can be explained by a more producer-friendly approach. Indeed, the right to cure is considered to counterbalance the rights of the consumer in the consumer sales instruments.

Secondly, as mentioned earlier, both systems even seem to reflect a divergent philosophy on contract law. One of the reasons might be the major influence of the law and economics scholarship in the US (see *supra*, para. 53) for several decades, which was not so much the case in the EU.[409] For decades, an important part of this scholarship – notwithstanding

---

408 Whitman, James Q., 'Consumerism Versus Producerism: A Study in Comparative Law', 177 *Yale L.J.* (2007), 340–406.

409 See, regarding the EU perspective, Sibony, Anne-Lise, and Alemanno, Alberto, 'The Emergence of Behavioural Policy Making: A European Perspective' in Alemanno, Alberto, and Sibony, Anne-Lise (eds.), *Nudge and the Law: A European Perspective* (Oxford: Hart Publishing, 2015), p. 22.

discordant voices – defended the irreparable injury rule, favoring damages over specific performance, as being the most efficient solution.

80 ... *yet so alike*. Both systems may seem very different; however, there are more similarities than one would assume at first sight.[410] If the *termination remedy* (also called cancellation or rescission) is compared in the different legal systems, it has to be concluded that a certain degree of 'seriousness' is often required, both in the EU and the US[411] system. Exceptions to this rule are the right to reject under UCC Article 2 (application of the perfect tender rule), if it does not concern an installment contract and termination under the ODSD Proposal. Another recurrent restriction to termination is the right to cure. In the EU system, this flows from the priority of specific performance. But the US system also often recognizes a right to cure of the defaulting party (the seller). So it has to be concluded that the termination remedy is often restricted in several ways. This can be explained by the radical impact of this remedy, leading to the unwinding of the contract.

In both EU and US law, the priority of the preferred remedy (specific performance or damages) is not absolute. If this were always the case, the other remedies would never be applicable. This observation indicates that EU and US law does not differ as much as might be thought at first sight.

In EU law, specific performance, as the preferred remedy, is often ruled out if its application is impossible or unlawful; if the seller has not completed repair or replacement within reasonable time; if repair or replacement would cause significant inconvenience to the consumer; or if it seems that the seller will not bring the goods in conformity within a reasonable time. This implies that, even though specific performance is the preferred remedy in the EU consumer sales *acquis*, an unfettered right of specific performance does not exist.

In US law, the damages rule is far from absolute. Indeed, if damages are inadequate the promisee can claim a specific remedy. Inadequacy, e.g. under UCC Article 2, will be present when the goods are 'unique' or in other proper circumstances. More generally, specific performance will be more readily available if there are few substitutes on the market. Also, contracts involving land will often lead to the application of specific performance. Insolvency and other difficulties in retrieving damages from

410 See also Mak, Vanessa, *Performance-oriented Remedies in European Sale of Goods Law* (Oxford: Hart Publishing, 2009), p. 77.

411 Llewellyn defends that consumer should be permitted rescission (termination) for minor defects: Llewellyn, Karl N., 'On Warranty of Quality, and Society: II', *Colum. L. Rev.* (1937), p. 388.

the defaulting party may also lead to the inappropriateness of damages. Difficulties in the assessment of damages – implying a risk of over- and under-compensation – will also more easily lead to specific performance. Some sellers will even prefer to offer specific performance, as a way to protect their reputation.

Of course, other situations will lead to a preference for damages under US law. Unsurprisingly, these situations often coincide with those in which the EU consumer sales systems accept an exception to the priority of specific performance.[412] One of the main similarities is that specific performance will not be granted in case of impossibility, unlawfulness, or if it implies a personal involvement of the defaulting party (*intuitu personae* contracts or personal service contracts). Whereas the EU system does not accept the priority of specific performance if it entails too much burden for the consumer (creditor), the US system attaches more importance to the societal costs[413] and is not willing to accept specific performance when it is difficult to administer and costly for society. In this regard, it is also important to take into account the consumer's faith in the seller. If the consumer no longer trusts the seller, this can also constitute a reason to prefer damages (or other remedies) over specific performance. Both systems seem to take into account disproportionate 'hardship' to the debtor; however, in the EU system the choice of the consumer is often restricted to either repair or replacement, whichever is not the most disproportionate vis-à-vis the other. In the US system, this can rule out specific performance altogether. The US system, moreover, does not accept specific performance in situations in which there is too much uncertainty to allow the scope of performance to be determined.

The important exceptions in both systems – to the damages rule or the specific performance rule – point out that the main difference between both systems is the initially preferred remedy. The starting point differs, but the exceptions to the rule bring both systems closer together than assumed at first sight. The important difference is that the creditor (here the consumer) will have a different burden of proof in each system, depending on which remedy he prefers.

Finally, it has to be mentioned that while assessing the US common law system, many arguments have been summed up *pro* and *contra* the

412 See also Mak, Vanessa, *Performance-oriented Remedies in European Sale of Goods Law* (Oxford: Hart Publishing, 2009), p. 102 *et seq*.

413 The public interest element is not so important in civilian systems compared to common law: ibid., p. 105.

preference of damages over specific performance (see *supra*, para. 50 *et seq.*): moral arguments, law and economics theories, and behavioral studies. However, none of the arguments assessed in this book conclusively demonstrate that one remedy should be preferred over the other.

3.2. PROPOSAL FOR A FREE CONSUMER CHOICE WHILE RESPECTING GOOD FAITH

3.2.1. A Free Choice

81 *No hierarchy between damages and specific performance.* As a consequence, it is clear that none of the remedies – whether damages or specific remedies – should be preferred over the other and that there should be a free choice between those remedies. This means that specific performance[414] should be, as a principle, be freely available for the consumer-buyer – contrary to the current US system.[415] Indeed, it has to be noted that the exceptions to both rules are so far-reaching (the damages rule/the specific performance rule) that the idea of a free choice between damages and specific performance does not seem so revolutionary. The idea of a free choice between damages and specific performance has also already been defended by many US scholars.[416] The conclusion that specific performance should be freely available is, moreover, supported by a survey of consumers requested by the EU Commission.[417] One of

---

414 Also referring to repair and replacement in the EU system: ibid., p. 120 *et seq.* (repair and replacement have the same objective compared to specific performance; therefore the balancing exercise, taking into account the economic interest of both parties, about the availability of specific performance will be similar).

415 Also defends a general availability of specific performance: ibid., p. 110.

416 See e.g. Laycock, Douglas, *The Death of the Irreparable Injury Rule* (New York: Oxford University Press, 1991), 356p.; Linzer, Peter, 'On the Amorality of Contract Remedies – Efficiency, Equity, and the Second *Restatement*', *Colum. L. Rev.* (1981), pp. 111–39; Schwartz, Alan, 'The Case for Specific Performance', *Yale L.J.* (1979), pp. 271–306. See also Corbin, Arthur Linton, et al., *Corbin on Contracts* (New Providence, San Francisco: Matthew Bender & Co., Inc., 2016), pp. 12–63, §63.4; Dawson, John P., 'Specific Performance in France and Germany', 57 *Mich. L. Rev.* (1959), p. 532; Farnsworth, E. Allan, 'Legal Remedies for Breach of Contract', 70 *Colum. L. Rev.* (1970), p. 1156.

417 See pp. 6–7 of the Qualitative Eurobarometer Study, Sales Remedies, Conducted by TNS Qual+ at the request of Directorate General for Health and Consumers, December 2009, http://ec.europa.eu/consumers/archive/rights/docs/aggregate%20report_dec2009_en.pdf.

its conclusions is that replacement is one of the most preferred remedies for consumers.[418] The chosen goods were often particularly desired and the fact that they were defective does not change this.[419] If products are bought very advantageously, consumers will be more likely to opt for replacement.[420] Repair is less popular, except in cases of durable goods which have been used for a while or when consumers are emotionally attached to the goods.[421]

Free choice between damages and specific performance: but what about termination? How does termination fit in this 'preferred' hierarchy of remedies? Termination is, as pointed out, often restricted to more serious breaches of contract and by the seller's right to cure. However, a free choice is to be preferred between performance, damages, and termination of the contract. Consequently, the consumer should also be able to choose for termination in case of minor defects.[422] This was also the choice of the European legislator in the recent ODSD Proposal/2017 Proposal (see *supra*, para. 34). A minor defect can indeed be very annoying to a consumer, up to the point of no longer wanting the product. Moreover, the seller's right to cure should not hinder the ability of a consumer to invoke termination of the contract if the shortcoming happens at or after the date of delivery (see *infra*, paras. 89–91). However, it has to be noted that a shortcoming *before* the delivery date will allow the seller to cure his shortcoming. The previously mentioned consumer survey requested by the EU Commission[423] even concludes that, next to replacement, termination is one of the most preferred remedies of a consumer. Termination is indeed felt to be more appropriate in cases where the consumer does not *trust* the seller anymore (see *infra*, para. 84). Moreover, the consumer may prefer termination over replacement if the consumer thinks that the replacement 82

418 See p. 100 *et seq.* of the same study.
419 See p. 35 of the same study.
420 See p. 44 of the same study (Latvia, second row).
421 See pp. 50 and 95 *et seq.* of the same study.
422 Llewellyn defends the argument that consumers should be permitted rescission (termination) for minor defects: Llewellyn, Karl N., 'On Warranty of Quality, and Society: II', *Colum. L. Rev.* (1937), p. 388.
423 See p. 6 and p. 105 *et seq.* of the Qualitative Eurobarometer Study, Sales Remedies, Conducted by TNS Qual+ at the request of Directorate General for Health and Consumers, December 2009, http://ec.europa.eu/consumers/archive/rights/docs/aggregate%20report_dec2009_en.pdf (see also p. 91: a UK consumer stated in the survey: 'This bit about the order it would be in [...] it doesn't make you feel great that they are not legally obliged to always give you the money back').

will also be faulty,[424] when there is no exact replacement possible, or when there is not time to look for an alternative.[425] Another situation in which the consumer may prefer termination over replacement is when he wants to be given a choice.[426] A consumer would not prefer repair and replacement if it would take too much time.[427] In cross-border situations, the refund remedy is even more popular, because the replacement remedy is thought to be complicated (costly and time consuming) in such situations.[428]

83 *And the right to cure?* The freedom to choose between damages and specific performance does not only imply the freedom to choose for specific performance. It also implies the freedom for the consumer to choose for damages or termination. This will imply that the seller has no right to cure after delivery (see extensively *infra*, para. 89 *et seq*.).

84 *General arguments pro a free choice.* Unsurprisingly, the majority of the EU consumer associations support a free choice of remedies.[429] This indicates that a free choice of remedies is at least considered by those associations to be consumer-friendly.[430] Many arguments which will be invoked for free choice between the remedies touch upon psychological and sociological aspects, which can be connected to a behavioral approach of the law.

Firstly, free choice prevents the consumer from the danger of making *a wrong choice* between the remedies, and being punished or slowed down

---

[424] See p. 23 of the same study (in case of clothing, consumers seek more often replacement if the goods are thought to be of a high quality, while they seek more often a refund for goods of a lower quality).

[425] See p. 105 of the same study.

[426] See p. 15 and 106 of the same study ('I'd like to be reimbursed. If I want the product I'll buy it, I don't want it forced on me').

[427] See p. 86 of the same study.

[428] See p. 36 and 107 of the same study.

[429] See Explanatory Memorandum ODSD Proposal, Results of Ex-Post Evaluations, Stakeholder Consultations and Impact Assessments, p. 9, however businesses are in favor of a hierarchy of consumer remedies; BEUC, BEUC Position Paper on the ODSD Proposal, 3 June 2016, http://www.beuc.eu/publications/beuc-x-2016-053_csc_beuc_position_paper_on_tangible_goods_proposal.pdf, pp. 11–3. See also Briefing of the EU Parliament, EU Legislation in Progress, February 2016, European Parliamentary Research Service by R. Mańko, p. 3 ('Arguably, especially in online [consumer] sales, a refund instead of repair/replacement may be a better remedy').

[430] Cf. Mak, Vanessa, *Performance-oriented Remedies in European Sale of Goods Law* (Oxford: Hart Publishing, 2009), p. 47 (she admits that the balance of interests might be different according to whether the sale is made in a consumer or commercial context, but argues that most arguments (in preferring one remedy over the other) are similar in both contexts).

for choosing the wrong remedy.[431] Insecurity about their entitlement to certain remedies and an inability to freely choose among them might reduce the consumer's confidence and bargaining position. It is thus more consumer-friendly to give the consumer free choice.

Furthermore, being given a free choice, a consumer can assess whether or not he still *trusts* the seller after defaulting. Distrust will more likely lead to the exclusion of specific performance. This is – in the opinion of the present author – one of the explanations why the Belgian customers of VW were not satisfied by a mere software update (repair). They had probably lost confidence in VW. When the consumer has lost confidence or trust in the product or the seller, termination will often be the only appropriate remedy.[432]

Also, a free choice would also take into account that a consumer's preference for one or the other remedy is *not static and evolves* over time and takes into account the relationship with the seller.

Another argument for a free choice between the remedies is explicitly drawn from *behavioral* insights. As explained above (para. 4) the very existence of EU consumer law is mainly explained by the will to protect consumers (as weaker parties) and to create a functioning and efficient internal market. Sibony and Helleringer[433] correctly point out that behaviorists have demonstrated that consumers will flourish and feel more confident to buy products in a certain market when there is certain degree of ease or simplicity.[434] Moreover, a simplified (consumer) contract law can also be a tool to increase the level of trust between parties.[435] Trust and simplicity are indeed also two key elements with regard to the hierarchy of remedies. A free choice of remedies will, of course, increase the level

---

431 See, however, footnote 3, and the mitigating effect of the *Duarte Hueros* case.

432 See also page 13 Explanatory memorandum Proposal for European Parliament and Council Directive on the sale of consumer goods and associated guarantees, Brussels 18 June 1996, COM(95) 520 final, 96/0161 (COD).

433 Although their paper is focused on information duties: Sibony, Anne-Lise, and Helleringer, Geneviève, 'EU Consumer Protection and Behavioural Sciences: Revolution or Reform?' in Alemanno, Alberto, and Sibony, Anne-Lise (eds.), *Nudge and the Law: A European Perspective* (Oxford: Hart Publishing, 2015), p. 226 *et seq*.

434 See also more generally: Sibony, Anne-Lise, and Alemanno, Alberto, 'The Emergence of Behavioural Policy Making: A European Perspective' in Alemanno, Alberto, and Sibony, Anne-Lise (eds.), *Nudge and the Law: A European Perspective* (Oxford: Hart Publishing, 2015), pp. 16–17.

435 Sibony, Anne-Lise, and Helleringer, Geneviève, 'EU Consumer Protection and Behavioural Sciences: Revolution or Reform?' in Alemanno, Alberto, and Sibony, Anne-Lise (eds.), *Nudge and the Law: A European Perspective* (Oxford: Hart Publishing, 2015), pp. 228–29.

of simplicity for consumers.[436] The mere fact that, today, consumers can make a 'wrong' choice (see *supra*, e.g. paras. 1 and 12 *et seq.*), demonstrates the complexity of the current system in the EU and in the US. Abolishing the hierarchy of remedies and allowing a consumer to choose freely between the given remedies will dramatically increase the level of simplicity of the remedial apparatus for consumers. Secondly, it would also enhance the level of trust of consumers in the system and the sellers. The fact that the consumer has a choice between remedies in case of a non-conformity would probably increase his trust in the salesperson(s) and the legal system.

A shift towards a free choice of remedies would thus imply a more consumer-friendly approach. This would mean for the EU a shift from 'producerism' towards 'consumerism' to speak with Whitman's model (see *supra*, para. 79 and 4 *in fine*).[437] Nevertheless, this would not necessarily amount to purely 'economic' interests of the consumers (to buy at the most competitive prices), but rather to substantive or 'procedural' protection of consumers.[438]

3.2.2. Limited by Good Faith

85 *Boundaries set by a good faith obligation.* Of course, this free choice should not be unfettered. It has to be restricted by the principles of good faith[439] and proportionality[440] (or similar doctrines, such as the abuse of

---

436 However it can also be argued that more choice has a paralyzing effect on consumers and thus does not increase simplicity: White, Alan M., 'Behavior and Contract', 27 *Law & Inequality: A Journal of Theory and Practice* 1 (2009), p. 153.

437 Whitman, James Q., 'Consumerism Versus Producerism: A Study in Comparative Law', 177 *Yale L.J.* (2007), pp. 340–406.

438 Which is described by Whitman as being more 'paternalistic'.

439 Being aware that 'good faith' is a problematic concept under European contract law (not every country interprets this concept in the same way): Zimmermann, Reinhard and Whittaker, Simon, *Good Faith in European Contract Law* (Cambridge: Cambridge University Press, 2000), 720p. See esp. Whittaker, Simon, and Zimmermann, Reinhard, 'Good Faith in European Contract Law: Surveying the Legal Landscape' in Zimmermann, Reinhard, and Whittaker, Simon (eds.), *Good Faith in European Contract Law* (Cambridge: Cambridge University Press, 2000), p. 57 and Whittaker, Simon, and Zimmermann, Reinhard, 'Coming to Terms with Good Faith' in Zimmermann, Reinhard, and Whittaker, Simon (eds.), *Good Faith in European Contract Law* (Cambridge: Cambridge University Press, 2000), pp. 699–700. See also recently: Navarretta, Emanuela, 'Good Faith and Reasonableness in European Contract Law' in Rutgers, Jacobien, and Sirena, Pietro (eds.), *Rules and Principles in European Contract Law* (Cambridge: Intersentia, 2015), pp. 151–59.

440 Poillot, Elise, 'The ECJ and General Principles Derived from the Acquis Communautaire' in Rutgers, Jacobien, and Sirena, Pietro (eds.), *Rules and Principles in European Contract Law* (Cambridge: Intersentia, 2015), p. 37 (next to the principle

rights).[441] Good faith should be understood to mean that a party cannot be allowed to count on rights flowing from a contract which would lead to an 'absurdity'.[442] This is also sometimes called the 'limitative' function of good faith, limiting the exercise of rights.[443] If exercising a right (e.g. the freedom to choose remedies) would lead to a manifest disproportion, it should be unenforceable or 'reduced'. This would imply a balancing of the (economic/procedural) interests of the seller and the consumer.[444] If the choice of the consumer did not happen in good faith, the chosen remedy should be denied and another remedy should be applied. This is the case if the advantages for the consumer are not in proportion with the disadvantages for the seller, in the case of impossibility to perform or unlawfulness of performing. Under Belgian contract law, the discretion of the judge would be limited by assessing good faith by the principle which prohibits a party from abusing his own rights. A judge will only dismiss a certain claim if a reasonable and careful person would *manifestly* not ask for it in the same circumstances. Such a 'limited role' of good faith would not be at odds with the sanctity of contract and party autonomy.[445]

---

of proportionality the principle of effectiveness can also be a guide when there is no hierarchy between the remedies). See also Cauffman, Caroline, 'The Principle of Proportionality and European Contract Law' in Rutgers, Jacobien, and Sirena, Pietro (eds.), *Rules and Principles in European Contract Law* (Cambridge: Intersentia, 2015), pp. 69–98.

441 The prohibition of abuse of rights is, according to Lenaerts, a general principle of EU law: Lenaerts, Annekatrien, 'The General Principle of the Prohibition of Abuse of Rights: A Critical Position on its Role in a Codified European Contract Law', *ERPL* (2010), pp. 1128–39 (uses the term '*abuse of rights*'). See also for this opinion, Ionescu, Raluca Nicoleta, *L'abus de droit en droit de l'Union européenne* (Brussels: Bruylant, 2012), pp. 357–490; Cf. Vogenauer, Stefan, 'The Prohibition of Abuse of Law: An Emerging General Principle of EU Law' in De La Feria, Rita, and Vogenauer, Stefan (eds.), *Prohibition of Abuse of Law. A New General Principle of EU Law?* (Oxford: Hart Publishing, 2011), pp. 563–71 ('*abuse of law*' is only to be considered an embryonic general principle). Cf. Cauffman, Caroline, 'The Principle of Proportionality and European Contract Law', Working Paper n° 2013/2', http://ssrn.com (2013), pp. 18–22 (critical). See, for the relation between the principle of good faith and the principle of the prohibition of abuse of rights: Lenaerts, Annekatrien, 'The General Principle of the Prohibition of Abuse of Rights: A Critical Position on its Role in a Codified European Contract Law', *ERPL* (2010), pp. 1145 *et seq.*

442 Whittaker, Simon, and Zimmermann, Reinhard, 'Coming to Terms with Good Faith' in Zimmermann, Reinhard, and Whittaker, Simon (eds.), *Good Faith in European Contract Law* (Cambridge: Cambridge University Press, 2000), p. 693.

443 Lenaerts, Annekatrien, 'The General Principle of the Prohibition of Abuse of Rights: A Critical Position on its Role in a Codified European Contract Law', *ERPL* (2010), pp. 1146 *et seq.*, and 1153.

444 See Mak, Vanessa, *Performance-oriented Remedies in European Sale of Goods Law* (Oxford: Hart Publishing, 2009), pp. 106–08.

445 See also ibid., p. 107.

86 *Instrumental use of a free choice between damages and specific performance?* Some arguments can be raised against the *free choice* between damages and specific remedies.[446] In some systems, a lawyer might, for example, influence the choice of the consumer, inducing him to prefer damages so as to ensure the collection of his own fees. It is also possible that the consumer will make a tactical choice for specific performance, fearing that a judge would not take seriously a claim for damages if specific performance was still possible. A choice for specific performance can have a signaling effect to stress the seriousness of the case. Without wanting to minimize these arguments, a judge can, depending on the civil procedural system, try to take these biases into account. However, a detailed study of the powers of intervention of a judge would lead us too far.

87 *Good faith and the termination remedy.* If a consumer manifestly infringes the principle of good faith, he can be denied the remedy of terminating the contract. Because termination is such a far-reaching and harsh remedy, this implies that the consumer must be extra careful. This means that there must exist a certain proportionality between the shortcoming and the remedy that the consumer invokes. Also, because termination is such a far-reaching remedy, under some circumstances, *a right to cure* will be appropriate (see *infra*, para. 90).[447] Think about extrajudicial termination, which also has to be notified (see *infra*, Chapters 3 and 4). This will be a safeguard for the seller, which will protect him from unreasonable consumer choices.

88 *Relationship between partial termination and price reduction.* In systems that accept partial termination (material, personal, and temporal), the statement that a free choice should be allowed is even easier to understand. Indeed, partial termination is not as radical as termination, because the contract will only be partially unwound. Of course, the choice of partial termination will also be subject to the principles of good faith and proportionality. The same is true for a proportional price reduction.

3.3. INFLUENCE OF THE SELLER'S RIGHT TO CURE?

89 *In principle there is no right to cure after delivery.* What is, furthermore, the implication of the seller's right to repair/replace or *to cure* if the

---

446 Arbel, Yonathan, A., 'Contract Remedies in Action: Specific Performance', *W. Va. L. Rev.* (2015), pp. 369–410.

447 Mak, Vanessa, *Performance-oriented Remedies in European Sale of Goods Law* (Oxford: Hart Publishing, 2009), p. 174 et seq.

consumer merely asks for damages, price reduction, or termination? The seller's right to cure is also called 'the mirror image of the buyer's entitlement to specific performance'.[448] Under the current consumer *acquis*, the hierarchy of remedies will allow the seller to repair or to replace (i.e. to cure), because those remedies are considered the 'primary' remedies: not only a right of the buyer, but also of the seller. The Volkswagen case shows that a consumer is not always interested in repair as a remedy. If the trust between the parties is gone, the buyer might legitimately prefer damages or termination over specific performance. Under US common contract law and the UCC, the right to cure also exists. In the UCC, the seller has, for example, a right to cure before the buyer can invoke his right to reject.

However, a free choice of remedies implies that the seller – in principle – does not have a right to cure. A judge might deny the buyer a chosen remedy, only if the choice for damages or termination would constitute a manifest infringement of the principle of good faith.

Mak has defended the argument that the seller has to have a right to cure, *before* and *after* the delivery date.[449] This proposal can be approved with regard to a right to cure up until the contractual delivery date – since good faith will require from the consumer to have patience up until the delivery date[450] – but not, in consumer cases, after the contractual delivery date. It can also be argued that, in principle, a shortcoming *before* the delivery date cannot be officially seen as a 'breach'[451] or a 'non-conformity'; but after the delivery date, this will be the case. A right to cure after the delivery date considerably weakens the level of consumer protection compared to a system in which the consumer has a free choice between specific performance, termination, damages, and price reduction. Mak remarks that the hierarchy of remedies in the Consumer Sales Directive seems – by preferring repair and replacement – to be more inspired by 'considerations of an economic nature rather than by consumer protection policy'.[452] In this view, performance-oriented remedies are considered to avoid economic waste and to be the more economically efficient remedy.[453] However, as seen earlier, law and economic arguments

---

448 Ibid., p. 187.

449 However, she admits that the seller's right to cure after the delivery date might be more controversial and must be limited: ibid., p. 149 *et seq.* (a right to cure *after* the delivery date may not be available if time is of the essence).

450 The possibility of an anticipatory breach is not being taken into account here.

451 In that case the seller is not in breach: ibid., p. 152.

452 Ibid., pp. 150–51.

453 Ibid., pp. 150–51, 164.

are not able to convincingly prove the economic efficiency of either remedy (see *supra*, para. 53). It can be concluded that a consumer-friendly approach would not, in principle, imply a general right to cure for the seller after the date for delivery.

90 *Right to cure after delivery and good faith*. However, one has to remain cautious and good faith will sometimes require, in certain circumstances – even after the due date – that the seller is allowed an attempt to cure. This situation will rise when remedies are invoked extrajudicially. Especially in case of far-reaching remedies, such as termination, which are applied extrajudicially, good faith will often require the buyer to allow the seller an attempt to cure (see also *supra*, para. 87). Of course, this means that in certain situations the performance-oriented remedies may take precedence over the other remedies, hence introducing a certain hierarchy of remedies.

91 *Creating a climate for informal cure*. Moreover, it is not unwise to create a climate in which informal attempts to cure are encouraged.[454] The buyer may choose to ask the seller to cure informally before invoking another remedy. Moreover, it will be shown later that the duties to notify of a shortcoming or relating to an extrajudicial remedy can also play a crucial role in this regard (*infra*, Chapter 4).

---

454 See, regarding informal attempts to cure, ibid., p. 176 *et seq*. (but prefers a statutory system over an informal one: p. 184).

CHAPTER 3
SELF-HELP

Self-help and the organization of remedies. The fact that a remedy/right can be applied without any court intervention also *de facto* influences the organization of remedies. The easier a remedy can be applied, the fewer hurdles a creditor (a consumer) has to take to be able to invoke a remedy, and the more consumer-friendly the organization of remedies will be. 92

Terminology. Another important aspect to consider is the terminology in this domain. In contributions about European (consumer) contract law, the terms 'extrajudicial remedies' or 'unilateral remedies' will often be encountered when describing a remedy for breach of contract that can be applied by the creditor without prior court intervention. A remedy that needs prior court intervention is often described as a 'judicial remedy'. Those terms are not used in US doctrine which makes a sharp distinction between, on the one hand, the so-called 'remedies' (such as damages and specific performance) that can only be applied judicially and require prior court intervention and, on the other hand, the so-called rights to self-help (such as suspension and termination of the contract) or 'privately administered remedies'.[455] 93

1. EU CONSUMER SALES *ACQUIS*

1.1. CONSUMER SALES DIRECTIVE PROVIDES NO CLEAR GUIDELINES

The doubtful case for self-help and termination. The 15th recital of the Consumer Sales Directive prescribes that it will be necessary to look at national law for the specific arrangement of the remedy of *termination.* 94

[455] See for this terminology: Katz, Avery W., 'Remedies for Breach of Contract under the CISG', 25 *Int. Rev. L. Econ.* (2006), p. 390, footnote 45.

Bianca is of the opinion that the remedy of *termination* can be invoked unilaterally in every case (whether national law prescribes it or not), and that this 15th recital only counts for 'secondary procedural aspects'.[456] However, in Belgian law for example, doctrine correctly follows a different approach: namely, that for this aspect (the judicial or unilateral character of this remedy), national law applies.[457] For Belgian law this means that termination must – in principle – be invoked judicially. Only in case of an express resolutory clause or in extraordinary circumstances can termination be applied without court intervention (unilateral or extrajudicial termination).

95 *Self-help for repair, replacement, and price reduction.* When focusing on the remedies of repair, replacement, and price reduction, it should be noted that these remedies are not mentioned in this 15th recital of the Directive. Does this mean that all those remedies can be invoked without any prior court intervention?

In case of *price reduction* it has to be taken into account that Belgian law does not provide the remedy of price reduction as a general remedy for non-conformity as provided for in the CSD.[458] Consequently, Bianca might be followed this time, assuming that the remedy of price reduction can be invoked *unilaterally*, but that the intervention of a judge will be necessary if there is a dispute concerning the amount of the reduction.[459] However, we must remain cautious in this respect.

---

456 Bianca, Cesare Massimo, 'Article 3. Droits et remèdes du consommateur' in Bianca, Cesare Massimo, et al. (eds.), *La directive communautaire sur la vente, Commentaire* (Brussels/Paris: Bruylant-LGDJ, 2004), p. 206.

457 Steennot, Reinhard, and Dejonghe, Sophie, *Consumentenbescherming en Handelspraktijken* (Antwerp: Intersentia, 2007), p. 540. See also Stijns, Sophie, 'De remedies van de koper bij niet-conformiteit' in Stijns, Sophie, and Jules Stuyck (eds.), *Het nieuwe kooprecht, De wet van 1 september 2004 betreffende de bescherming van de consumenten bij verkoop van consumptiegoederen* (Antwerp: Intersentia, 2005), pp. 74–6. Wéry, Patrick, 'Les droits légaux du consommateur en cas de défaut de conformité' in Biquet-Mathieu, Christine, and Patrick Wéry (eds.), *La nouvelle garantie des biens de consommation et son environnement légal* (Brussels: die Keure, 2005), pp. 152–53: the author is, however, critical about the fact that the legislator has not provided for a unilateral termination-option for the consumer.

458 In Belgian law, the remedy of price reduction is currently only accepted in cases of hidden defects of a sold good '*actio quanti minoris*' (see Art. 1644 B.W.) and in commercial sales contracts if there is a minor difference in quality or quantity. See also extensively: Jansen, Sanne, *Prijsvermindering: remedie tot bijsturing van contracten* (Antwerp: Intersentia, 2015), 1200p.

459 Bianca, Cesare Massimo, 'Article 3. Droits et remèdes du consommateur' in Bianca, Cesare Massimo, et al. (eds.), *La directive communautaire sur la vente, Commentaire* (Brussels/Paris: Bruylant-LGDJ, 2004), p. 206. Zimmermann is of the opinion that the purchaser (buyer) cannot unilaterally terminate (or reduce the price) under

Also with regard to *repair and replacement*, Bianca advocates that a consumer must be allowed to apply these remedies without any prior intervention of a court.[460] The CSD does not provide something specifically, but prescribes that the consumer may 'require' the seller to repair the goods or to replace them.[461] This seems to allow the consumer to ask the seller for extrajudicial repair or replacement. Only if the seller does not react and comply, a judicial intervention will be necessary to force the seller to perform specifically.

1.2. CESL PROVIDES SEVERAL EXTRAJUDICIAL REMEDIES

Termination by notification. The CESL is very favorable towards self-help remedies. Termination can be exercised by notification (Article 118 CESL). However, Article 119 CESL makes it clear that the buyer, if he is not a consumer, loses his right to terminate the contract if notice is not given within a reasonable time (see also *infra*, para. 120). 96

Other remedies. The wording of the CESL does not make clear whether or not price reduction can be invoked without prior intervention of a judge.[462] Nevertheless, the terms of Article 120.1 CESL are the following: 'A buyer [...] may reduce the price'. Consequently, it can be considered that this remedy can be applied without prior intervention of a judge, as a self-help remedy.[463] It is not clear whether this extrajudicial variant must 97

the Consumer Sales Directive ('by his own act'), but that he has only a claim for termination (or price reduction): Zimmermann, Reinhard, *The New German Law of Obligations* (Oxford: Oxford University Press, 2004), pp. 107 and 113–14.

460 Bianca, Cesare Massimo, 'Article 3. Droits et remèdes du consommateur' in Bianca, Cesare Massimo, et al. (eds.), *La directive communautaire sur la vente, Commentaire* (Brussels/Paris: Bruylant-LGDJ, 2004), pp. 205–06.

461 See Art. 3.3 Consumer Sales Directive and the 10th–11th recitals.

462 See, on how to exercise the price reduction remedy, Feltkamp, Regine, and Vanbosselе, Frederic, 'Remedies Under the Optional Common European Sales Law – A Good Alternative for Belgian Sales Law?' in Claeys, Ignace, and Feltkamp, Regine (eds.) *The Draft Common European Sales Law: Towards an Alternative Sales Law?* (Antwerp: Intersentia, 2013), n° 50 ('Article 120 does not indicate further how the price reduction is to be determined and by whom').

463 Jansen, Sanne, 'Price Reduction as a Remedy in European Contract Law and the Consumer Acquis' in Keirse, Anne L.M., and Loos, Marco B.M. (eds.), *Alternative Ways to Ius Commune. The Europeanisation of Private Law* (Antwerp: Intersentia, 2012), p. 193; Jansen, Sanne, *Prijsvermindering: remedie tot bijsturing van contracten* (Antwerp: Intersentia, 2015), n° 434.

also be exercised upon notice, which is the case for termination; however, this probably will also be necessary.[464] For the sake of completeness, Article 113 must also be mentioned, prescribing an extrajudicial right to withhold performance, which will not be discussed further. Furthermore, Article 110 CESL prescribes that the buyer is entitled to 'require' performance of the seller's obligations. This also (*cf. supra*, para. 95) seems to allow the consumer to ask the seller for extrajudicial specific performance. It is only if the seller does not react and comply, that a judicial intervention will be necessary to force the seller to perform specifically.

1.3. ODSD/2017 PROPOSAL PROVIDES SEVERAL EXTRAJUDICIAL REMEDIES

98 *Termination upon notice.* Article 13.1 ODSD/2017 Proposal explicitly prescribes a termination upon notice by the consumer to the seller: 'The consumer shall exercise the right to terminate the contract by notice to the seller given by any means'. This means that the consumer can apply the termination remedy without prior intervention of a judge.[465] It thus goes a step further than the current Consumer Sales Directive, which leaves it to the Member States to design the termination remedy (see *supra*, para. 94).

99 *Other remedies.* Article 12 ODSD/2017 Proposal dedicated to price reduction does not hint towards whether it can be applied extrajudicially: 'The reduction of the price shall be proportionate to [...]'. Unfortunately, Article 9 ODSD/2017 Proposal does not hint towards extrajudicial application of price reduction: 'The consumer shall be *entitled*

464 Schmidt-Kessel, Martin, 'Art. 120 GEK-E' in Schmidt-Kessel, Martin (ed.), *Der Entwurf für ein Gemeinsames Europäisches Kaufrecht* (Munich: Sellier, 2014), p. 604; Schulze, Reiner, and Zoll, Fryderyk (eds.), *European Contract Law* (Munich: Beck, 2016), p. 262; Zoll, Fryderyk, 'Article 120' in Schulze, Reiner (ed.), *Common European Sales Law (CESL)* (Munich: Beck, 2012), p. 527.

465 See also Claeys, Ignace, and Vancoillie, Jonas, 'Remedies, Modification of Digital Content and Right to Terminate Long-Term Digital Content Contracts' in Claeys, Ignace, and Terryn, Evelyne (eds.), *Digital Content & Distance Sales* (Cambridge: Intersentia, 2017), pp. 189–90; Straetmans, Gert, and Meys, Shana, 'The New Proposals for Directives Concerning Digital Content and Online/Distance Sales' in Claeys, Ignace, and Terryn, Evelyne (eds.), *Digital Content & Distance Sales* (Cambridge: Intersentia, 2017), p. 333.

to a proportionate reduction of the price [...]'.[466] Furthermore, Article 9.4 ODSD/2017 Proposal prescribes an extrajudicial right for the consumer to withhold the payment of any outstanding part of the price, until the seller has brought the goods into conformity with the contract. Finally, Article 9.1 ODSD/2017 Proposal does not make clear whether specific performance can be applied without any prior intervention by a judge: 'In the case of a lack of conformity with the contract, the consumer shall be entitled to have the goods brought into conformity by the seller, free of charge, by repair or replacement in accordance with Article 11'. The term 'shall be entitled' does not really hint towards an extrajudicial application of remedies. When comparing this with the CSD, the wording of which hints towards the possibility of extrajudicial price reduction, repair, and replacement, the ODSD/2017 Proposal loses on clarity and consumer-friendliness.

2. COMMON LAW APPROACH

Rights to self-help. Interestingly, the US (common law) system explicitly 100
provides for statutory self-help rights under the UCC[467] (sales)[468] and implicitly provides for such rights by the 2nd restatement[469] of contract law.[470] They are seen as opposed to so-called 'judicial' remedies such as damages, specific performance, and injunctions (see also *supra*, para. 93).

---

466 Emphasis added. See also about this question Straetmans, Gert, and Meys, Shana, 'The New Proposals for Directives Concerning Digital Content and Online/Distance Sales' in Claeys, Ignace, and Terryn, Evelyne (eds.), *Digital Content & Distance Sales* (Cambridge: Intersentia, 2017), p. 332 (but the authors do not provide the answer either).

467 UCC is the abbreviation for Uniform Commercial Code. Consulted version: https://www.law.cornell.edu/ucc.

468 See, e.g., UCC §2-601 (extrajudicial termination: 'perfect tender rule'), §2-712 ('cover') and §2-717 (deduction of damages from the price).

469 http://www.lexinter.net/LOTWVers4/restatement_(second)_of_contracts.htm.

470 See, for detail, Taylor, Celia R., 'Self-help in Contract Law: An Exploration and Proposal', 33 *Wake Forest L. Rev.* (1998), pp. 839–907. See also on self-help remedies Gergen, Mark P., 'A Theory of Self-help Remedies in Contract', 89 *B.U L. Rev.* (2009), pp. 1397–449. See more generally on self-help (and its constitutional aspects) Pozen, David E., 'Self Help and the Separation of Powers', 124 *Yale L.J.* (2014), pp. 2–90. See also on the UK and Australia with regard to termination: Musgrave, Thomas D., 'Comparative Contractual Remedies', *U.W. Austl. L. Rev.* (2008–09), p. 338 *in fine.*

Often the general term of 'self-help' is defined by US scholarship as follows: 'legally permissible conduct that individuals undertake absent the compulsion of law and without the assistance of a government official in efforts to prevent or remedy a legal wrong'.[471] This definition clearly transcends the right to self-help in case of breach of contract and encompasses behavior such as self-defense, arbitration, and abatement. This book will be confined to the right to self-help in case of breach of contract, whereby the creditor reacts appropriately to a breach of contract without a prior court intervention.[472] This implies that the creditor reacts in a unilateral way.[473] Of course, this reaction can always be subject to a final determination by a court when challenged by the counterparty.[474]

101 *Self-help as an 'ugly duckling'?* In common contract law, self-help remedies are not often discussed. More commonly, the judicial remedies such as damages, injunctions, and specific performance attract the attention. Only a few scholars, such as Gergen and Taylor, have devoted attention to this particular category of remedies – not requiring any prior intervention by a judge.[475]

---

[471] Brandon, Douglas I., et al., 'Special Project: Self-Help: Extrajudicial Rights, Privileges and Remedies in Contemporary American Society', 37 *Vand. L. Rev.* (1984), p. 850. See also: Badawi, Adam B., 'Self-Help and the Rules of Engagement', 29 *Yale J. On Reg.* (2012), pp. 7–8 (reframing it as 'situations where someone has the right or privilege to do something that could also be done through an agent of the state once a court or other state entity has verified the claim'); Corbin, Arthur Linton, et al., *Corbin on Contracts* (New Providence, San Francisco: Matthew Bender & Co., Inc., 2016), §63.22; Sinel, Zoë, 'De-Ciphering Self-Help', 67 *U. Toronto L.J.* (2017), p. 32 (but this author refines this definition as a 'privilege arising from a wrong').

[472] See also: Gergen, Mark P., 'A Theory of Self-help Remedies in Contract', 89 *B.U L. Rev.* (2009), p. 1397 ('by which I mean actions a party may take to obtain redress for breach of contract without going to court').

[473] See, regarding the difference between cooperative and non-cooperative (unilateral) self-help: Taylor, Celia R., 'Self-help in Contract Law: An Exploration and Proposal', 33 *Wake Forest L. Rev.* (1998), pp. 853–54.

[474] See also about the importance of this aspect: Sinel, Zoë, 'De-Ciphering Self-Help', 67 *U. Toronto L.J.* (2017), p. 67; Taylor, Celia R., 'Self-help in Contract Law: An Exploration and Proposal', 33 *Wake Forest L. Rev.* (1998), p. 846.

[475] Gergen, Mark P., 'A Theory of Self-help Remedies in Contract', 89 *B.U L. Rev.* (2009), pp. 1397–449; Taylor, Celia R., 'Self-help in Contract Law: An Exploration and Proposal', 33 *Wake Forest L. Rev.* (1998), pp. 839–907. See also: Brandon, Douglas I., et al., 'Special Project: Self-Help: Extrajudicial Rights, Privileges and Remedies in Contemporary American Society', 37 *Vand. L. Rev.* (1984), p. 911 *et seq.*; Farnsworth, E. Allan, *Farnsworth on Contracts* (New York: Kluwer, 2004), §8.19a.

Delimitation – This book will not deal with each and every manifestation of self-help in contract law. Therefore, it will not deal topics such as the doctrine of adequate assurances, the repossession of goods,[476] and set-off. 102

2.1. SUSPENSION AND TERMINATION UNDER COMMON CONTRACT LAW

Suspension and termination/cancellation. Under common contract law, two important self-help remedies are suspension and termination/cancellation in case of breach of contract.[477] We have seen before under which circumstances both remedies can be invoked (see *supra*, para. 58). Their application has been made difficult by requiring a material/total breach of contract and – reserved to termination – a right to cure for the debtor. Once these difficult requirements have been fulfilled, the creditor does not need to wait for a prior intervention of the court and can – at his own risk[478] – suspend or terminate the contract. However, the difficulty of invoking these self-help remedies lies precisely in the vague nature of the concept of a 'material breach of contract'.[479] If the creditor decides to rely on a self-help remedy, and misjudges the concept of a 'material breach of contract', he risks being himself found at breach.[480] As unilaterally 103

476 See e.g. Badawi, Adam B., 'Self-Help and the Rules of Engagement', 29 *Yale J. On Reg.* (2012), p. 23 *et seq.*; Brandon, Douglas I., et al., 'Special Project: Self-Help: Extrajudicial Rights, Privileges and Remedies in Contemporary American Society', 37 *Vand. L. Rev.* (1984), p. 916 *et seq.*

477 See e.g. Farnsworth, E. Allan, *Farnsworth on Contracts* (New York: Kluwer, 2004), §8.15. See for the historical background of these self-help remedies: Taylor, Celia R., 'Self-help in Contract Law: An Exploration and Proposal', 33 *Wake Forest L. Rev.* (1998), pp. 860–62. See also about suspension as a self-help and 'indirect' remedy: Lewinsohn-Zamir, Daphna, 'Do the Right Thing: Indirect Remedies in Private Law', 94 *B.U L. Rev.* (2014), p. 63 *et seq.*

478 See, regarding this aspect, Taylor, Celia R., 'Self-help in Contract Law: An Exploration and Proposal', 33 *Wake Forest L. Rev.* (1998), p. 850. See also Ferriell, Jeff, *Understanding Contracts* (New Providence, San Francisco: Matthew Bender & Co., Inc., 2009), p. 532.

479 Taylor, Celia R., 'Self-help in Contract Law: An Exploration and Proposal', 33 *Wake Forest L. Rev.* (1998), p. 864. See also Badawi, Adam B., 'Self-Help and the Rules of Engagement', 29 *Yale J. On Reg.* (2012), p. 39 *et seq.* (the breach has to be clear in order to allow a party to withhold his performance, this means that doctrine creates incentives to perform rather than to withhold).

480 Taylor, Celia R., 'Self-help in Contract Law: An Exploration and Proposal', 33 *Wake Forest L. Rev.* (1998), p. 864.

terminating a contract is the most invasive form of self-help, one has to be careful not to treat the debtor unfairly and it will be necessary to assess carefully whether there is effectively a material breach of contract.[481]

104 *Other self-help remedies.* Apart from extrajudicial termination of the contract, other self-help remedies are also applied under common contract law.[482] A party can exercise its power to repair a defect in performance or to obtain an equivalent of the promised performance and then collect the cost of repair or the equivalent. This is often called an 'incomplete' form of self-help.[483] Another self-help remedy is the power to complete performance on repudiation and to collect the contract price.

105 *The 2nd restatement of contract law.* Although the 2nd restatement does not explicitly mention the concept of 'self-help remedy', it gives some implicit guidance with regard to some such remedies.[484]

With regard to termination, we have already seen that §237 acknowledges the right of the creditor to terminate unilaterally the contract if the breach of contract amounts to a material breach (see *supra*, para. 58). The assessment of this material breach (see also §241) is at the risk of the non-breaching party, who will face the consequence of being at breach himself if termination is wrongly applied. The difficulty of this assessment might reduce the effectiveness of the termination self-help remedy in this regard.[485] Also, the seller's right to cure, which is present in §237 of the 2nd restatement (see also *supra*, para. 58) has to be considered.[486] This means that the buyer's right to unilaterally terminate the contract upon a material breach can be stopped by the seller's successfully applied right to cure. This seller's right to cure has also to be considered a 'self-help' remedy, because it does not require any prior intervention by a judge. This second hurdle, the fact that the debtor has a right to cure and that the creditor must give the latter a period to effect cure, makes it even harder to

[481] See e.g.: Murray, John E., *Murray on Contracts* (Durham: Carolina Academic Press, 2011), §108.

[482] Gergen, Mark P., 'A Theory of Self-help Remedies in Contract', 89 *B.U L. Rev.* (2009), p. 1436.

[483] Corbin, Arthur Linton, et al., *Corbin on Contracts* (New Providence, San Francisco: Matthew Bender & Co., Inc., 2016), §63.22.

[484] Taylor, Celia R., 'Self-help in Contract Law: An Exploration and Proposal', 33 *Wake Forest L. Rev.* (1998), p. 878.

[485] Ibid., p. 879.

[486] See also extensively on the concrete application of the right to cure under the 2nd restatement of contract law: ibid., pp. 880–81.

unilaterally terminate the contract. This all shows the 'unwillingness of the restatement to encourage self-help'.[487]

With regard to the 'deduction of damages' the introductory note to Chapter 16 of the 2nd restatement on remedies states that it does 'not deal with the extent to which a party to a contract is empowered to protect himself or to obtain satisfaction by methods not involving recourse to a court, such as deducting damages that he claims from the price that he owes'.[488] This indicates that the 2nd restatement does not provide any guidelines with regard to this kind of self-help remedy.

2.2. REJECTION, REVOCATION, AND CURE UNDER UCC ARTICLE 2

Rejection and cure. As this book focuses upon the buyer's remedies in 106
(consumer) sales law, it has to be taken into account that the common law remedy of termination is clearly regulated in UCC Article 2 for sales contracts. It has to be noted that the UCC does not explicitly label the remedies of rejection and revocation (or the subsequent right to cancel the contract) as self-help remedies.[489] Nevertheless, it allows the buyer in many occasions to take action without a prior court intervention.[490]

We have seen that – in principle – the perfect tender rule applies when the buyer wants to *reject* the performance and cancel the contract (UCC §2-601, see *supra*, para. 70). This high standard implies – contrary to the material breach rule – that it is easy for the buyer to invoke this remedy.[491] However, UCC §2-508 tempers a potential harsh treatment of the seller by allowing the latter a 'right to cure' (see *supra*, para. 69). The seller's right to cure can also be considered a self-help remedy, but a self-help remedy that is exercised by the seller (and not by the buyer).[492]

---

487 Taylor, Celia R., ibid., p. 881.

488 Introductory note to Chapter 16, 2nd restatement of contract law, pp. 99–100.

489 Taylor, Celia R., 'Self-help in Contract Law: An Exploration and Proposal', 33 *Wake Forest L. Rev.* (1998), p. 868 *et seq.*

490 Ferriell, Jeff, *Understanding Contracts* (New Providence, San Francisco: Matthew Bender & Co., Inc., 2009), p. 751 ('Cancellation is the unilateral termination of the contract due to breach'). See also Speidel, Richard E., 'Buyer's Remedies of Rejection and Cancellation under the UCC and the Convention', 6 *J. Contract L.* (1993), p. 131.

491 Taylor, Celia R., 'Self-help in Contract Law: An Exploration and Proposal', 33 *Wake Forest L. Rev.* (1998), p. 869.

492 Ibid., pp. 873–75.

107 *Revocation*. The above-mentioned perfect tender rule is not applicable after acceptance of the goods, because the right to revoke acceptance and to cancel the contract requires a 'substantial impairment' of the value of the goods to the buyer (see *supra*, para. 70).[493] In addition, revocation and the subsequent cancellation of the contract – as is the case for termination under common law – can be invoked by the buyer without prior intervention by the court.[494]

108 *Cover*. Another self-help remedy under UCC Article 2 is 'cover' in §2-712. The buyer who has not received the promised performance can go out on the market and buy substitute goods. The action to 'cover' is considered a self-help remedy, although further legal action might have to be undertaken to recover the amounts invested in the cover transaction (i.e. damages; cover is an incomplete form of self-help, see *supra*, para. 104).[495] The authorization of the self-help remedy of cover in UCC Article 2 and the ease with which it can be invoked (also due to the perfect tender rule) is considered to demonstrate the UCC's strong support for self-help'.[496]

109 *Deduction of damages*. UCC §2-717 allows the buyer to deduce damages from the contract price, which is an application of the common law principle of set-off. The details of this self-help remedy will not be explored, but it might be risky to invoke this remedy unilaterally because the buyer has to make a correct assessment of the proper amount that he would deduce from the price.[497]

110 *Other self-help remedies*. Very briefly, the self-help remedies of identification and recovery of the goods to the contract[498] and resale of goods in the buyer's possession upon a rejection or justifiable revocation of acceptance[499] also have to be mentioned. An elaborate discussion of these remedies goes beyond the scope of this book.

---

493 However, it is challenged whether judges apply this last rule so strictly: Gergen, Mark P., 'A Theory of Self-help Remedies in Contract', 89 *B.U L. Rev.* (2009), p. 1414 ('courts are very protective of buyers' rights').

494 Fonseca, Patricia F., and Fonseca, John R., *Williston on Sales* (Eagan: West, 2006), p. 737 ('Revocation is unilateral in nature [...]. The assent of the seller is not needed').

495 See Taylor, Celia R., 'Self-help in Contract Law: An Exploration and Proposal', 33 *Wake Forest L. Rev.* (1998), p. 869.

496 Ibid., p. 870.

497 Ibid., p. 871.

498 UCC §2-711(2)(a).

499 UCC §2-711(3).

3. COMPARATIVE ANALYSIS: MOVING TOWARDS MORE SELF-HELP

Self-help as consumer emancipator. A self-help/extrajudicial remedy is positive for consumers and has to be considered as a consumer protective measure. It changes things for consumers, because if the consumer invokes a certain remedy without prior court intervention, it is often up to the seller to ask a judge to intervene if he disagrees.[500] If the consumer has already paid – which makes it more difficult for a consumer to apply, for example, price reduction or termination without the prior intervention of a judge – one must not underestimate the *psychological* advantage of extrajudicial remedies. The mere fact that the consumer has the right to extrajudicially invoke a remedy, enables consumers to claim their rights and to speak up. It enhances the consumers' *bargaining position*. It can actually be seen – in the present author's opinion – as an emancipator for consumers. 111

Termination as an extrajudicial remedy. Almost under all EU instruments discussed here, termination can be applied extrajudicially. One exception is the EU Consumer Sales Directive, in which the 15th recital leaves the Member States free to regulate the elaboration of the termination remedy. Some Member States, such as Belgium, which still do not allow a general right to extrajudicial termination, are thus not obliged to introduce this possibility. Termination can also be invoked extrajudicially in the US system. This free availability of an extrajudicial termination is, however, often offset by the more stringent requirements that have to be fulfilled in order to invoke this remedy. The requirement for a certain degree of seriousness of the breach and a right to cure will often make it more difficult to invoke termination. 112

Indeed, termination is the most invasive remedy, allowing the whole contract to be unwound. When allowing this remedy extrajudicially, good faith (see also *supra*, para. 87) will often require a certain proportionality with the breach of contract and a certain period for the seller in which he can still perform (i.e. right to cure). However, this last aspect (a right to cure) is of specific importance if the termination remedy is invoked extrajudicially, and is of lesser importance if this remedy is invoked in judicial proceedings, given that the seller often has already had ample of opportunity to cure his breach in the latter situation. But even in case of

500 This is, of course, not the case if the consumer has already paid in case of price reduction or termination of the contract.

an extrajudicial termination, a situation of urgency can prevent the seller from invoking his right to cure. Therefore, no harsh rules are recommended, but rather the principle of good faith that can be applied in a flexible manner in order to fit all situations.

113 *(Extra)judicial application of specific performance.* The EU instruments do not explicitly foresee or prescribe an extrajudicial application of specific performance (repair or replacement). Nevertheless, the consumer protection background of these instruments and their wording often seem to allow that the consumer can unilaterally invoke specific performance. However, if the seller does not comply, the consumer will be obliged to ask a judge to enforce specific performance.

In the US system, specific performance is certainly not considered a self-help right. A consumer would have to go to the judge to enforce it. Nevertheless, similar to the EU system, nothing stops a consumer from asking the seller for specific performance without first going to a judge.

114 *Damages are never applied extrajudicially.* The damages remedy is typically, under all systems, applied judicially because of the necessary assessment of the amount of damages by a judge. Therefore, damages are understandably never mentioned when examining self-help or extrajudicial remedies.

CHAPTER 4
NOTIFICATION DUTIES

Influence of notification duties. Notification duties directly influence the hierarchy of remedies. Remedies are easier to invoke if they are not subject to a duty of notification. Consequently, stringent notification duties will often limit the ability of consumers to invoke their remedies. On the other hand, the stricter the notification and examination duties, the more the stability of the contract is promoted.[501] 115

Different kinds of notification duties. A first category of notification duties deals with warning the debtor of the fact that there is a shortcoming. Some systems require that the creditor 'puts his debtor in default' ('*mise en demeure/ingebrekestelling*', see *infra*, para. 139). Other systems introduce a 'notification duty' of the creditor, obliging the latter to inform his debtor that there is a shortcoming in the contract. A second category is the notification duties that deal with the remedies themselves. Certain remedies (especially extrajudicial remedies) require that the creditor must warn the debtor of his intention to invoke the remedy. 116

1. EU CONSUMER SALES *ACQUIS*

1.1. CONSUMER SALES DIRECTIVE

1.1.1. Optional Duty to Notify of Shortcomings

Facultative notification duty. In its 19th recital, the Consumer Sales Directive mentions a possibility for Member States to set a period within which the consumer must inform the seller of any lack of conformity, which may not be less than *two months* after the consumer has *detected* 117

501 Zoll, Fryderyk, 'Article 106' in Schulze, Reiner (ed.), *Common European Sales Law (CESL)* (Munich: Beck, 2012), p. 491.

(or discovered) it (see also Article 5.2 CSD). The notification duty only runs after the actual discovery of the non-conformity, implying that the buyer is not under a duty to examine the delivered goods.[502] It also allows Member States to ensure a higher level of protection for the consumer by not introducing such an obligation. Member States have currently regulated this possibility of a notification duty in various ways.[503]

The Belgian law maker has decided that parties may agree to set a period within which the consumer must inform the seller of any lack of conformity, which may not be less than two months as from the day the consumer has discovered the defect.[504] The Belgian implementation of the Consumer Sales Directive does not mention any sanction if (the agreed period for) the duty to notify has not been respected.[505] Belgian commentators report that contracts between consumers and sellers often state that the consumer is no longer allowed to claim a remedy if he fails to notify a lack of conformity within the contractual period of time that was stipulated.[506]

1.1.2. No Regulation Governing the Duty to Notify of Remedies

118 *Regulation left to national order.* The Consumer Sales Directive does not comment on the duty to notify the application of the chosen remedies.[507] In Belgium, legal doctrine is clear that the choice of the consumer to invoke a remedy must be *notified* to the seller; the consumer must make

---

[502] Jeloschek, Christoph, *Examination and Notification Duties in Consumer Sales Law* (Munich: Sellier, 2006), p. 49 (footnote 74).

[503] See e.g. Explanatory Memorandum ODSD Proposal, p. 6 (in 11 Member States the consumer does not have to notify, in 12 Member States there is a possibility to notify within 2 months, and in 5 Member States the consumer has to notify within a different period of time).

[504] Art. 1649*quater*, §2 CC.

[505] Some Belgian commentators claim that the consumer will be contractually liable towards the seller: Delforge, Catherine, et al., 'De quelques délais emblématiques du contrat de vente' in X., *Contrats spéciaux* (Limal: Anthemis, 2013), n° 71.

[506] Claeys, Ignace, and Vancoillie, Jonas, 'Remedies, Modification of Digital Content and Right to Terminate Long-Term Digital Content Contracts' in Claeys, Ignace, and Terryn, Evelyne (eds.), *Digital Content & Distance Sales* (Cambridge: Intersentia, 2017), p. 179.

[507] Jansen, Sanne, 'Price Reduction as a Remedy in European Contract law and the Consumer Acquis' in Keirse, Anne L.M., and Loos, Marco B.M. (eds.), *Alternative Ways to Ius Commune. The Europeanisation of Private Law* (Antwerp: Intersentia, 2012), pp. 183–84.

clear which remedy he has chosen.[508] Article 1649*quinquies*, §2 and §3 CC states that the consumer has the right to 'claim' ('*eisen*' or '*verlangen*'/'*exiger*') a remedy.[509] This term is not by any means clarified. Wéry holds the opinion that repair or replacement (§2) has to be 'claimed' orally or in writing, without going to court. This implies, if the judge does not intervene *a priori*, a *choice* for one of the four remedies and its *notification* to the debtor.[510] This notification must be clear and the consumer may leave no doubt about his choice.[511] In many cases, the consumer will not have a *real* choice, taking into account the hierarchy of the remedies, prescribed by the Consumer Sales Directive. If the seller does not act upon the notification, the consumer has to put the seller in default,[512] if he has

---

508 Stijns, Sophie, 'De remedies van de koper bij niet-conformiteit' in Stijns, Sophie, and Stuyck, Jules (eds.), *Het nieuwe kooprecht, De wet van 1 september 2004 betreffende de bescherming van de consumenten bij verkoop van consumptiegoederen* (Antwerp: Intersentia, 2005), p. 68; Wéry, Patrick, 'Les droits légaux du consommateur en cas de défaut de conformité' in Biquet-Mathieu, Christine, and Wéry, Patrick (eds.), *La nouvelle garantie des biens de consommation et son environnement légal* (Brussels: die Keure, 2005), pp. 143–44.

509 See extensively: Wéry, Patrick, 'Les droits légaux du consommateur en cas de défaut de conformité' in Biquet-Mathieu, Christine, and Wéry, Patrick (eds.), *La nouvelle garantie des biens de consommation et son environnement légal* (Brussels: die Keure, 2005), pp. 136–37.

510 Ibid., n° 13 and 20. See also: Jansen, Sanne, 'Price Reduction as a Remedy in European Contract Law and the Consumer Acquis' in Keirse, Anne L.M., and Loos, Marco B.M. (eds.), *Alternative Ways to Ius Commune. The Europeanisation of Private Law* (Antwerp: Intersentia, 2012), pp. 183–84; Steennot, Reinhard, and Dejonghe, Sofie, *Consumentenbescherming en Handelspraktijken* (Antwerp: Intersentia, 2007), n° 1080; Stijns, Sophie, 'De remedies van de koper bij niet-conformiteit' in Stijns, Sophie, and Stuyck, Jules (eds.), *Het nieuwe kooprecht, De wet van 1 september 2004 betreffende de bescherming van de consumenten bij verkoop van consumptiegoederen* (Antwerp: Intersentia, 2005), n° 38. See similarly: Bianca, Cesare Massimo, 'Article 3. Droits et remèdes du consommateur' in Bianca, Cesare Massimo, et al. (eds.), *La directive communautaire sur la vente, Commentaire* (Brussels/Paris: Bruylant-LGDJ, 2004), n° 65 (about the choice between repair and replacement).

511 Stijns, Sophie, 'De remedies van de koper bij niet-conformiteit' in Stijns, Sophie, and Stuyck, Jules (eds.), *Het nieuwe kooprecht, De wet van 1 september 2004 betreffende de bescherming van de consumenten bij verkoop van consumptiegoederen* (Antwerp: Intersentia, 2005), n° 38; Stijns, Sophie, 'De consumentenkoop: actuele knelpunten' in Tilleman, Bernard, and Verbeke, Alain (eds.), *Knelpunten verkoop roerende goederen* (Antwerp: Intersentia, 2009), n° 58; Wéry, Patrick, 'Les droits légaux du consommateur en cas de défaut de conformité' in Biquet-Mathieu, Christine, and Wéry, Patrick (eds.), *La nouvelle garantie des biens de consommation et son environnement légal* (Brussels: die Keure, 2005), n° 13.

512 This raises the question of the relation between a notification of a shortcoming and a *mise en demeure* (see *infra*, para. 139).

not already done this.[513] The same reasoning applies to an extrajudicial price reduction[514] or a termination in §3 (the latter can only be invoked extrajudicially in extraordinary circumstances). The consumer must inform the seller about the (extrajudicial) remedy chosen.

1.2. CESL

1.2.1. No Duty to Notify of Shortcomings

119 *No examination and notification duties for consumers.* The CESL does not provide for any examination or notification duty for consumers with regard to shortcomings. Article 106.3 CESL excludes any notification or examination duty by a consumer (as it also excludes the seller's right to cure if the buyer is a consumer).[515] Some commentators welcome this absence of notification and examination duties, claiming it enhances consumer protection and increases the quality of the performance. Consumers might not know that they have such an obligation, thereby losing their remedies if they fail to observe it. Others are critical and argue that this might be disproportionate, taking into account the seller's interests.[516]

However, the CESL prescribes that the buyer or customer – when he is *not* a consumer – must examine the goods or the service and notify within a *reasonable period of time*.[517] The buyer or customer must first '*examine* the goods within a reasonable time or cause them to be examined, not exceeding 14 days from the date of delivery of the goods, supply of digital

---

513 Wéry, Patrick, 'Les droits légaux du consommateur en cas de défaut de conformité' in Biquet-Mathieu, Christine, and Wéry, Patrick (eds.), *La nouvelle garantie des biens de consommation et son environnement légal* (Brussels: die Keure, 2005), n° 20.

514 See, regarding extrajudicial price reduction in consumer sales: Jansen, Sanne, 'Price Reduction as a Remedy in European Contract Law and the Consumer Acquis' in Keirse, Anne L.M., and Loos, Marco B.M. (eds.), *Alternative Ways to Ius Commune. The Europeanisation of Private Law* (Antwerp: Intersentia, 2012), pp. 177–78.

515 See also *supra*, para. 27.

516 Proposes an 'explicit information duty on the seller in this respect' (informing the consumer of his notification duties): Feltkamp, Regine, and Vanbossele, Frederic, 'Remedies Under the Optional Common European Sales Law – A Good Alternative for Belgian Sales Law?' in Claeys, Ignace, and Feltkamp, Regine (eds.), *The Draft Common European Sales Law: Towards an Alternative Sales Law?* (Antwerp: Intersentia, 2013), n° 37.

517 Art. 106.2, 121–122, and 155.5–156 CESL.

content or provision of related services'. Further, the buyer or customer must *notify* the debtor, specifying the nature of the lack of conformity, within a reasonable period, which starts to run from the moment when the goods are supplied or when the buyer discovers or could be expected to discover the lack of conformity, whichever is later, with a maximum period of two years. The buyer may not rely on the lack of conformity if he did not give notice to the seller within a reasonable time, specifying the lack of conformity (Article 122(1) CESL). This Article was later amended by the EU Parliament on 26 February 2014. The first version of the Article stated that the buyer may not rely on the lack of conformity if he did not give notice to the seller within a reasonable time, specifying the lack of conformity (in a contract between traders). However, Parliament proposed amending this Article and added that the buyer may still reduce the price or claim damages, except for loss of profit, if he has a reasonable excuse for his failure to give the required notice. This means that some remedies can still be invoked if the buyer has a reasonable excuse for omitting his obligation to notify. The buyer loses his right to invoke the lack of conformity (and all his remedies) if he fails to give notice within a period of two years from the time at which the goods were handed over to the buyer according to the contract.

1.2.2. Duty to Notify in Case of Termination

Notification of termination. Under the CESL, there is no general principle to notify the debtor in order to invoke a remedy. Articles 118 and 138 of the CESL establish a duty to notify the seller should *the buyer* wish to invoke the right to terminate the contract, which is also the case under the PECL and the DCFR.[518] The fact that the *buyer* can terminate the contract upon notice, means that this remedy can be invoked *extrajudicially* (see *supra*, para. 96). Consumers and other buyers alike must thus notify the seller before the contract can be terminated. However, if the buyer is *not* a consumer (or if no performance at all has been tendered), the buyer will lose his right to invoke termination if he does not notify *within a reasonable time* as from the moment the right arose or he could be expected to have 120

[518] See also Art. 10 of the CESL, which elaborates on the notification. If the creditor does not notify the debtor within a reasonable time, he loses his right to terminate. See also Arts. 115 and 135 CESL: termination for delay in delivery after a notice fixing an additional time for performance.

become or became aware of the non-performance (Article 119 CESL). No specific form is required for this notification of termination if taking into account Articles 6 and 10 CESL.[519]

A notice of the remedy by the *buyer* is logical in case of an *extrajudicial* termination. But what about a termination that is invoked judicially? A judicial termination implies that the buyer asks for it in his writ of summons or in his conclusions. This should be sufficient to count as a 'notice' of termination.

121 *Other remedies?* This obligation to notify is not provided for in the case of other remedies (e.g. price reduction) and some concerns in relation to the practical applicability of those other remedies might be raised.

Is a duty to notify the debtor *to invoke a remedy* necessary if there is a duty to notify *a non-conformity*? First of all, there is not always a duty under the CESL to notify *a non-conformity*: this is not the case when the creditor is a consumer. Consequently, it is, in the present author's view, advisable that the consumer informs the debtor about a *non-conformity* with the contract within a reasonable period, for reasons of proof concerning the passing of risk (did the non-conformity of the good appear before or after the passing of risk?). Furthermore, it is advisable that the creditor informs the debtor somehow about his intention to invoke an *extrajudicial* remedy. This might also be necessary for reasons of proof about the question of which remedy the creditor has chosen[520] (in case the judge exercises an *a posteriori* control after the extrajudicial or unilateral use of a remedy). Indeed, the judge must be able to examine the consumer's choice with regard to the conditions of application of the remedy. A notification of the application of an extrajudicial remedy will facilitate this task.

---

519 Criticize the fact that Art. 10(2) unclearly states that 'a notice may be given by any means appropriate to the circumstances': Feltkamp, Regine, and Vanbosselе, Frederic, 'Remedies Under the Optional Common European Sales Law – A Good Alternative for Belgian Sales Law?' in Claeys, Ignace, and Feltkamp, Regine (eds.), *The Draft Common European Sales Law: Towards an Alternative Sales Law?* (Antwerp: Intersentia, 2013), n° 48.

520 Confusion is possible between e.g. partial termination or price reduction, suspension or price reduction, damages or price reduction. Müller-Chen correctly points out the ambiguity if the creditor just pays a reduced price with a notice of defect, since this only makes clear that there is a temporary retention of part of the price, but not a final selection of a remedy: Müller-Chen, Markus, 'Art. 50 CISG' in Schlechtriem, Peter, and Ingeborg Schwenzer (eds.), *Commentary on the CISG* (Oxford: Oxford University Press, 2005), p. 598, n° 4.

1.3. ODSD/2017 PROPOSAL

1.3.1. No Duty to Notify of Shortcomings

No notification duty as a consumer protective measure. The Explanatory Memorandum of the ODSD/2017 Proposal makes it clear that consumers would not have the duty – which they currently have under a number of national laws – to notify a defect in the goods to the seller within a certain period of time from its discovery.[521] Also, recital 25 of the ODSD/2017 Proposal states clearly that a notification obligation with regard to a lack of conformity should not be established. 122

The fact that no notification duty can be required from the consumer was forecast by the evolution of the two previous instruments. Article 5.2 of the oldest instrument, the CSD, does not require a harmonized notification duty, but provides that the Member States could introduce or maintain a requirement that the consumer must inform the seller of the lack of conformity within a period of two months from the date on which he detected such lack of conformity, in order to benefit from his rights (see *supra*, para. 117). The CESL only provides for a duty to examine and notify of a lack of conformity in contracts between traders, it is not required when the buyer is a consumer (see *supra*, para. 119).

1.3.2. Duty to Notify Only in the Case of Termination

Notification of termination. Article 13.1 ODSD/2017 Proposal makes clear that the remedy of termination must be exercised by the consumer by *notice* to the seller, given by any means. This means two things. First, this means that the consumer can apply, without prior intervention of a judge, the termination remedy (see, regarding the extrajudicial application of termination, *supra*, para. 98). Secondly, it means that the consumer is obliged to notify the seller of his intention to invoke the remedy of termination. 123

[521] Explanatory Memorandum ODSD Proposal, pp. 3 and 13 and recital 25 ODSD/2017 Proposal. It is indeed sufficient that only the recital/Memorandum refers to this, and that it is not explicitly mentioned in a provision of the ODSD, because of the maximum harmonization-character of the proposed directive: Claeys, Ignace, and Vancoillie, Jonas, 'Remedies, Modification of Digital Content and Right to Terminate Long-Term Digital Content Contracts' in Claeys, Ignace, and Terryn, Evelyne (eds.), *Digital Content & Distance Sales* (Cambridge: Intersentia, 2017), p. 180.

The question of whether the notification is reserved for an *extrajudicial* termination arises. In other words: does a judicial termination require a prior notification by the consumer or is notification solely necessary in case of an extrajudicial termination? A judicial termination implies that the buyer asks for it in his writ of summons or in his conclusions. This should be sufficient to count as a 'notice' of termination.

If this is compared with the Consumer Sales Directive – which does not regulate this aspect of termination – it is clear that the Commission has finally chosen a harmonized regime of termination regarding this aspect in the ODSD/2017 Proposals (see *supra*, para. 118). Like the CESL, it imposes a notification duty on the consumer when invoking the termination remedy (see *supra*, para. 120).

Article 13 ODSD/2017 Proposal, however, does not prescribe any sanction if the consumer does not notify the termination remedy *within a certain period* of time. Consequently, the consumer will not lose his right to invoke termination if he does not notify within a reasonable time as from the moment the right arose, or could be expected to have become or became aware of the non-performance. The consumer is only obliged to notify of termination if he is intending to invoke it, and not within a certain period of time.

With regard to the notification duty, the ODSD/2017 Proposal makes clear that no specific *form* is required: 'notice to the seller given by *any means*'. This is also the case under the CESL (see *supra*, para. 120). So this means that this notification of termination can be done by, for example, phone, e-mail,[522] letter or registered letter. Of course, one has to provide the means to prove this notification, which can be more difficult in case of a merely oral notification.

124 *Other remedies?* This obligation to notify is not provided for in the case of other remedies (e.g. price reduction) and the same concerns in relation to the practical applicability of those remedies appear if the consumer would be allowed to invoke them extrajudicially (see also under the CESL, para. 120).

522 See also Claeys, Ignace, and Vancoillie, Jonas, 'Remedies, Modification of Digital Content and Right to Terminate Long-Term Digital Content Contracts' in Claeys, Ignace, and Terryn, Evelyne (eds.), *Digital Content & Distance Sales* (Cambridge: Intersentia, 2017), p. 189.

2. COMMON LAW APPROACH

2.1. COMMON CONTRACT LAW

2.1.1. No General Duty to Notify of Shortcomings

125 *No general duty to notify of shortcomings.* In common law there is no general rule, as is the case under the UCC (see *supra*, para. 130), obliging a creditor to notify his debtor of a breach of contract (upon acceptance).[523] Moreover, courts are reluctant to transplant the UCC rule to notify a shortcoming after acceptance.[524]

126 *Notification of the defect, cure, and termination of the contract.* As discussed earlier, the (extrajudicial remedy of) termination can only be invoked (in absence of a breach of an express promissory condition) if (1) there a material (total) breach of a reciprocal contract; and often (2) a period of time to cure the breach has passed (see *supra*, para. 58). If a material breach can be established, the question whether a period of time to cure has to be set by means of a notice of the shortcoming arises. The answer to this question is not straightforward. First of all, this will depend on whether or not time is of the essence for the performance of the contract and whether or not the defect can be cured.[525] If time is of the essence or the defect is not curable, the notification of such a period of time is most likely not required. If time is not of the essence[526] and the defect is curable, such a notice of a 'period of time to cure' may be useful.[527] This most likely requires a *notice of the defect*, allowing the debtor

---

523 Reitz, John C., 'Against Notice: A Proposal to Restrict the Notice of Claims Rule in U.C.C. §2-607 (3) (a)', 73 *Cornell L. Rev.* (1987–88), p. 535. The first restatement of contract law of 1932 did incorporate a notice rule (for buyers) in §412; the 2nd restatement not anymore; perhaps the introduction in the first restatement can be explained by the fact that professor Williston (who also introduced such a rule in §49 of the Uniform Sales Act) was the reporter for the first restatement (see for this explanation the previously cited article of Reitz, footnote 5).

524 Even in cases where there is a transplant of the UCC Art. 2 warranties in other domains such as leases and delivery of services. Clark, Barkley, 'The First Line of Defense in Warranty Suits: Failure to Give Notice of Breach', 15 *UCC L.J.* (1982), pp. 117–18.

525 See also comment of the 2nd restatement of contract law §242, a).

526 In sales contracts, even if time is of the essence, the contract may not be immediately be terminated without giving a chance to cure: Farnsworth, E. Allan, *Farnsworth on Contracts* (New York: Kluwer, 2004), §8.18.

527 Describes it as an option 'where a party is not proceeding with performance in accordance with the terms of the contract but is not yet guilty of a total breach': Perillo, Joseph M., *Contracts* (St. Paul: West Academic, 2014), p. 397.

a reasonable opportunity to cure.[528] Indeed, it is logical that the creditor has to notify the debtor of the shortcoming, to enable the debtor to exercise his right to cure.

2.1.2. *No General Duty to Notify of Remedies*

127 *Election of remedies*. The most important act that the aggrieved party has to do in order to elect a remedy is to bring a suit for it. However, in either situation, the aggrieved party has no duty to notify in advance his election of remedies to the other party.[529] If the aggrieved party notifies his choice of one remedy, it will not be binding, except if the other party detrimentally relies on this choice.[530] The same holds true for a suit for one remedy rather than another remedy; this choice is not deemed to be irrevocable unless the other party changes his position in reliance to the chosen remedy.[531] Corbin finally holds that the doctrine of election can be

Cf.: Farnsworth, E. Allan, *Farnsworth on Contracts* (New York: Kluwer, 2004), §8.17 ('It would therefore seem that if cure is possible, notice of suspension, and perhaps of the breach relied on to justify it, ought to be required if the party in breach would not otherwise be aware of them') and §8.19a ('Furthermore, an aggrieved party can gain at least some advantage by making the other party aware of a claimed breach if the aggrieved party later claims that the breach is material and has not been cured in time').

528 Ferriell, Jeff, *Understanding Contracts* (New Providence, San Francisco: Matthew Bender & Co., Inc., 2009), pp. 536–37. Cf.: Hillman, Robert A., *Principles of Contract Law* (St. Paul: West Academic, 2014), p. 331 ('It is also important to consider whether the injured party gave reasonable notice of his grievance').
See also comment of the 2nd restatement of contract law §242, b) ('The reasonableness of the injured party's conduct in communicating his grievances and in seeking satisfaction is a factor to be considered in this connection [cure]').

529 Corbin, Arthur Linton, et al., *Corbin on Contracts* (New Providence, San Francisco: Matthew Bender & Co., Inc., 2016), §66.3. Also Pesando, Marie K., 'Election of Remedies', 25 *Am. Jur. 2d* (2017), §4. See also *Federal Life Ins. Co. v. Maxam*, 70 Ind. App. 266 (1919); *Indianapolis v. Twin Lakes Enterprises, Inc.* 568, N.E.2d 1073 (Ind. Ct. App. 1991).

530 2nd restatement of contract law, §378. Corbin, Arthur Linton, et al., *Corbin on Contracts* (New Providence, San Francisco: Matthew Bender & Co., Inc., 2016), §66.3 and §66.5; Pesando, Marie K., 'Election of Remedies', 25 *Am. Jur. 2d* (2017), §15.

531 2nd restatement of contract law, §378. Corbin, Arthur Linton, et al., *Corbin on Contracts* (New Providence, San Francisco: Matthew Bender & Co., Inc., 2016), §66.5. See however Pesando, Marie K., 'Election of Remedies', 25 *Am. Jur. 2d* (2017), §16 (some jurisdictions hold that the commencement of an action can be considered as an act of election, some do not hold this view). See, e.g., in line with the 2nd restatement of contract law §378: *Ripple v. Wold*, 1996 SD 68 (1996); *Quality Components Corp. v. Kel-Keef Enters*, 316 Ill. App. 3d 998 (2000); *Hill v. Raffone*, 103 Conn. App. 737 (2007); *Homeland Training Ctr., LLC v. Summit Point Auto. Research Ctr.*, 594 F.3d 285 (4th Cir. 2010); *PHL Variable Ins. v. Charter Oak Trust*, 2011 Conn. Super. LEXIS 610 (2011).

explained by the estoppel[532] principle: everything is about the conduct of the parties.[533]

With regard to damages and specific performance, the so-called judicial remedies, the choice for one or the other remedy will be considered a 'notice' or an 'election'. Suing for one remedy rather than the other is considered 'giving notice' or 'a manifestation of election' of that remedy.[534] This choice for one or the other remedy is not irrevocable.[535] Choosing the wrong remedy (e.g. because of limitation periods or conditions of application that are not fulfilled) will not bar the plaintiff from choosing another remedy.[536] Also a suit for specific performance or damages is not necessarily definitive, and does not prevent the aggrieved party from changing the action; unless the other party relies on it and changes his position (estoppel principle).[537]

In case of a material breach of contract, and if the conditions of a total breach of contract are fulfilled (see *supra*, para. 58), the non-breaching party can choose to terminate the contract because of a total breach, or he can choose to keep the contract and recover damages because of a partial breach.[538] This is also called the 'election doctrine'.[539] Consequently, the contract is not automatically and *ipso facto* terminated or ended by such a breach.[540] But what will constitute such an election?[541] Often, it is held that once a party continues to perform despite a material breach, this party has elected a remedy and can no longer terminate. Consequently, one strand contends that a continued performance can constitute such an election for

---

532 This is the principle that prevents a person from claiming something that is in contradiction with previous positions held before a court.

533 Corbin, Arthur Linton, Perillo, et al., *Corbin on Contracts* (New Providence, San Francisco: Matthew Bender & Co., Inc., 2016), §66.6.

534 Ibid., n° 12–66, §66.5.

535 2nd restatement of contract law, §378 (see also *supra*).

536 Corbin, Arthur Linton, et al., *Corbin on Contracts* (New Providence, San Francisco: Matthew Bender & Co., Inc., 2016), n° 12–66, §66.5.

537 See extensively ibid., §66.9. See *contra: Davis v. Beury*, 134 Va. 322, 114 S.E. 773 (1922).

538 See, e.g.: *Cities Serv. Helex, Inc. v. United States*, 211 Ct. Cl. 222 (Fed. Cl. 1976); *Dunkin' Donuts of America, Inc. v. Minerva, Inc.*, 956 F.2d 1566 (11th Cir. 1992); *ESPN, Inc. v. Office of the Comm'r of Baseball*, 76 F. Supp. 2d 383 (S.D.N.Y. 1999); *Gillard v. Martin*, 13 A.3d 482 (Pa. Super. Ct. 2010); *Old Stone Corp. v. United States*, 450 F.3d 1360 (Fed. Cir. 2006); *Precision Pine & Timber, Inc. v. United States*, 72 Fed. Cl. 460 (Fed. Cl. 2006); *Westlands Water Dist. v. United States*, 109 Fed. Cl. 177 (Fed. Cl. 2013); *Transact, Inc. v. D'Errico (In re Transact, Inc.)*, 2014 U.S. Dist. LEXIS 109746, (C.D. Cal. 2014).

539 Lord, Richard A., *A Treatise on the Law of Contracts by Samuel Williston* (Westlaw, 2013), §39:32.

540 *Dunkin' Donuts of America, Inc. v. Minerva, Inc.*, 956 F.2d 1566 (11th Cir. 1992).

541 See, regarding this question describing the strict and lenient standard, without making a choice: *Cities Serv. Helex, Inc. v. United States*, 211 Ct. Cl. 222 (Fed. Cl. 1976); *Old Stone Corp. v. United States*, 450 F.3d 1360 (Fed. Cir. 2006).

keeping the contract in force (lenient standard).[542] This rule would deviate from the previously treated 'estoppel' rule. However, others propose a detrimental reliance of the breaching party on the continued performance as a yardstick (strict standard, estoppel rule).[543] The 'conduct' of the parties seems to be one of the most important factors and not a 'formal' notification duty or notice.[544]

128 *Deadline for performance after which termination is allowed.* The Vienna Sales Convention (CISG) foresees in Articles 47 and 63 the possibility to 'fix an additional period of time of reasonable length for performance'. During this period of time the aggrieved party may suspend its performance and if it expires, he may terminate the contract. Although US common law does not know such a rule, some courts have accepted that the aggrieved party can give the other party a reasonable deadline by notification within which he must perform.[545]

2.2. UCC ARTICLE 2

2.2.1. General Duty to Notify of a Breach (Shortcomings) after Acceptance

129 *Inspection and stating defects (to establish breach or) to justify rejection (before acceptance).* The buyer has a right to inspect the goods 'at any reasonable place and time and in a reasonable manner' (UCC §2-513). Acceptance of the goods only happens after a reasonable opportunity to inspect the goods (UCC §2-606(1)(a)). According to UCC §2-605(1) the buyer *must state all the particular defects* which he discovers upon

---

542 Lord, Richard A., *A Treatise on the Law of Contracts by Samuel Williston* (Westlaw, 2013), §39:32. *Westlands Water Dist. v. United States*, 109 Fed. Cl. 177 (Fed. Cl. 2013).

543 See stricter: Corbin, Arthur Linton, et al., *Corbin on Contracts* (New Providence, San Francisco: Matthew Bender & Co., Inc., 2016), §66.7 ('[...] but the need for an estoppel is as pragmatically indicated in this situation as is indicated in others'). 2nd restatement of contract law, §378.

544 *Dunkin' Donuts of America, Inc. v. Minerva, Inc.*, 956 F.2d 1566 (11th Cir. 1992) ('If he decides to close the contract and so conducts himself, both parties are relieved of their further obligations and the injured party is entitled to damages to the end of the contract term (to put him in the position he would have occupied if the contract had been completed). If he elects instead to continue the contract, the obligations of both parties remain in force and the injured party may retain only a claim for damages for partial breach'; the court does not mention a notification duty).

545 See Farnsworth, E. Allan, *Farnsworth on Contracts* (New York: Kluwer, 2004), §8.19a. See e.g. *Kasarsky v. Merit Sys. Prot. Bd.*, 296 F.3d 1331 (Fed. Cir. 2002).

reasonable inspection. If he fails to state defects he will not be able to rely on the defect to *reject* or to establish a breach of contract if the seller could have cured that defect seasonably (see also *infra*, para. 131).[546] This duty to notify for discoverable defects has to be read in conjunction with the seller's right to cure (see *supra*, para. 69). The Official Comment clarifies that this section enables the buyer to give a 'quick and informal' notice of defects. It is aimed at balancing the interests of the buyer and the seller.[547] The seller may be misled if the buyer omits to state curable defects.

General notice of defects after acceptance. UCC §2-607(3)(a) requires 130
that where a tender has been accepted, the buyer must notify the seller of the breach of contract[548] within a reasonable time *after discovering* or after he should have discovered the breach. In the case of a lack of such a notification, the buyer will be barred from his remedies (such as damages).[549] The post-2003 amended UCC Article 2 does not prescribe an automatic bar from any remedy if the buyer does not notify, but only if the seller is prejudiced by the failure to notify.[550] However, here reference will be made to the pre-2003 version, because this is the version of the UCC most widely adopted by the different US States.

The first hurdle is to know *who* the buyer must notify.[551] What is the meaning of 'notify *the* seller' in UCC §2-607(3)(a)? Must the buyer only

---

546 If both parties are merchants a more stringent rule applies: when after rejection the seller requests in writing a 'full and final written statement of all defects on which the buyer proposes to rely' the buyer cannot rely on unstated defects that could have been reasonably discovered: Perillo, Joseph M., *Contracts* (St. Paul: West Academic, 2014), p. 404.

547 See Official Comment UCC §2-605. See also Ferriell, Jeff, *Understanding Contracts* (New Providence, San Francisco: Matthew Bender & Co., Inc., 2009), p. 550.

548 According to the following case this notification duty is not only applicable to non-conformity but also to delays in performance: *Eastern Air Lines, Inc. v. McDonnell Douglas Corp.*, 532 F.2d 957 (US Court of Appeals, Fifth Circuit 1976).

549 This rule is not applicable to rejection and revocation because they are subject to shorter cut-off rules (see also below, paras. 131 and 132): Reitz, John C., 'Against Notice: A Proposal to Restrict the Notice of Claims Rule in U.C.C. §2-607 (3) (a)', 73 *Cornell L. Rev.* (1987–88), p. 534. *Contra*: Clark, Barkley, 'The First Line of Defense in Warranty Suits: Failure to Give Notice of Breach', 15 *UCC L.J.* (1982), p. 107 (also includes revocation of acceptance) and p. 112 (failure to give timely notice bars the buyer from damages and revocation of acceptance); White, James J., and Summers, Robert S., *Uniform Commercial Code* (St. Paul: West Academic), §11–10, p. 417 (UCC §2-607(3)(a) also includes the right to revoke acceptance). Considers this penalty 'harsh': Reitz, John C., 'Against Notice: A Proposal to Restrict the Notice of Claims Rule in U.C.C. §2-607 (3) (a)', 73 *Cornell L. Rev.* (1987–88), p. 534.

550 Fonseca, Patricia F., and Fonseca, John R., *Williston on Sales* (Eagan: West, 2006), p. 779.

551 See regarding this topic: Leete, Burt A., 'The Notice Booby-Trap of U.C.C. Section 2-607(3)(a)', 22 *Am. Bus. LJ* (1984), pp. 109–24; Prince, Harry G., 'Overprotecting

notify his immediate seller or also others in the chain of distribution? The answer differs from state to state.[552] Doctrine is also divided with regard to the correct answer to this question.[553] Therefore, it is most prudent to notify all the relevant actors in the chain of distribution.[554]

---

the Consumer? Section 2-607(3)(a) Notice of Breach in Nonprivity Contexts', 66 *N.C. L. Rev.* (1987–88), pp. 107–69; Reitz, John C., 'Against Notice: A Proposal to Restrict the Notice of Claims Rule in U.C.C. §2-607 (3) (a)', 73 *Cornell L. Rev.* (1987–88), pp. 544–45 (footnote 34).

See, regarding the question whether it is sufficient to give notice to a *third party* who has a close relationship with the seller or with the intent that the third party will inform the seller of the defects: Prince, Harry G., 'Overprotecting the Consumer? Section 2-607(3)(a) Notice of Breach in Nonprivity Contexts', 66 *N.C. L. Rev.* (1987–88), p. 118.

552 See, e.g., *contra* notification of others in the chain of distribution (many other cases are available from different jurisdictions): *Firestone Tire & Rubber Co. v. Cannon*, 53 Md. App. 106; *Cooley v. Big Horn Harvestore Systems*, Inc., 813 P.2d 736 (Colo. 1991). See e.g. *pro* notification of others in the chain of distribution (many other cases are available from different jurisdictions): *Morrow v. New Moon Homes, Inc.*, 548 P.2d 279 (Alaska 1976); *Berry v. G.D. Searle & Co.*, 56 Ill. 2d 548, (Ill. 1974).

553 Favors the opinion that the buyer has to notify only his immediate seller: Keeton, Page W., et al., *Prosser and Keeton on Torts* (St. Paul: West, 1984), p. 691; Leete, Burt A., 'The Notice Booby-Trap of U.C.C. Section 2-607(3)(a)', 22 *Am. Bus. LJ* (1984), p. 123 (an unsophisticated buyer may be unaware of the fact that he has to notify others in the distribution chain and the literal interpretation of the term 'seller' in UCC §2-607(3)(a) points at the immediate seller). As Dean Prosser pointed out with respect to §49 in: Prosser, William L., 'The Assault upon the Citadel (Strict Liability to the Consumer)', 69 *Yale L.J.* (1960), p. 1130.

The consumer also has to notify the breach in non-privity contexts (i.e. if the consumer is a remote vendee pursuing an action against a manufacturer or seller with whom there has not been a direct sales transaction): Prince, Harry G., 'Overprotecting the Consumer? Section 2-607(3)(a) Notice of Breach in Nonprivity Contexts', 66 *N.C. L. Rev.* (1987–88), p. 109 *et seq.* (notice gives a seller the possibility to correct the defect or to minimize damages; to negotiate settlement or to prepare litigation and gives protection against stale claims; moreover, the so-called argument of 'consumer naiveté' has been overstated). See also Chavis, Marvin, 'Notice of Breach and the Uniform Commercial Code', 25 *U. Fla. L. Rev.* (1972–73), pp. 529–32; Phillips, Jerry J., 'Notice of Breach in Sales and Strict Tort Liability Law: Should There Be a Difference?', 47 *Ind. L.J.* (1971–72), p. 464 (also in case of a claim by a third party beneficiary); White, James J., and Summers, Robert S., *Uniform Commercial Code* (St. Paul: West Academic), §11-10, pp. 420–21 (notification required of a remote manufacturer). Cf. Clark, Barkley, 'The First Line of Defense in Warranty Suits: Failure to Give Notice of Breach', 15 *UCC L.J.* (1982), pp. 126–29 (or the buyer notifies his immediate seller and the latter passes the notification on or the buyer should notify the remote manufacturer himself).

See extensively, without taking a clear stance: Fonseca, Patricia F., and Fonseca, John R., *Williston on Sales* (Eagan: West, 2006), pp. 788–91 (however, seem to favor the opinion that is not requiring a notification when there is no privity: pp. 788–89).

554 See for this advice Leete, Burt A., 'The Notice Booby-Trap of U.C.C. Section 2-607(3)(a)', 22 *Am. Bus. L.J.* (1984), p. 123.

With regard to the *form* of this notification duty, it can be said that the notice does not need to be written and may be oral.[555] Of course, for reasons of proof, it will be prudent to notify by means of a written document.[556] It may be given in a single communication or derived from different communications.[557] It has to be communicated to a responsible person, which means that a notice to an employee might not be sufficient.[558]

Notification has to be done within 'reasonable' time.[559] According to the Official Comment, for a merchant buyer the *timing* of the notification is dependent on commercial standards.[560] However, for a retail consumer – which is our case study – this has to be judged by different standards: 'in this case it [reasonable time] will be extended, for the rule of requiring notification is designed to defeat commercial bad faith, not to deprive a good faith consumer of his remedy'.[561] Generally, time to notify will be limited in the case of perishable goods.[562] Reitz defends the argument that a notice is only too late if the delay in notice prejudices the seller.[563] The time for

---

555 See e.g. *T. J. Stevenson & Co. v. 81,193 Bags of Flour*, 629 F.2d 338 (5th Cir. 1980); *K & M Joint Venture v. Smith International, Inc.*, 669 F.2d 1106 (6th Cir. 1982); *Pay Tel Sys. v. Seiscor Technologies*, 899 F. Supp. 152 (S.D.N.Y. 1995) (phone call is sufficient). See also Chavis, Marvin, 'Notice of Breach and the Uniform Commercial Code', 25 *U. Fla. L. Rev.* (1972–73), p. 536; Clark, Barkley, 'The First Line of Defense in Warranty Suits: Failure to Give Notice of Breach', 15 *UCC L.J.* (1982), p. 119; Fonseca, Patricia F., and Fonseca, John R., *Williston on Sales* (Eagan: West, 2006), p. 809; Hammond, George F., 'Notification of Breach Under Uniform Commercial Code Section 2-607(3)(a): A Conflict, A Resolution', 70 *Cornell L. Rev.* (1984–85), p. 526; Prince, Harry G., 'Overprotecting the Consumer? Section 2-607(3)(a) Notice of Breach in Nonprivity Contexts', 66 *N.C. L. Rev.* (1987–88), p. 117; White, James J., and Summers, Robert S., *Uniform Commercial Code* (St. Paul: West Academic), §11-10, pp. 421–22.

556 See also Prince, Harry G., 'Overprotecting the Consumer? Section 2-607(3)(a) Notice of Breach in Nonprivity Contexts', 66 *N.C. L. Rev.* (1987–88), pp. 117–18.

557 *T. J. Stevenson & Co. v. 81,193 Bags of Flour*, 629 F.2d 338 (5th Cir. 1980); *K & M Joint Venture v. Smith International, Inc.*, 669 F.2d 1106 (6th Cir. 1982). See also Prince, Harry G., 'Overprotecting the Consumer? Section 2-607(3)(a) Notice of Breach in Nonprivity Contexts', 66 *N.C. L. Rev.* (1987–88), p. 118.

558 Chavis, Marvin, 'Notice of Breach and the Uniform Commercial Code', 25 *U. Fla. L. Rev.* (1972–73), p. 536.

559 See Fonseca, Patricia F., and Fonseca, John R., *Williston on Sales* (Eagan: West, 2006), p. 794 *et seq.*

560 See extensively Prince, Harry G., 'Overprotecting the Consumer? Section 2-607(3)(a) Notice of Breach in Nonprivity Contexts', 66 *N.C. L. Rev.* (1987–88), pp. 125–27.

561 Official Comment UCC §2-607. See also e.g. Chavis, Marvin, 'Notice of Breach and the Uniform Commercial Code', 25 *U. Fla. L. Rev.* (1972–73), p. 539.

562 Clark, Barkley, 'The First Line of Defense in Warranty Suits: Failure to Give Notice of Breach', 15 *UCC L.J.* (1982), pp. 131–32 and 134.

563 Reitz, John C., 'Against Notice: A Proposal to Restrict the Notice of Claims Rule in U.C.C. §2-607 (3) (a)', 73 *Cornell L. Rev.* (1987–88), p. 548, 579 *et seq.* and 590, 593–594 (the buyer would only lose its remedies if a delay in notification prejudices the seller).

notice starts to run, according to UCC §2-607(3)(a), after the buyer discovers or should have discovered the breach of contract.[564] Finally, it has to be noted that opinions are divided as to the question whether a 'notice through legal papers' is sufficient (e.g. by filing a claim or a complaint).[565]

The requirements as to the *content* of such a notification do not seem elaborate at first sight. Anyhow, the notice should first identify the transaction or goods involved in the breach.[566] There is more discussion about the intensity of the complaints of the buyer in the notification.[567] According to the Official Comment, it is sufficient to let the seller know that there are some troubles with regard to the transaction and that the buyer must only inform the seller that the transaction involves a breach.[568] This is rather confusing: is merely a statement that the transaction is 'troublesome' required, or is it necessary to notify a 'breach of contract'? The Comment makes it clear that there is no requirement of a clear statement with all the objections – as is required under UCC §2-605 with regard to

564 See regarding latent defects: *Q. Vandenberg & Sons, v. Siter*, 204 Pa. Super. 392, 204 A.2d 494 (1964).

565 A pre-litigation notice is required: e.g., *Lynx, Inc. v. Ordnance Products, Inc.*, 273 Md. 1, 327 A.2d 502 (1974); *Armco Steel Corp. v. Isaacson Structural Steel Co.*, 611 P.2d 507 (Alaska 1980); *Whitesell Corp. v. Whirlpool Corp.*, 2009 U.S. Dist. LEXIS 95111 (W.D. Mich. 2009). See also: Fonseca, Patricia F., and Fonseca, John R., *Williston on Sales* (Eagan: West, 2006), pp. 788, 791–92, 803, 808–09, 812 (however, points to some exceptions); Henning, William H., and Lawrence, William H., 'A Unified Rationale for Section 2-607(3)(a)', 46 *San Diego L. Rev.* (2009), p. 584 (one out of the two authors is of this opinion).

Contra in a consumer case (filing a complaint is sufficient): *Shooshanian v. Wagner*, 672 P.2d 455 (Alaska 1983); *Owens v. Glendale Optical Co.*, 590 F. Supp. 32 (S.D. Ill. 1984); *In re Bridgestone/Firestone, Inc. v. Wilderness Tires Prods. Liab. Litig.*, 155 F. Supp. 2d 1069, (S.D. Ind. 2001). Also contra (filing a complaint is sufficient if all the requirements of the notice rule are fulfilled): Henning, William H., and Lawrence, William H., 'A Unified Rationale for Section 2-607(3)(a)', 46 *San Diego L. Rev.* (2009), p. 584 (one out of the two authors is of this opinion); Prince, Harry G., 'Overprotecting the Consumer? Section 2-607(3)(a) Notice of Breach in Nonprivity Contexts', 66 *N.C. L. Rev.* (1987–88), pp. 128–32; Reitz, John C., 'Against Notice: A Proposal to Restrict the Notice of Claims Rule in U.C.C. §2-607 (3) (a)', 73 *Cornell L. Rev.* (1987–88), p. 581.

566 *Lynx, Inc. v. Ordnance Products, Inc.*, 273 Md. 1, 327 A.2d 502 (1974); Prince, Harry G., 'Overprotecting the Consumer? Section 2-607(3)(a) Notice of Breach in Nonprivity Contexts', 66 *N.C. L. Rev.* (1987–88), p. 119.

567 See extensively: Prince, Harry G., 'Overprotecting the Consumer? Section 2-607(3)(a) Notice of Breach in Nonprivity Contexts', 66 *N.C. L. Rev.* (1987–88), pp. 119–25. See also Reitz, John C., 'Against Notice: A Proposal to Restrict the Notice of Claims Rule in U.C.C. §2-607 (3) (a)', 73 *Cornell L. Rev.* (1987–88), p. 543 and footnote 31.

568 Official Comment UCC §2-607, 4.

rejection (see *supra*, and *infra*, paras. 129 and 131).[569] Furthermore, for this notification it is sufficient to inform the seller of the shortcoming; it is not necessary to choose a remedy (such as damages) in the notification.[570] Finally, it has to be noted that actual knowledge of the breach by the seller (independent from any notice), does not do away with the duty to notify of the buyer: the seller still has to know whether or not the buyer wants redress.[571]

As mentioned, the UCC comments are rather unclear about the strictness of the content of the notification.[572] It is not surprising that, in the case law, there is discussion about the strictness of the content of the notification duty of the buyer. Some courts consider it sufficient that the notification establishes a 'complaint about the transaction', i.e. that it is 'troublesome' (lenient standard of notification).[573] Some courts use a

---

569 Official Comment UCC §2-607, 4.

570 Official Comment UCC §2-607.

571 Prince, Harry G., 'Overprotecting the Consumer? Section 2-607(3)(a) Notice of Breach in Nonprivity Contexts', 66 *N.C. L. Rev.* (1987–88), p. 125. See, e.g., *American Manufacturing Co. v. United States Shipping Board Emergency Fleet Corp.*, 7 F.2d 565 (2d Cir. 1925) ('The notice 'of the breach' required is not of the facts, which the seller presumably knows quite as well as, if not better than, the buyer, but of buyer's claim that they constitute a breach'); *Standard Alliance Industries, Inc. v. Black Clawson Co.*, 587 F.2d 813; *In re Frite-Lay N. Am., Inc.*, 2013 U.S. Dist. LEXIS 123824 (E.D.N.Y. 2013); *Singleton v. Fifth Generation, Inc.*, U.S. Dist. LEXIS 14000 (N.D.N.Y. 2016). Cf.: Fonseca, Patricia F., and Fonseca, John R., *Williston on Sales* (Eagan: West, 2006), pp. 792–94 (generalized knowledge of a possible defect is not sufficient as a notice of defect; actual knowledge of a defect can be). *Contra*: Reitz, John C., 'Against Notice: A Proposal to Restrict the Notice of Claims Rule in U.C.C. §2-607 (3) (a)', 73 *Cornell L. Rev.* (1987–88), pp. 576–77 ('notice should not apply at all in cases in which the seller knows the factual basis for the buyer's claim'). Also *contra*: *Hays v. General Elec. Co.*, 151 F.Supp.2d 1001, 45 U.C.C. Rep. Serv.2d 449 (N.D. Ill. 2001). Cf.: White, James J., and Summers, Robert S., *Uniform Commercial Code* (St. Paul: West Academic), §11-10, p. 418 (there is split in authority when it concerns a late delivery).

572 See very extensively on this uncertainty Clark, Barkley, 'The First Line of Defense in Warranty Suits: Failure to Give Notice of Breach', 15 *UCC L.J.* (1982), pp. 119–23; Hammond, George F., 'Notification of Breach Under Uniform Commercial Code Section 2-607(3)(a): A Conflict, a Resolution', 70 *Cornell L. Rev.* (1984–85), pp. 525–56.

573 See e.g. *Northern States Power Co. v. ITT Meyer Industries*, Div. of ITT Grinnell Corp., 777 F.2d 405 (8th Cir. 1985); *United States ex rel. Conroy v. Southern Contracting*, 862 F. Supp. 107 (D.S.C. 1994); *Munch v. Sears Roebuck & Co.*, 2007 WL 2461660 (N.D. Ill. 2007). Similarly (taking heavily into account the context of the notification): *Chainworks, Inc. v. Webco Indus.*, 2006 U.S. Dist. LEXIS 9194 (W.D. Mich. 2006). See also for this opinion Henning, William H. and Lawrence, William H., 'A Unified Rationale for Section 2-607(3)(a)', 46 *San Diego L. Rev.* (2009), p. 582; Milberger, Patrick A., 'Section 2-607(3)(a): Effective Notification of Breach under the Uniform Commercial Code', 44 *U. Pitt. L. Rev.* (1983), p. 748; Phillips, Jerry J., 'Notice of Breach

stricter test and require that the buyer must let the seller know that he considers the seller to be in breach (strict standard of notification).[574] The *Peavey* case stresses, however, that the strict standard of notification is only applicable between merchants.[575] A careful buyer who does not want to take chances, will always notify the seller of the fact that he finds the seller in breach of the contract.[576] Prince finds a middle ground between both approaches and says that an adequate notice requires that the seller is put on notice of a possible lawsuit.[577] This means that it will depend on the concrete situation whether an explicit statement of breach of contract has to be given in the notice of the buyer. Hammond proposes a similar approach and claims that the content of the notification depends on an evaluation

---

in Sales and Strict Tort Liability Law: Should There Be a Difference?', 47 *Ind. L.+J.* (1971–72), p. 477; Reitz, John C., 'Against Notice: A Proposal to Restrict the Notice of Claims Rule in U.C.C. §2-607 (3) (a)', 73 *Cornell L. Rev.* (1987–88), pp. 575–76 ('the only notice that the rule should require the buyer to give the seller is either notice of the factual basis for its claim of breach of sufficient notice of the buyer's dissatisfaction so that the seller knows that it may have breached'). See also PEB Study Group, Uniform Commercial Code Article 2: Preliminary Report 168 (1990) ('Literal interpretations of the notice requirement should be rejected. Either the text of §2-607(3)(a) or the comments should be revised to require only that the notice inform the seller that problems have arisen or continue to exist with regard to the accepted goods').

574 See e.g. *Eastern Air Lines v. McDonnell Douglas Corp.*, 532 F.2d 957 (5th Cir. 1976); *Southern Illinois Stone Co. v. Universal Engineering Corp.*, 592 F.2d 446 (8th Cir. 1979); *T. J. Stevenson & Co. v. 81,193 Bags of Flour*, 629 F.2d 338 (5th Cir. 1980); *K & M Joint Venture v. Smith International, Inc.*, 669 F.2d 1106 (6th Cir. 1982); *Roth Steel Products v. Sharon Steel Corp.*, 705 F.2d 134 (6th Cir. 1983); *Industrial Fiberglass v. Jandt*, 361 N.W.2d 595, (N.D. 1985); *C.R. Daniels, Inc. v. Yazoo Mfg. Co.*, 641 F. Supp. 205 (S.D. Miss. 1986); *Quaker Alloy Casting Co. v. Gulfco Industries, Inc.*, 686 F. Supp. 1319 (N.D. Ill. 1988).

575 Between merchants, a stricter standard of notification might be applied implying that a notice indicating a mere 'troublesome' transaction is not sufficient: *Peavey Elecs. Corp. v. Baan U.S.A., Inc.*, 10 So. 3d 945 (Miss. App. 2009) ('it is not enough under section 2-607 that a seller has knowledge of the facts constituting a nonconforming tender; he must also be informed that the buyer considers him to be in breach of contract'; 'only the 'strict standard of notification' [...] can be justly applied where both parties are merchants under the UCC'). See also: *Industrial Fiberglass v. Jandt*, 361 N.W.2d 595, (N.D. 1985). *Accord* Fonseca, Patricia F., and Fonseca, John R., *Williston on Sales* (Eagan: West, 2006), p. 785. About the fact that a stricter standard is applicable between merchants in comparison to consumers, see also Chavis, Marvin, 'Notice of Breach and the Uniform Commercial Code', 25 *U. Fla. L. Rev.* (1972–73), p. 537.

576 Clark, Barkley, 'The First Line of Defense in Warranty Suits: Failure to Give Notice of Breach', 15 *UCC L.J.* (1982), pp. 122–23.

577 Prince, Harry G., 'Overprotecting the Consumer? Section 2-607(3)(a) Notice of Breach in Nonprivity Contexts', 66 *N.C. L. Rev.* (1987–88), p. 124.

of the concrete facts of the case in light of the goals of UCC §2-607(3)(a) (i.e. good faith, negotiations, cure, and preparing for litigation).[578]

If a buyer does not comply with the strict requirements of UCC §2-605 (stating all the particular defects, see *supra*, para. 129), he still has his right to damages if he has complied with the less strict requirements of UCC §2-607(3)(a), merely indicating that there is a problem with the performance of the transaction or a breach of contract (depending on which case law has to be followed).[579]

2.2.2. *Notifying the Remedies of Rejection, Revocation, and Notifying Cure*

Notifying the remedy of rejection. We have already seen that UCC §2-602(1) 131
prescribes that rejection has to be done within a reasonable time after delivery or tender and that the buyer has to seasonably notify[580] the seller of his rejection (see *supra*, para. 70).[581] Without a seasonable notification, the rejection is ineffective.[582] Indeed, the Official Comments state that it 'requires affirmative action by the buyer to avoid acceptance'. The lack of a timely and unequivocal notice of rejection will deprive the buyer from rejecting the goods.[583] However, he will not be deprived automatically from his damages remedy, which is subject to the notification duty of UCC §2-607(3)(a) (*supra*, para. 130).[584]

The first question that arises is *who* the buyer has to notify: his immediate seller or also others in the chain of distribution? Does the same problem arise as in case of UCC §2-607(3)(a) (*supra*, para. 130)? It is probably the immediate seller whom the buyer has to notify of the rejection. Moreover, with regard to UCC §2-606, doctrine[585] accepts that the term 'seller' (concerning acceptance) refers to the buyer's immediate seller.

---

578 Hammond, George F., 'Notification of Breach Under Uniform Commercial Code Section 2-607(3)(a): A Conflict, a Resolution', 70 *Cornell L. Rev.* (1984–85), p. 555.

579 See also Ferriell, Jeff, *Understanding Contracts* (New Providence, San Francisco: Matthew Bender & Co., Inc., 2009), p. 558.

580 Official Comment UCC §2-602, 1: the concept of notification is defined in UCC §1-201; nevertheless, it seems that §1-202 actually defines the concept of notification.

581 See also: Perillo, Joseph M., *Contracts* (St. Paul: West Academic, 2014), p. 403.

582 Official Comment UCC §2-602, 1. See regarding ineffectiveness: White, James J., and Summers, Robert S., *Principles of Sales Law* (St. Paul: Thomson Reuters, 2009), p. 492.

583 Ferriell, Jeff, *Understanding Contracts* (New Providence, San Francisco: Matthew Bender & Co., Inc., 2009), p. 550.

584 Henning, William H., and Lawrence, William H., 'A Unified Rationale for Section 2-607(3)(a)', 46 *San Diego L. Rev.* (2009), pp. 574–75.

585 Leete, Burt A., 'The Notice Booby-Trap of U.C.C. Section 2-607(3)(a)', 22 *Am. Bus. L.J.* (1984), p. 114.

With regard to the *form* of the notice, the UCC does not prescribe that it has to be a written notice.[586] However, for reasons of proof it is recommended that a written notice should be sent to the seller.[587]

As to the *timing* of the notice, UCC §2-602(1) requires that the buyer 'seasonably' notifies the seller. Courts are not likely to approve a 'notice through legal papers'.[588] The timeliness of the notice is related with the timeliness of the rejection itself.[589] Often it is stated that timeliness depends on the nature, purpose, and circumstances of the action.[590] In comparison with the notice specified in UCC §2-607(3)(a), the timing of a notice of rejection is more stringent than a notice for breach to recover damages.[591] A rejection notice should normally be earlier than the notice for breach.

With regard to the *content* of the notice, it has already been mentioned that it has to be an unequivocal notice.[592] It goes further than a notification of breach of contract according to UCC §2-607(3)(a) (*supra*, para. 130).[593]

---

586 See e.g. *Western Conference Resorts, Inc. v. Pease*, 668 P.2d 973 (Colo.App. 1983) (phone call); *Pomerantz Paper Corp. v. New Community Corp.*, 207 N.J. 344 (2011): ('Nothing in the statute's reference to the obligation to reject by 'seasonably notif[ying] the seller,' N.J.S.A. 12A:2-602(1), or in the definition of notification, N.J.S.A. 12A:1-201(26), demands that notification be in writing. On the contrary, the form of notice need only be reasonable in the context of the course of dealing between the parties').

587 See also White, James J., and Summers, Robert S., *Principles of Sales Law* (St. Paul: Thomson Reuters, 2009), p. 488 ('[...] those who have depended on non-written or equivocal notice, have not fared well in the courts').

588 Ibid., p. 488.

589 Ibid., p. 488.

590 See UCC §1-205. White, James J., and Summers, Robert S., *Principles of Sales Law* (St. Paul: Thomson Reuters, 2009), pp. 488–89 (considers this as a 'disheartening platitude' and proposes to take into account: the difficulty of discovering defects, the terms of the contract, the perishability of the goods and the course of performance after sale and before formal rejection) See also Ferriell, Jeff, *Understanding Contracts* (New Providence, San Francisco: Matthew Bender & Co., Inc., 2009), p. 557 (a 'timely' notification depends on the nature of the goods and the complexity or elaborateness of testing and examining the goods). See e.g. *Miron v. Yonkers Raceway, Inc.*, 400 F.2d 112 (2d Cir. 1968) taking into account the 'perishability' of the goods: 'a live animal is more prone to rapid change in condition and to injury than is an inanimate object').

591 White, James J., and Summers, Robert S., *Uniform Commercial Code* (St. Paul: West Academic), §11-10, p. 422.

592 Merely 'grumbling' that the quality of the goods is insufficient: *Van Dorn Co v. Future Chem. & Oil Corp.*, 753 F.2d 565, 575 (7th Cir. 1985). See also: Ferriell, Jeff, *Understanding Contracts* (New Providence, San Francisco: Matthew Bender & Co., Inc., 2009), p. 557.

593 Henning, William H., and Lawrence, William H., 'A Unified Rationale for Section 2-607(3)(a)', 46 *San Diego L. Rev.* (2009), p. 574. Cf. *Midwest Generation, LLC v. Carbon Processing & Reclamation, LLC*, 445 F. Supp. 2d 928, (N.D. Ill. 2006) ('Mere complaints are not enough to meet the UCC standard for rejection').

It is not sufficient to merely notify a defect of the goods. The notice of rejection must make clear that the goods are *unacceptable* and must include the *grounds* for rejection, which is the nature of the defects.[594]

This duty to notify also has to be understood in relation to the seller's right to cure (see *supra*, para. 69).[595] After the notification of rejection, the seller often has a right to cure.[596] The notification may give the seller a second chance to perform the contract. This implies that the buyer must also state all the particular defects which he discovers upon reasonable inspection if he wants to reject the goods (UCC §2-605(1)) (see also *supra*, para. 129).[597] If he fails to state the defects, he will not be able to rely on a defect to reject or to establish a breach of contract if the seller could have cured that defect seasonably.[598]

Notifying the remedy of revocation of acceptance. UCC §2-608(2) 132
prescribes, alongside to its other demanding conditions of application (see *supra*, para. 70), that revocation of acceptance must happen within a reasonable time after the buyer discovers or ought to have discovered the reasons for revoking acceptance (and before the goods undergo a substantial change not caused by their own defects). Moreover, revocation of acceptance is not effective until the buyer notifies[599] the seller of this. This notification has to be done timely and unequivocally.[600] However, even if he fails to notify revocation of acceptance he will – similarly to the

594 See Ferriell, Jeff, *Understanding Contracts* (New Providence, San Francisco: Matthew Bender & Co., Inc., 2009), p. 557.

595 White, James J., and Summers, Robert S., *Principles of Sales Law* (St. Paul: Thomson Reuters, 2009), p. 487. See also Henning, William H., and Lawrence, William H., 'A Unified Rationale for Section 2-607(3)(a)', 46 *San Diego L. Rev.* (2009), p. 574; Phillips, Jerry J., 'Notice of Breach in Sales and Strict Tort Liability Law: Should There Be a Difference?', 47 *Ind. L. J.* (1971–72), pp. 465–66.

596 See also Perillo, Joseph M., *Contracts* (St. Paul: West Academic, 2014), p. 403.

597 Ferriell, Jeff, *Understanding Contracts* (New Providence, San Francisco: Matthew Bender & Co., Inc., 2009), p. 550.

598 If both parties are merchants, a more stringent rule applies: when the seller requests after rejection in writing a 'full and final written statement of all defects on which the buyer proposes to rely' the buyer cannot rely on unstated defects that could have been reasonably discovered: Perillo, Joseph M., *Contracts* (St. Paul: West Academic, 2014), p. 404.

599 Official Comment UCC §2-608, definitional cross references: the concept of notification is defined in UCC §1-201; nevertheless, UCC §1-202 actually defines the concept of notification.

600 Ferriell, Jeff, *Understanding Contracts* (New Providence, San Francisco: Matthew Bender & Co., Inc., 2009), p. 562.

case of rejection (see *supra*, para. 131) – not automatically be deprived of his damages remedy, which is subject to the notification duty of UCC §2-607(3)(a). Some authors qualify the notification duty in case of revocation of acceptance as the second duty, because the buyer first has to notify the shortcoming under UCC §2-607(3)(a).[601] Perhaps not all authors mention the 'double notification duty' because both notifications can be done in the same *instrumentum*, if the conditions applying to each notification duty are fulfilled.[602]

With regard to the *form* of the notification, it is clear that this notification does not require any particular form.[603] An oral notification would be sufficient; nevertheless, for reasons of proof an unequivocal written notification is to be preferred.[604]

Next, it has to be noted that the notification has to be done in a *timely* manner.[605] However, contrary to UCC §2-602(1) about rejection, which requires that the buyer 'seasonably' notifies the seller, UCC §2-608(2) does not explicitly prescribe this. Nevertheless, revocation of acceptance has to be done within a reasonable time, which is interconnected with the timeliness of the notice of revocation.[606] Revocation must be done within a reasonable time after the buyer discovers, or should have discovered, the ground for it, and before any substantial change in the goods has

---

601 Clark, Barkley, 'The First Line of Defense in Warranty Suits: Failure to Give Notice of Breach', 15 *UCC L.J.* (1982), pp. 112–13; Stolzenberg, Doreen, 'UCC Section 2-608: Reasonable Time for Revocation of Acceptance', 44 *Fordham L. Rev.* (1976), p. 994.

602 It can be done in one *instrumentum*: Clark, Barkley, 'The First Line of Defense in Warranty Suits: Failure to Give Notice of Breach', 15 *UCC L.J.* (1982), p. 113 (calls it a 'double duty notice'). *Stofman v. Keenan Motors, Inc.*, 1973 Pa. Dist. & Cnty. Dec. LEXIS 289 (1973) (implicitly); *Christopher v. Larson Ford Sales*, 577 P.2d 1009 (Utah 1976) (implicitly, about a defective motor home).

603 Perillo, Joseph M., *Contracts* (St. Paul: West Academic, 2014), p. 406. See also *Hays Merch. v. Dewey*, 78 Wn.2d 343 (Wash. 1970); *Peckham v. Larsen Chevrolet-Buick Oldsmobile*, 99 Idaho 675, 587 P.2d 816 (1978); *Luson Int'l Distributors, Inc. v. Fabricating & Production Machinery, Inc.*, 966 F.2d 9 (1st Cir. 1992).

604 Cf. White, James J., and Summers, Robert S., *Principles of Sales Law* (St. Paul: Thomson Reuters, 2009), p. 505. *DeVoe Chevrolet-Cadillac, Inc. v. Cartwright*, 526 N.E.2d 1237, 7 UCC2d 792 (Ind. App. 1988) ('Notice of revocation should be in writing. […] Nonwritten notice or equivocal notice of revocation does not fare well in the courts […], the buyer's act of returning goods was not adequate notice of revocation.').

605 See extensively on the timeliness of the revocation Fonseca, Patricia F., and Fonseca, John R., *Williston on Sales* (Eagan: West, 2006), p. 739 *et seq.* and p. 744; Stolzenberg, Doreen, 'UCC Section 2-608: Reasonable Time for Revocation of Acceptance', 44 *Fordham L. Rev.* (1976), p. 991 *et seq.*

606 White, James J., and Summers, Robert S., *Principles of Sales Law* (St. Paul: Thomson Reuters, 2009), p. 505.

happened and is not caused by their own defects.[607] It is clear that the buyer will have a longer period to revoke acceptance compared to a notification of breach under UCC §2-607 and longer than the period of time to notify rejection.[608] It is also accepted that, with regard to consumers, a more lenient standard applies for the timeliness of the notice of revocation compared to a merchant buyer, which is also the case under UCC §2-607(3)(a).[609] Judges will take different factors into account when determining the reasonableness of the timeliness of the notice of revocation.[610] Difficulties in discovering the defect will, for example, prolong the period of time in which the buyer may revoke acceptance.[611] Furthermore, the assurances the seller gives with regard to the cure he will offer play an important role, since the buyer is generally required to offer the seller a possibility to cure (see *supra*, para. 69).[612]

With regard to the *content* it has to be noted that the notice has to be unequivocal. Similarly to the notification of rejection, the buyer's notice to revoke acceptance may not merely indicate that there is a problem with the transaction or a breach of contract.[613] This notice must make clear that the buyer does not want to keep the goods because they are unacceptable.[614]

---

607 UCC §2-608(2).

608 UCC §2-608, Comment 4. Stolzenberg, Doreen, 'UCC Section 2-608: Reasonable Time for Revocation of Acceptance', 44 *Fordham L. Rev.* (1976), p. 994; White, James J., and Summers, Robert S., *Principles of Sales Law* (St. Paul: Thomson Reuters, 2009), p. 505.

609 Stolzenberg, Doreen, 'UCC Section 2-608: Reasonable Time for Revocation of Acceptance', 44 *Fordham L. Rev.* (1976), p. 995.

610 See for an overview Stolzenberg, Doreen, 'UCC Section 2-608: Reasonable Time for Revocation of Acceptance', 44 *Fordham L. Rev.* (1976), p. 997 *et seq.*

611 See e.g. *Henry v. Don Wood Volkswagen, Inc.*, 526 S.W.2d 483, 16 U.C.C. Rep. Serv. 991 (Tenn. Ct. App. 1974). Stolzenberg, Doreen, 'UCC Section 2-608: Reasonable Time for Revocation of Acceptance', 44 *Fordham L. Rev.* (1976), pp. 1000–04.

612 *Stroh v. American Recreation & Mobile Home Corp.*, 35 Colo. App. 196, 530 P.2d 989 (1975). Stolzenberg, Doreen, 'UCC Section 2-608: Reasonable Time for Revocation of Acceptance', 44 *Fordham L. Rev.* (1976), pp. 997–99.

613 Official Comment UCC §2-608, 5.: 'More will generally be necessary than the mere notification of breach required under the preceding section'. See also *Connecticut Inv. Casting Corp. v. Made-Rite Tool Co.*, 382 Mass. 603, 416 N.E.2d 966, 31 UCC 531 (1981); *DeVoe Chevrolet-Cadillac, Inc. v. Cartwright*, 526 N.E.2d 1237, 7 UCC2d 792 (Ind. App. 1988) ('Merely complaining about the quality of goods, without more, does not adequately inform the seller the buyer has revoked'); *Golden Needles Knitting & Glove Co. v. Dynamic Marketing Enterprises, Inc.*, 766 F. Supp. 421 (W.D.N.C. 1991); *Luson Int'l Distributors, Inc. v. Fabricating & Production Machinery, Inc.*, 966 F.2d 9 (1st Cir. 1992).

614 Ferriell, Jeff, *Understanding Contracts* (New Providence, San Francisco: Matthew Bender & Co., Inc., 2009), p. 563; Fonseca, Patricia F., and Fonseca, John R., *Williston on Sales* (Eagan: West, 2006), pp. 742–53; White, James J., and Summers, Robert S.,

However, the Official Comment also provides that the notification requirements are less stringent if the buyer is a consumer.[615]

133 *No notice to subsequently cancel the contract.* After rejection and revocation of acceptance, the buyer may (even extrajudicially) cancel the contract if all the required conditions of application are fulfilled (see *supra*, paras. 69–70: e.g. the seller did not cure the shortcoming). The UCC does not provide for a process or a notification of the right to subsequently 'cancel' (terminate) the contract by the buyer.[616]

134 *Notification, rejection, and revocation in a judicial context.* As discussed previously, rejection, and revocation are considered typical self-help remedies, not requiring a prior intervention of a judge. What happens if the buyer invokes the right to reject or to revoke for the first time in a judicial context (i.e. before a judge); e.g. as a defense to a payment claim of the seller or in his summons? What happens if the buyer has not notified the rejection or revocation of acceptance and he first asks for it in a judicial context? Would this mean that the buyer has not notified seasonably? As mentioned, the buyer should notify rejection and revocation of acceptance within a reasonable time (*supra*, para. 131 and 132). It is clear that if these notification obligations are not satisfactorily fulfilled by the buyer, he will not be able to reject or to revoke[617] acceptance. In the case of rejection,

---

Principles of Sales Law (St. Paul: Thomson Reuters, 2009), p. 503. See *Lynx, Inc. v. Ordnance Products, Inc.*, 273 Md. 1, 327 A.2d 502 (1974) ('The criterion of good faith and the consideration that a speedy inexpensive method of operation is desirable, lead to the conclusion that the form and content of such notice of revocation should inform the seller that the buyer has revoked, identify the particular goods as to which he has revoked and set forth the nature of the non-conformity since such notice would corroborate the buyer's good faith and give the seller an opportunity to make a substitute performance to maintain good will or to avoid litigation'); *Connecticut Inv. Casting Corp. v. Made-Rite Tool Co.*, 382 Mass. 603, 416 N.E.2d 966, 31 UCC 531 (1981); *Golden Needles Knitting & Glove Co. v. Dynamic Marketing Enterprises, Inc.*, 766 F. Supp. 421 (W.D.N.C. 1991); *Luson Int'l Distributors, Inc. v. Fabricating & Production Machinery, Inc.*, 966 F.2d 9 (1st Cir. 1992). See also *Malul v. Capital Cabinets, Inc.*, 191 MIsc. 2d 399, 740 N.Y.S.2d 828 (2002) (it may not be a mere request to cure).

Often a notice of rescission is considered to operate as a notice of revocation: *Jensen v. Seigel Mobile Homes Group*, 105 Idaho 189 (1983).

615 Official Comment UCC §2-608, 5.

616 Speidel, Richard E., 'Buyer's Remedies of Rejection and Cancellation under the UCC and the Convention', 6 *J. Contract L.* (1993), p. 131 (with regard to rejection).

617 E.g. if the buyer fails to give notice of revocation because of a failure to discover the defects as soon as reasonably possible: Phillips, Jerry J., 'Revocation of Acceptance and the Consumer Buyer', 75 *Com. L.J.* (1970), p. 356.

the problem of the seller's right to cure will also play an important role. The question remains whether or not a summons, an action, or a defense before a court can constitute such a notification. A prior notification duty – separate from a summons, legal action, or defense – seems to be a condition without which rejection and revocation cannot be administered. In the case of rejection this is understandable. Rejection does not require a prior notification of a breach of contract (according to UCC §2-607(3)(a)). Thus, if the buyer has to give the seller a period of time to cure the defect, he should notify the seller of the rejection in advance. In the case of revocation of acceptance, the seller will be often already be notified by the notification duty of the buyer under UCC §2-607(3)(a) (notification of a breach of contract). In this case, it actually seems unnecessary to require a prior notification of a judicial revocation of acceptance (separate from a summons, legal action, or defense).

Notifying the right to cure. As discussed earlier, in the case of 135
rejection by the buyer, the seller often has a right to cure (see *supra*, para. 69). While it has to be admitted that the seller's right to cure cannot be considered a real 'remedy', it interferes with the organization of the remedies. If the right to cure is subject to a duty on the seller to notify that he wishes to invoke the right the cure, it will be harder to invoke this right.

As discussed earlier, UCC §2-508 distinguishes between two situations according to whether or not the time for performance has expired. If the time for performance has *not yet expired* and the buyer rejects the performance, the seller has a right to cure *if he promptly notifies the buyer* and cures within the contract time. The Official Comment specifies that the closer it is to the contract date, the more important it is for the seller to act with promptness with regard to this notification duty.[618] If time for performance *has expired* and the buyer rejects the performance, the seller may only exercise his right to cure if he had 'reasonable grounds to believe that the goods would be acceptable'[619] (with or without money allowance),

618 Official Comment UCC §2-508, 1.

619 See regarding the interpretation of such 'reasonable grounds': Lawrence, William H., 'Cure After Breach of Contract Under the Restatement (Second) of Contracts: An Analytical Comparison with the Uniform Commercial Code', 70 *Minn. L. Rev.* (1986), p. 720 (taking into account the prior course of dealing, the course of performance or a usage, and the surrounding market conditions; see also p. 745 *in fine*); Schwartz, Alan, and Scott, E. Robert, *Sales Law and the Contracting Process* (New York: Foundation Press, 1991), pp. 274–76 (believe that this rule in UCC §2-508(2) cannot be applied in real life because if a seller would be surprised by a rejection, the rejection must be

if he promptly notifies the buyer, and exercises his right to cure within a reasonable time.

With regard to *timing*, in both situations a 'prompt' notification is required. If the seller notifies his intention to cure at the moment of the notice of rejection by the buyer, it will often be considered 'timely'.[620] It will not be timely if the seller has already given the buyer the opportunity to arrange for buying substitute goods or repair, and then claims his right to cure.[621]

With regard to *content*, this notification has to be clear and unequivocal.[622] The notice has to make clear that the seller acknowledges the defect and will try to cure it.[623]

3. COMPARATIVE ANALYSIS

3.1. 'NOTIFICATION LIGHT' FOR SHORTCOMINGS?

3.1.1. EU Consumer Sales Approach Moving Towards an (Unjustified) Abolishment

136 *Tendency towards the abolishment of a notification duty of shortcomings.* First, it has to be noted that a consumer has, under the current EU consumer sales system, no real duty to examine the goods (see *supra*, para. 117). Moreover, the legislator is gradually shifting towards a notification-free system. Indeed, the EU legislator is slowly adhering to a system in which consumers do not have any obligation to notify their

---

wrongful because the goods will then conform to the contract; they also believe that there are good reasons to limit the seller's cure opportunities because the buyer can be affected by intangible losses such as lost confidence); Sebert, John A., 'Legal Theory: Rejection, Revocation, and Cure under Article 2 of the UCC: Some Modest Proposals', 84 *Nw. U.L. Rev.* (1990), p. 391.

620 White, James J., and Summers, Robert S., *Principles of Sales Law* (St. Paul: Thomson Reuters, 2009), p. 513–14. *Traynor v. Walters*, 342 F. Supp. 455, 10 UCC 965 (M.D.Pa 1972).

621 *National Fleet Supply, Inc. v. Fairchild*, 540 N.E.2d 1015, 36 UCC 480 (Ind. App. 1983). White, James J., and Summers, Robert S., *Principles of Sales Law* (St. Paul: Thomson Reuters, 2009), pp. 513–14.

622 White, James J., and Summers, Robert S., *Principles of Sales Law* (St. Paul: Thomson Reuters, 2009), p. 513. *T& S Brass & Bronze Works, Inc. v. Pic-Air, Inc.*, 790 F.2d 1098, 1 UCC2d 433 (4th Cir. 1986).

623 *T& S Brass & Bronze Works, Inc. v. Pic-Air, Inc.*, 790 F.2d 1098, 1 UCC2d 433 (4th Cir. 1986).

seller of a shortcoming. Whereas the Consumer Sales Directive still gave the national legislator the opportunity to introduce such a notification duty within certain boundaries, the CESL and the newest Commission Proposals (ODSD/2017 Proposal) do away with such a notice.

3.1.2. *Common Law Approach and the UCC Standard*

137 *Notification of shortcomings: not a typical common law requirement.* As previously discussed, under common law the notification of a shortcoming is not typically required. Nevertheless, the UCC has introduced an important duty to notify of a shortcoming in the case where the buyer has accepted the goods and wants to claim damages for a defect (*supra*, para. 130). This notification duty has been extensively discussed in US doctrine (see also *infra*, para. 140); however, where consumers are involved, many commentators do not believe that the benefits of the notification for the seller balance the disadvantages for the consumer.

138 *Different standards under the UCC.* Under the UCC, it is clear that buyers who are consumers will be treated more favorably compared to professionals. To comply with the notification requirement of UCC §2-607(3)(a), they will be granted more time to notify and the notification's content will be judged in a less strict way.[624] A corporate player buying a sophisticated machine and merely suffering economic loss will have to be more wary about the notification duty. However, this does not mean that the consumer is considered exempted from this duty.

3.1.3. *Relation with 'Mise en Demeure'*

139 *Mise en demeure and notification of breach.* Something which has not appeared in the discussion of the EU consumer sales *acquis* and the common law is the concept of '*mise en demeure*', which is a typical French and Belgian concept. It literally means to put your debtor 'in default' and has similar functions to a notification of breach. An important ruling of the Belgian Court of Cassation established a 'general principle' of putting the debtor in default.[625] The concept of *mise en demeure* is not limited to informing the other party of the fact that you want the obligation to be

---

624 See also Clark, Barkley, 'The First Line of Defense in Warranty Suits: Failure to Give Notice of Breach', 15 *UCC L.J.* (1982), p. 116.

625 Cass. 9 April 1976, *Arr. Cass.* 1976, 921, *Pas.* 1976, 887 and *RW* 1976–77, 921, note.

performed. It is also the starting point of interests that start to run, and it transfers the risk to the creditor (in sales contracts). In 1988–89, Reitz wrote about the 'mysteries' of the *mise en demeure* in French contract law, doubting its usefulness in modern US contract law.[626] This rule is unknown in common law, and considered extremely mild towards debtors. However, we have seen that the UCC requires in certain circumstances a notification of the breach of contract (after acceptance) or of a certain remedy (rejection and revocation) (see *supra*, para. 129). Notification only fulfills one of the roles of the *mise en demeure*, i.e. the role providing information. Belgian contract law also prescribes some notification duties, separate from the *mise en demeure* – e.g., in sales and tenancy law.[627] Although the content of the notification might differ – instead of informing the debtor of the fact that performance of the contract is requested, a notification will inform the debtor of the defects, troubles, the breach, or the remedy that the creditor wishes to invoke – both instruments provide the debtor with information about the (non-)performance of the contract.

Notwithstanding the fact that both – a *mise en demeure* and a notification of a shortcoming – can sometimes fulfill a similar role, the present author has previously defended the argument that they have a separate right of existence under Belgian contract law. Nevertheless, their scopes of application may have important overlapping areas, which might lead to confusion. Perhaps, it would be better to redefine the goals of both instruments of systems that contain – next to a duty to notify – a *mise en demeure*. In what follows, the reasoning distinguishing a notification of a shortcoming and a *mise en demeure* under Belgian contract law is set out.

On the one hand, a *notification* of a shortcoming (such as the duty to notify in case of sale or tenancy contracts, as mentioned before) is particularly aimed at *informing* the debtor about the shortcoming in the performance of a contract. Additionally, the duty to notify seems to enable the debtor to *remedy the contract* by means of performance in kind. On the other hand, a *default notice (mise en demeure)* enables the creditor to invoke a sanction to remedy an unexcused shortcoming of the contract. This implies that a default notice aims to warn the debtor.[628] From the

---

626 Reitz, John C., 'The Mysteries of the *mise en demeure*', 63 *Tul. L. Rev.* (1988–89), pp. 85–120.

627 See for tenancy law e.g. Art. 1721 and 1726 CC.

628 Demeyere, Luc, and Visser, Maaike, 'Ingebrekestellingsclausules' in Ballon, Gabriël-Luc, et al., *Contractuele Clausules* (Antwerp: Intersentia, 2013), 1005.

moment the debtor has been put in default, the creditor can call upon any sanction. Whereas a *notification* merely informs the debtor about the shortcoming in performance, a *default notice* also will make clear that the creditor is able (and perhaps also willing) to invoke a sanction.[629] As Largarde puts it rightly with regard to a notification, as opposed to a default notice: '*Il s'agit en effet d'aviser le débiteur et non de l'avertir*'.[630] It has to be concluded that, indeed, both mechanisms overlap with each other, but seem to have a separate right to exist.

When examining this reasoning in the light of the comparative findings from common law, it is important to immediately point to the core of the matter. Under Belgian contract law, a *mise en demeure* and a notification of a shortcoming can be distinguished based on, on the one hand, the aim to inform the seller of the fact that one is going to invoke a remedy and, on the other hand, to merely inform the seller about a shortcoming. This is a difficult point in the UCC §2-607(3)(a) reasoning about the content of the notification duty: is a mere notification of the defect or the fact that the transaction is troublesome enough, or should it be clear that the party is held in breach and that the other party will invoke remedies (see *supra*, para. 130)?

Both systems seem to struggle with the same difficulties, although on different levels (general contract law – special contracts) and in different terms (*mis en demeure* – notification).

3.1.4. Arguments in Favor of and Against a Notification Duty of Shortcomings

Lively debate. In the US and in the EU, the buyer's notification duty of shortcomings is the subject of a lively debate.[631] In both jurisdictions some 140

See for France: Brès, Aurélie, *La résolution du contrat par dénonciation unilatérale* (Paris: Litec, 2009), n° 779; Libchaber, Rémy, 'Demeure et mise en demeure en droit français' in Fontaine, Marcel, and Viney, Geneviève (eds.), *Les sanctions de l'inexécution des obligations contractuelles* (Brussels: Bruylant, 2001), n° 15.

629 See Delahaye, Thierry, *Résiliation et résolution unilatérales en droit commercial belge* (Brussels: Bruylant, 1984), n° 235 ('Elle peut se comparer à un ultime avertissement 'avant les poursuites"). See also for France: Lagarde, Xavier, 'Remarques sur l'actualité de la mise en demeure', JCP G (1996), n° 2 et seq; Popineau-Dehaullon, Catherine, *Les remèdes de justice privée à l'inexécution du contrat* (Paris: LGDJ, 2008), n° 841 and 868.

630 Lagarde, Xavier, 'Remarques sur l'actualité de la mise en demeure', *JCP G* (1996), n° 12.

631 See for the EU Jeloschek, Christoph, *Examination and Notification Duties in Consumer Sales Law* (Munich: Sellier, 2006), 234p. See e.g. for the US Reitz, John C., 'Against Notice: A Proposal to Restrict the Notice of Claims Rule in U.C.C. §2-607 (3) (a)', 73 *Cornell L. Rev.* (1987–88), pp. 534–95.

authors defend a duty to notify and others would applaud an abolishment of any notification duty. It is not surprising that the same arguments are invoked in favor or against this instrument.

141 *Conflict of interest between buyers and sellers.* This discussion reveals a fundamental conflict of interest between buyers (consumers) and sellers. Indeed, often the whole discussion boils down to comparing the interests of the buyer and the seller. The buyer does not want to be overburdened with obligations before he can invoke his remedies for non-conformity; while the seller wants to make it as difficult as possible for the buyer to invoke his remedies. Hence, a notification duty will hurt a buyer and be beneficial for a seller.

3.1.4.1. Opponents of a Notification Duty

142 *General.* Many authors have pleaded against notification duties of shortcomings, especially when consumers are involved. In a chapter about the 2008 proposal on the CRD, Loos has, for example, expressed his vigorous aversion to such a duty to notify of a lack of conformity by the consumer.[632] The European Consumer Organization (BEUC) also rejects such an obligation to notify a defect within a certain period of time after discovery as being 'burdensome and unsubstantiated'.[633] Therefore, many authors welcome the new approach of the ODSD/2017 Proposal, banning a notification duty for consumers with regard to a lack of conformity.[634] The arguments they invoke are sometimes not confined to whether the buyer is a consumer or a commercial buyer. Their most important arguments are (1) consumer naiveté (which is a specific argument); and (2) the harsh

---

632 Loos, Marco B.M., 'Sales Law in the DCFR', *SSRN, Centre for the Study of European Contract Law Working Paper Series No. 2010/04* (2010), pp. 33–4. See also for detail on the examination and notification duties under the PEL (S) and the DCFR: Loos, Marco B.M., 'Sales Law in the DCFR', *SSRN, Centre for the Study of European Contract Law Working Paper Series No. 2010/04* (2010), pp. 21–5.

633 BEUC response, p. 25.

634 Also welcoming this approach Loos, Marco B.M., 'Not Good But Certainly Content: The Proposals For European Harmonisation of Online and Distance Selling of Goods and the Supply of Digital Content' in Claeys, Ignace, and Terryn, Evelyne (eds.), *Digital Content & Distance Sales* (Cambridge: Intersentia, 2017), pp. 22–3 (doubts whether a duty to notify is especially problematic in cross-border transactions compared to other situations). See also Straetmans, Gert, and Meys, Shana, 'The New Proposals for Directives Concerning Digital Content and Online/Distance Sales' in Claeys, Ignace, and Terryn, Evelyne (eds.), *Digital Content & Distance Sales* (Cambridge: Intersentia, 2017), pp. 326–27 (merely state that it is consumer-friendly).

sanction of losing all the remedies if not complying with the notification duty (which is a general argument). US lawyers also invoke the fact that a notification for a shortcoming is not a typical common law feature.

Consumer naiveté. The first argument against the buyer's duty to notify a shortcoming is called the 'consumer naiveté'.[635] A consumer would often not be aware of his duty to notify the seller of a shortcoming.[636] A consumer may not automatically think to inform his seller of a shortcoming, and will frequently wait for a long time before consulting a lawyer. Some consumers do not even have the means to consult a lawyer. Some US scholars describe the duty of a consumer to notify the seller as a 'booby trap'.[637] 143

Harsh sanction. The second argument is that the consumer would face a very harsh sanction if he forgets to notify or does not notify (within a reasonable time).[638] He would lose all his remedies for breach of contract. In some systems, the duty to notify is triggered even by the fact that you, as a buyer, *ought* to have known the non-conformity or the defect.[639] In this case, it can be said that the buyer is even able to lose his rights without knowing about the defect. This sanction is indeed not always in proportion with the losses of the seller. Moreover, it was the seller – and not the buyer – who failed in the first place to perform properly. Often the loss of the full amount of the claim is too harsh.[640] Reitz correctly points out that it is better to bar damages for the consumer only to the extent necessary to overcome the seller's prejudice due to the lack of notice of the shortcoming.[641] 144

---

635 (Only about the remote seller) Keeton, Page W., et al., *Prosser and Keeton on Torts* (St. Paul: West, 1984), p. 691; Reitz, John C., 'Against Notice: A Proposal to Restrict the Notice of Claims Rule in U.C.C. §2-607 (3) (a)', 73 *Cornell L. Rev.* (1987–88), pp. 534 *et seq* (esp. p. 539).

636 Jeloschek, Christoph, *Examination and Notification Duties in Consumer Sales Law* (Munich: Sellier, 2006), pp. 118 *et seq.*; Loos, Marco B.M., 'Sales Law in the DCFR', *SSRN, Centre for the Study of European Contract Law Working Paper Series No. 2010/04* (2010), p. 24. With regard to Art. III.-3:107 DCFR: Von Bar, C. and Clive, E., *Draft Common Frame of Reference (DCFR)*, 6 V. (Munich: Sellier, 2009), p. 807. See also BEUC response, p. 25.

637 Esp. in the context of a remote seller.

638 Reitz, John C., 'Against Notice: A Proposal to Restrict the Notice of Claims Rule in U.C.C. §2-607 (3) (a)', 73 *Cornell L. Rev.* (1987–88), p. 534.

639 See, regarding this argument, Jeloschek, Christoph, *Examination and Notification Duties in Consumer Sales Law* (Munich: Sellier, 2006), pp. 117–18.

640 Reitz, John C., 'Against Notice: A Proposal to Restrict the Notice of Claims Rule in U.C.C. §2-607 (3) (a)', 73 *Cornell L. Rev.* (1987–88), p. 578 *et seq.*

641 Ibid., p. 582. See also Milberger, Patrick A., 'Section 2-607(3)(a): Effective Notification of Breach under the Uniform Commercial Code', 44 *U. Pitt. L. Rev.* (1983), pp. 733–34.

145 *Corrosion of public respect.* Somewhat linked with the previous argument, some authors point out that such a harsh regime for consumers would lead to the corrosion of the public respect for law, because people expect reasonableness from the law.[642] Losing all remedies because of a rigid rule has not been respected will not be accepted by the public.

146 *Easy escape for the seller.* In some situations, the buyer's notification duties will serve as a 'mere escape for the seller', without discussing the crux of the case, the non-conformity.[643] It is often the first line of defense that the seller will invoke. This might seem unfair, because it is the seller who has not complied with his obligation to perform, and not the buyer.

147 *Costs for the buyer.* Moreover, this approach to notification can have, according to Reitz, negative economic effects.[644] If the consumer always has to bear the cost of the seller's breach if he is barred from any remedy due to a lack of notification, it will eventually lead to the protection and shielding of poorly performing sellers. Furthermore, it is also contended that notification duties will lead to other extra costs for the buyer, for example, the cost of consulting experts.[645]

148 *No common law feature.* A notification duty for a shortcoming is not considered a typical common law feature.[646] Under common contract law, there does not exist a general duty to notify one's debtor of a shortcoming (see also *supra*, para. 125). Williston introduced the duty to notify in the 1906 draft of the Uniform Sales Act §49.[647] This later became the notification rule under UCC §2-607(3)(a).

149 *Alternatives?* Some authors propose an alternative. They do not wish to abolish the notification duty all together, but to preserve it for the cases where it is really necessary. Often they propose to keep only the notification

642 Reitz, John C., 'Against Notice: A Proposal to Restrict the Notice of Claims Rule in U.C.C. §2-607 (3) (a)', 73 *Cornell L. Rev.* (1987–88), p. 539, footnote 16.

643 See e.g. Jeloschek, Christoph, *Examination and Notification Duties in Consumer Sales Law* (Munich: Sellier, 2006), p. 113 *et seq.*

644 Reitz, John C., 'Against Notice: A Proposal to Restrict the Notice of Claims Rule in U.C.C. §2-607 (3) (a)', 73 *Cornell L. Rev.* (1987–88), p. 539, footnote 15.

645 Jeloschek, Christoph, *Examination and Notification Duties in Consumer Sales Law* (Munich: Sellier, 2006), p. 119.

646 See e.g. Reitz, John C., 'Against Notice: A Proposal to Restrict the Notice of Claims Rule in U.C.C. §2-607 (3) (a)', 73 *Cornell L. Rev.* (1987–88), pp. 534–35.

647 Ibid., pp. 534–35.

duty for a shortcoming if the seller can establish (significant) prejudice by the lack of notification.[648]

3.1.4.2. In Defense of a Notification Duty

General. Specifically with regard to consumer sales, some authors have criticized the abolition of a consumer's notification duty.[649] Although they are often concerned about consumer protection, a total abolition would swing the balance in the opposite direction. Different arguments are invoked to keep the notification duty. The most important are that such a notification (1) gives the seller the opportunity to minimize damages and to cure; (2) gives both parties the opportunity to negotiate and to settle their dispute; (3) gives the seller the opportunity to investigate the shortcoming; (4) protects the seller from 'stale' claims; (5) will encourage good faith; and (6) is not at odds with consumer protection because the consumer 'naiveté' is often overestimated. Moreover, some authors propose – as a compromise – a longer or maximum time limit to notify to avoid stale claims.[650] 150

Before going into the details of the different arguments, the general '*information providing*' role of the notification duty has also been stressed.[651] A notification of a shortcoming provides the seller with useful information: he now knows that he did not perform properly and can offer a solution to solve the problem in the particular case. He can also try to

648 Henning, William H., and Lawrence, William H., 'A Unified Rationale for Section 2-607(3)(a)', 46 *San Diego L. Rev.* (2009), p. 578; Reitz, John C., 'Against Notice: A Proposal to Restrict the Notice of Claims Rule in U.C.C. §2-607 (3) (a)', 73 *Cornell L. Rev.* (1987–88), pp. 534–94.

649 Claeys, Ignace, and Vancoillie, Jonas, 'Remedies, Modification of Digital Content and Right to Terminate Long-Term Digital Content Contracts' in Claeys, Ignace, and Terryn, Evelyne (eds.), *Digital Content & Distance Sales* (Cambridge: Intersentia, 2017), p. 180 and 230; Jansen, Sanne, and Stijns, Sophie, 'Proposal for a Directive on Certain Aspects Concerning Contracts for the Online and Other Distance Sale of Goods. Scope of Application, Definitions, and Conformity' in Claeys, Ignace, and Terryn, Evelyne (eds.), *Digital Content & Distance Sales* (Cambridge: Intersentia, 2017), pp. 92–3. See in the context of the CESL: Feltkamp, Regine, and Vanbossele, Frederic, 'Remedies under the Optional Common European Sales Law – A Good Alternative for Belgian Sales Law?' in Claeys, Ignace, and Feltkamp, Regine (eds.), *The Draft Common European Sales Law: Towards an Alternative Sales Law?* (Antwerp: Intersentia, 2013), p. 228.

650 Claeys, Ignace, and Vancoillie, Jonas, 'Remedies, Modification of Digital Content and Right to Terminate Long-Term Digital Content Contracts' in Claeys, Ignace, and Terryn, Evelyne (eds.), *Digital Content & Distance Sales* (Cambridge: Intersentia, 2017), p. 180.

651 See extensively Jeloschek, Christoph, *Examination and Notification Duties in Consumer Sales Law* (Munich: Sellier, 2006), p. 108 *et seq.*

avoid future non-conformities by changing from suppliers and passing on this information to the manufacturers (who can adapt their manufacturing process). The seller can also opt for a product recall to avoid future losses of consumers. This information duty and the results therefrom tie into the arguments bundled here under the common denominator of '*mitigation*'.

151 *Mitigation.* Indeed, many arguments have to do with the 'duty to mitigate damages'. A notification of a shortcoming often gives the seller the opportunity to correct (cure) the breach and to minimize damages.[652] Under the Consumer Sales Directive and the ODSD/2017 Proposal, for example, the seller has the 'right' (and the duty) to repair or to replace the goods. It is considered a primary remedy for the buyer, but it is also a right of the seller. The sooner the seller is able to repair or to replace, the more likely it is that extra losses will be avoided. A notification of a shortcoming will enable the seller to react as soon as possible and to mitigate losses. Some authors have criticized this argument by pointing out that a cure is of special relevance when the buyer choses for termination.[653] Moreover, there will be no minimizing of damages if the buyer has no confidence in the seller's cure[654] or if the seller does not offer the cure with the lowest cost.[655] Another counterargument is that not every case of non-conformity has the tendency to become worse.[656] Nevertheless, this does not mean that this argument is totally empty of meaning.

Other mitigation arguments can also be invoked. A timely notification will, for example, allow the seller to reuse or to dispose of returned goods

---

652 See for the US e.g., *Marshall v. Bryant Air Conditioning Co.*, 650 F.2d 724 (5th Cir. 1981); *Maybank v. S.S. Kresge Co.*, 302 N.C. 129, 273 S.E.2d 681 (1981). Chavis, Marvin, 'Notice of Breach and the Uniform Commercial Code', 25 *U. Fla. L. Rev.* (1972–73), pp. 522–23; Fonseca, Patricia F., and Fonseca, John R., *Williston on Sales* (Eagan: West, 2006), pp. 781 and 812–13; Prince, Harry G., 'Overprotecting the Consumer? Section 2-607(3)(a) Notice of Breach in Nonprivity Contexts', 66 *N.C. L. Rev.* (1987–88), p. 142; White, James J., and Summers, Robert S., *Uniform Commercial Code* (St. Paul: West Academic), §§11-10, p. 418.

653 UCC §2-607(3)(a) gives the seller no right to cure but they can agree to it: Henning, William H., and Lawrence, William H., 'A Unified Rationale for Section 2-607(3)(a)', 46 *San Diego L. Rev.* (2009), p. 590.

654 Reitz, John C., 'Against Notice: A Proposal to Restrict the Notice of Claims Rule in U.C.C. §2-607 (3) (a)', 73 *Cornell L. Rev.* (1987–88), pp. 560–61.

655 Henning, William H., and Lawrence, William H., 'A Unified Rationale for Section 2-607(3)(a)', 46 *San Diego L. Rev.* (2009), p. 592; Reitz, John C., 'Against Notice: A Proposal to Restrict the Notice of Claims Rule in U.C.C. §2-607 (3) (a)', 73 *Cornell L. Rev.* (1987–88), pp. 560–61.

656 Jeloschek, Christoph, *Examination and Notification Duties in Consumer Sales Law* (Munich: Sellier, 2006), p. 105.

after termination or replacement.[657] Moreover, a side effect of a notification duty is that it often ensures that the goods will only have been used for a limited amount of time; avoiding deterioration of the goods.[658]

Mitigation (2). A less frequently invoked argument is that a notification of a buyer could protect the seller from prejudice from loss of claims against supplier or carriers (pass-on claims) because of limitation periods. Indeed, the absence of a notification duty will decrease the chances of the seller to have redress towards his seller.[659] Also, loss of opportunity for the seller to avoid similar liability to other buyers is invoked.[660] A seller could make adjustments to the manufacturing process and make product recalls to avoid further losses. A problem with this argument is that the causal link for these kind of mitigating effects of a notification duty becomes highly uncertain and speculative.[661] 152

Quick settlement. The second argument that is invoked is closely linked with the first. A notification of a shortcoming gives the parties the opportunity to attempt a settlement through negotiations.[662] This has been 153

657 However, Jeloschek argues that professional parties are repeat-players and should be well equipped/prepared to address problems with regard to claims based on non-conformity with the contract Jeloschek, Christoph, *Examination and Notification Duties in Consumer Sales Law* (Munich: Sellier, 2006), p. 89.

658 Jeloschek counters this argument by stating that other instruments can be used to reach the same goal, such as specific restrictions to apply a certain remedy (such as termination) if the goods are substantially deteriorated: Jeloschek, Christoph, *Examination and Notification Duties in Consumer Sales Law* (Munich: Sellier, 2006), p. 90.

659 Jeloschek argues that the redress issue cannot be left alone to a regime of notification and examination and requires autonomous rules on redress of the final seller towards the other links in the chain: Jeloschek, Christoph, *Examination and Notification Duties in Consumer Sales Law* (Munich: Sellier, 2006), p. 101.

660 Clark, Barkley, 'The First Line of Defense in Warranty Suits: Failure to Give Notice of Breach', 15 *UCC L.J.* (1982), p. 111. This is criticized by Reitz, John C., 'Against Notice: A Proposal to Restrict the Notice of Claims Rule in U.C.C. §2-607 (3) (a)', 73 *Cornell L. Rev.* (1987–88), pp. 573–74 (these are often also tort cases (because of bodily harm) in which there is no notice rule; moreover such a prejudice is speculative).

661 I.e., there is perhaps no direct causal relation or link between the failure to notify and the further losses.

662 UCC §2-607 comment 4. *Eastern Air Lines Inc. v. McDonnell Douglas Corp.*, 532 F.2d 957 (5th Cir. 1976); *T.J. Stevenson & Co. v. 81, 193 Bags of Flour*, 629 F.2d 338, (5th Cir. 1980). Chavis, Marvin, 'Notice of Breach and the Uniform Commercial Code', 25 *U. Fla. L. Rev.* (1972–73), pp. 522 and 524–25; Clark, Barkley, 'The First Line of Defense in Warranty Suits: Failure to Give Notice of Breach', 15 *UCC L.J.* (1982), p. 110; Hammond, George F., 'Notification of Breach Under Uniform Commercial Code Section 2-607(3)(a): A Conflict, a Resolution', 70 *Cornell L. Rev.* (1984–85), p. 541; Milberger, Patrick A., 'Section 2-607(3)(a): Effective Notification of Breach

criticized by different authors who challenge the idea that early negotiations after a breach will automatically lead to a speedier settlement and that negotiations before litigation would always be better than negotiations during litigation.[663]

154 *Evidence and investigation.* The proponents of a notification duty also argue that it gives the seller an opportunity to investigate the facts (to test and inspect the goods, to interview people and to preserve evidence or information) and to prepare for litigation.[664] This argument has been criticized by authors who claim that this disadvantage of the seller has often no practical consequence. This would be the case if the seller knows of the defects: e.g., in case of late delivery;[665] if the seller knows of the defect upon delivery; if the seller has admitted the defects; and in the case of delivery of the wrong goods. This means that only in special circumstances, such as rotten fruit, there is a significant effect resulting from the information imbalance.[666] It has also been argued that this 'investigation and evidence'

under the Uniform Commercial Code', 44 *U. Pitt. L. Rev.* (1983), p. 737; Phillips, Jerry J., 'Notice of Breach in Sales and Strict Tort Liability Law: Should There Be a Difference?', 47 *Ind. L. J.* (1971–72), pp. 468–69; Prince, Harry G., 'Overprotecting the Consumer? Section 2-607(3)(a) Notice of Breach in Nonprivity Contexts', 66 *N.C. L. Rev.* (1987–88), pp. 140–41.

663 Reitz, John C., 'Against Notice: A Proposal to Restrict the Notice of Claims Rule in U.C.C. §2-607 (3) (a)', 73 *Cornell L. Rev.* (1987–88), p. 550 *et seq*. See also *Shooshanian v. Wagner*, 672 P.2d 455 (Alaska 1983) ('the filing of a complaint is certainly not a bar to the negotiation and settlement of claims. To the contrary, the prospect of going to trial is often a powerful incentive to a defendant to investigate the claims against it and to arrive at a reasonable agreement').

664 *Owen v. Sears, Roebuck & Co.*, 273 F.2d 140 (9th Cir. 1959); *Eastern Air Lines Inc. v. McDonnell Douglas Corp.*, 532 F.2d 957 (5th Cir. 1976); *Cole v. Keller Indus.*, 872 F. Supp. 1470 (E.D. Va. 1994). Chavis, Marvin, 'Notice of Breach and the Uniform Commercial Code', 25 *U. Fla. L. Rev.* (1972–73), pp. 522 and 523–24; Clark, Barkley, 'The First Line of Defense in Warranty Suits: Failure to Give Notice of Breach', 15 *UCC L.J.* (1982), p. 111; Hammond, George F., 'Notification of Breach Under Uniform Commercial Code Section 2-607(3)(a): A Conflict, a Resolution', 70 *Cornell L. Rev.* (1984–85), p. 541; Milberger, Patrick A., 'Section 2-607(3)(a): Effective Notification of Breach under the Uniform Commercial Code', 44 *U. Pitt. L. Rev.* (1983), p. 737; Phillips, Jerry J., 'Notice of Breach in Sales and Strict Tort Liability Law: Should There Be a Difference?', 47 *Ind. L. J.* (1971–72), pp. 466–468; Prince, Harry G., 'Overprotecting the Consumer? Section 2-607(3)(a) Notice of Breach in Nonprivity Contexts', 66 *N.C. L. Rev.* (1987–88), pp. 140–141; White, James J., and Summers, Robert S., *Uniform Commercial Code* (St. Paul: West Academic), §§11-10, p. 418.

665 See also Henning, William H., and Lawrence, William H., 'A Unified Rationale for Section 2-607(3)(a)', 46 *San Diego L. Rev.* (2009), p. 583.

666 Reitz, John C., 'Against Notice: A Proposal to Restrict the Notice of Claims Rule in U.C.C. §2-607 (3) (a)', 73 *Cornell L. Rev.* (1987–88), pp. 562–63 *et seq.*

argument has no value because often only the *buyer* has the burden of proof, and not the seller.[667] However, it will also become increasingly difficult *for the buyer* to prove when a certain shortcoming has taken place, how it happened, and what the initial state of the goods was, etc. Therefore, although this might sound contradictory, the notification duty can also been seen as an important instrument to safeguard the interests of the buyer.

Avoidance of 'stale claims'. The next important argument of some 155
proponents of the notification rule is that it would protect the seller from so-called 'stale' claims.[668] Some authors call it 'mind balm' or 'repose' for the seller.[669] Others refer to 'legal certainty'.[670] A duty to notify within a reasonable time assures the seller that there are no more future claims; it increases his ability to plan the future. Nevertheless, this argument has been heavily criticized by doctrine. First and foremost, it has been advanced that 'repose' is a function of the statute of limitations and not of a notification.[671] Moreover, even if a duty to notify would offer some peace of mind for the seller this can be severely undermined because of the uncertainty of the interpretation of judges of the 'reasonableness' with regard to the timing of the notification.[672] Moreover, 'mind balm' can never

---

667 See for this opinion: Jeloschek, Christoph, *Examination and Notification Duties in Consumer Sales Law* (Munich: Sellier, 2006), p. 94 (however, he starts from the premise of the burden of proof in a very static system in which the parties have no obligation to cooperate in good faith).

668 *Pollard v. Saxe & Yolles Dev. Co.*, 12 Cal. 3d 374 (1974); *Eastern Air Lines Inc. v. McDonnell Douglas Corp.*, 532 F.2d 957 (5th Cir. 1976); *Cole v. Keller Indus.*, 872 F. Supp. 1470 (E.D. Va. 1994); *Brookings Mun. Utils., Inc. v. Amoco Chem. Co.*, 103 F. Supp. 2d 1169 (D.S.D. 2000). Chavis, Marvin, 'Notice of Breach and the Uniform Commercial Code', 25 *U. Fla. L. Rev.* (1972–73), p. 525; Clark, Barkley, 'The First Line of Defense in Warranty Suits: Failure to Give Notice of Breach', 15 *UCC L.J.* (1982), p. 111; Phillips, Jerry J., 'Notice of Breach in Sales and Strict Tort Liability Law: Should There Be a Difference?', 47 *Ind. L.J.* (1971–72), pp. 469–70; Prince, Harry G., 'Overprotecting the Consumer? Section 2-607(3)(a) Notice of Breach in Nonprivity Contexts', 66 *N.C. L. Rev.* (1987–88), pp. 141–42.

669 White, James J., and Summers, Robert S., *Uniform Commercial Code* (St. Paul: West Academic), §§11-10, pp. 418–19 ('mind balm').

670 Jeloschek, Christoph, *Examination and Notification Duties in Consumer Sales Law* (Munich: Sellier, 2006), p. 134 *et seq.*

671 Henning, William H., and Lawrence, William H., 'A Unified Rationale for Section 2-607(3)(a)', 46 *San Diego L. Rev.* (2009), p. 593.
Nevertheless, there is a difference between a lawsuit and a notification. See, regarding this difference: Reitz, John C., 'Against Notice: A Proposal to Restrict the Notice of Claims Rule in U.C.C. §2-607 (3) (a)', 73 *Cornell L. Rev.* (1987–88), p. 553.

672 Ibid., Reitz, John C., p. 554.

be offered in respect of latent defects, because notification is only required upon the 'discovery' of the defect.[673]

156 *Good faith.* Proponents also claim that a notification duty prevents the seller from commercial bad faith.[674] Notifying the seller of a shortcoming would be an expression of good faith by the buyer-consumer. Good faith has to be analyzed, according to some authors, taking into account the communication between both parties, the nature of their contractual relation, and the commercial context. Nevertheless, this argument is sometimes tackled by stating that the good faith reasoning is not well-elaborated and often given no meaning which is independent from mitigation, staleness, the right cure, settlement, and investigation arguments.[675]

157 *Overestimation of consumer naiveté.* When assessing the arguments against the notification of a shortcoming, the argument that highlighted the consumer's unprofessionalism and naiveté stands out (*supra*, para. 143). Those features would make the consumer unfit to notify a seller of a shortcoming. An important argument of the proponents of a notification duty stresses the overestimation of consumer naiveté or unwariness.[676] They advance that a consumer is not always lacking knowledge.[677] Some doubt that consumers would remain silent when clearly being aware of a defect.[678] And if they would remain silent in such a situation, education of consumers of their rights and duties seems to be the answer.[679] Consumers are, according to them, not always so helpless and often have the help of

---

673 Henning, William H., and Lawrence, William H., 'A Unified Rationale for Section 2-607(3)(a)', 46 *San Diego L. Rev.* (2009), p. 593.

674 See also UCC §2-607 comment 4; *Eastern Air Lines Inc. v. McDonnell Douglas Corp.*, 532 F.2d 957 (5th Cir. 1976). *K & M Joint Venture v. Smith International, Inc.*, 669 F.2d 1106, (6th Cir. 1982). Hammond, George F., 'Notification of Breach Under Uniform Commercial Code Section 2-607(3)(a): A Conflict, a Resolution', 70 *Cornell L. Rev.* (1984–85), p. 540. Cf.: Milberger, Patrick A., 'Section 2-607(3)(a): Effective Notification of Breach under the Uniform Commercial Code', 44 *U. Pitt. L. Rev.* (1983), pp. 733–49 (but mainly addresses good faith to favor the lenient approach towards the content of the notification of breach, *supra*, para. 130).

675 Henning, William H., and Lawrence, William H., 'A Unified Rationale for Section 2-607(3)(a)', 46 *San Diego L. Rev.* (2009), pp. 587–89.

676 Prince, Harry G., 'Overprotecting the Consumer? Section 2-607(3)(a) Notice of Breach in Nonprivity Contexts', 66 *N.C. L. Rev.* (1987–88), p. 143 *et seq.*

677 Ibid., p. 144.

678 White, James J., and Summers, Robert S., *Uniform Commercial Code* (St. Paul: West Academic), §§11-10, p. 418.

679 Phillips, Jerry J., 'Notice of Breach in Sales and Strict Tort Liability Law: Should There Be a Difference?', 47 *Ind. L.J.* (1971–72), p. 476.

an attorney.[680] The most reasonable argument of this strand is that it is often enough to give the consumer more 'reasonable' time to notify the shortcoming.[681] So the consumer unwariness can be counterbalanced by giving the consumer more time to notify (and consult a lawyer) compared to a commercial buyer. This method of reasoning can also be fruitful with regard to the content of the notification duty: a consumer should just make clear, in an informal way, that there is something wrong with the transaction; without having to claim a certain remedy or to point at a breach of contract.

Notification by lawsuit? Finally, some authors defend the duty of the buyer to notify because they do not consider it difficult to comply with this requirement. They consider that an initiation of a lawsuit is sufficient as a notice of breach.[682] This is criticized by those who consider that a notification duty of the buyer is primarily meant to give the seller a reasonable opportunity to cure.[683] 158

Benefits for the consumer. As stated earlier (*supra*, para. 154), if the burden of proof lies on the buyer, a notification can help him to prove when a certain shortcoming has taken place, how it happened, and what the initial state of the goods was. Moreover, a notification duty can also have benefits for the buyer, such as being able to decide whether or not to pay the price, to incite the seller to deliver conforming goods, and to settle any problems in his transaction quickly.[684] 159

3.1.5. *Fair Balance under a 'Notification Light'*

Consumer context. After examining the arguments in favor of and against a notification duty, the question whether a notification duty is useful in the 160

680 Prince, Harry G., 'Overprotecting the Consumer? Section 2-607(3)(a) Notice of Breach in Nonprivity Contexts', 66 *N.C. L. Rev.* (1987–88), p. 145. See also Chavis, Marvin, 'Notice of Breach and the Uniform Commercial Code', 25 *U. Fla. L. Rev.* (1972–73), p. 530 (thus an extension of the 'reasonable time to notify' should suffice to protect the consumer).

681 Prince, Harry G., 'Overprotecting the Consumer? Section 2-607(3)(a) Notice of Breach in Nonprivity Contexts', 66 *N.C. L. Rev.* (1987–88), pp. 145–46.

682 See for US (UCC) law: Prince, Harry G., 'Overprotecting the Consumer? Section 2-607(3)(a) Notice of Breach in Nonprivity Contexts', 66 *N.C. L. Rev.* (1987–88), p. 128 *et seq.* (see also about this controversy *supra*, para. 130).

683 Fonseca, Patricia F., and Fonseca, John R., *Williston on Sales* (Eagan: West, 2006), p. 813.

684 Jeloschek, Christoph, *Examination and Notification Duties in Consumer Sales Law* (Munich: Sellier, 2006), pp. 129–30.

consumer context has to be examined. Most agree that a consumer case must at least be treated more leniently than a case in which two traders conclude a sales contract. Indeed, one has to take into account that the consumer must be considered the 'weaker' party.[685] However, in the EU system, the balance has totally shifted in favor of the consumer and does away with the notification duty for a shortcoming, at least in its latest instruments. In the US sales law system, commentators struggle with the notification requirement and make exceptions when consumers are involved.

161 *Balancing of interests.* In the opinion of the present author,[686] the buyer's and seller's interests have to be balanced. It is true that the lack of a duty to notify the seller about a non-conformity might result in a greater flexibility to invoke a non-conformity by the consumer (and later on, to apply remedies), but at the same time, it significantly reduces the protection of the seller.[687] However, it is essential that a creditor (consumer or not) always informs the debtor about a *lack of conformity* with the contract within a reasonable period after its discovery, mainly for reasons of proof concerning the passing of risk (did the non-conformity of the goods appear before or after the passing of risk?).[688] This can be useful both for the consumer and for the seller, depending on whom the burden of proof rests. If it is true that consumers are not aware of this duty – which is often questionable: how can a consumer expect that something would improve without telling the seller? – a large-scale consumer campaign should be launched to raise awareness. Although a notice of a shortcoming will not always necessarily lead to a quicker settlement of disputes, it will at least open a dialogue between both parties. This might lead to an exchange of the expectations of both parties. This dialogue might then lead (indirectly)

---

685 See also ibid., pp. 145–46.

686 See for the same opinion Jansen, Sanne, and Stijns, Sophie, 'Proposal for a Directive on Certain Aspects Concerning Contracts for the Online and Other Distance Sale of Goods. Scope of Application, Definitions, and Conformity' in Claeys, Ignace, and Terryn, Evelyne (eds.), *Digital Content & Distance Sales* (Cambridge: Intersentia, 2017), pp. 92–3.

687 See, regarding the DCFR (but about the requirement to notify remedies): Samoy, Ilse, and Dang Vu, Tâm, 'Performance and Non-performance in the DCFR' in Sagaert, Vincent, et al. (eds.), *The Draft Common Frame of Reference: A National and Comparative Perspective* (Antwerp: Intersentia, 2012), para. 69.

688 See for the same opinion: Feltkamp, Regine, and Vanbosselе, Frederic, 'The Optional Common European Sales Law: Better Buyer's Remedies for Seller's Non-Performance in Sales of Goods?', *ERPL* (2011), pp. 896–97.

to a mitigation of damages (for both parties). At the very least, under some circumstances, the duty to perform one's obligations in good faith would require such a notification duty. Nevertheless, it has to be admitted that the sanction for not notifying, which is often 'losing all remedies' altogether, is quite harsh for a consumer and should be mitigated.

It is interesting to note in this regard that one of the earlier versions of the Consumer Sales Directive Proposals actually did require a notification of the lack of conformity (within one month from the date of detection or when the consumer ought to have detected the lack of conformity).[689] It was supposed to balance the consumer's freedom to choose between the four rights in that Proposal (only later the hierarchy of remedies was introduced, *supra*, para. 10). However, after the introduction of the hierarchy of remedies – emitting the priority of repair and replacement – these provisions on the duty to notify a lack of conformity were removed, because they were no longer needed to balance the rights between the consumer and the seller.[690]

Notification 'light' as compromise. A fair balance might be struck by providing for a so-called 'light-version' notification duty. The consumer need not comply with the same requirements as a commercial buyer. According to Jeloschek: 'In other words, examination and notification duties may be reconciled with the idea of consumer protection, provided that the harshest consequences for the buyer are defused'.[691] Several elements of the notification requirement could be alleviated.[692] 162

1. The *'examination duty'* of the buyer has not been studied here in detail.[693] A separate examination duty, next to a notification duty, will render it even more difficult for a buyer to invoke his remedies.

689 See Art. 4 Proposal for European Parliament and Council Directive on the sale of consumer goods and associated guarantees, Brussels 18 June 1996, COM(95) 520 final, 96/0161 (COD).

690 Page 4 of the Explanatory Memorandum of the Amended proposal for a European Parliament and Council Directive on the sale of consumer goods and associated guarantees, Brussels 31 March 1998, COM(1998) 217 final, 96/0161 (COD). See also Zollers, Frances E., et al., 'Consumer Protection in the European Union: An Analysis of the Direction on the Sale of Consumer Goods and Associated Guarantees', *U. Pa. J. Int'l Econ. L.* (1999), footnote 85.

691 In his PhD thesis about examination and notification duties: Jeloschek, Christoph, *Examination and Notification Duties in Consumer Sales Law* (Munich: Sellier, 2006), p. 177.

692 See for a well fleshed-out alternative: ibid., p. 217.

693 See, e.g., for the EU Consumer Sales Context: ibid., p. 40 *et seq.*

An express examination duty is not foreseen under the current EU consumer sales *acquis*. But an implied duty to examine – which will be triggered when a buyer ought to have discovered the defect within a certain period of time – is also currently not allowed. Member States have, under the CSD, only the possibility to introduce a notification duty, which may not be shorter than two months after the buyer has 'discovered' the defect.[694] This means after the *actual* discovery of the defect, and not when the consumer 'ought' to have discovered a defect. This means that the consumer does not have an implied duty to examine. Also, the other EU consumer sales instruments do not require the consumer to examine the goods. In US sales law, there exists, for certain remedies, a duty to examine the goods. Indeed, under the UCC, the buyer has a right to inspect the goods 'at any reasonable place and time and in a reasonable manner' (UCC §2-513). According to UCC §2-605(1), the buyer must, moreover, state all the particular defects which he discovers upon reasonable inspection. If he fails to state those defects he will not be able to rely on the defect to reject or to establish a breach of contract if the seller could have cured that defect seasonably. Taking into account the consumer perspective, it is reasonable *not* to require from a consumer to examine the goods upon delivery – even not implicitly.[695]

2. The question *when* the consumer has to notify the seller arises. If the seller is aware of the shortcoming or ought to be aware of it, it would be unfair to require from the consumer to notify the – already known – defect to the seller.
3. Furthermore, the notification of the shortcoming often has to be done within a 'reasonable time' after discovery of the defect (e.g., a period of at least two months).[696] From a consumer perspective, at least the 'reasonableness' of the *period of time to notify*, starting from the actual

694 Calls, hence, the notification duty a mere 'passive duty': ibid., p. 146.

695 *Contra*: ibid., p. 179 ('[...] a notification duty solely based on actual discovery, as introduced by the Sales Directive, loses out to its fully-fledged sibling. The main concern is that it will be virtually impossible for the seller to prove that the buyer has detected the non-conformity') and pp. 208–09.

696 In most cases, a two-month period of time will be within the consumer's expectations. See p. 8 of the Qualitative Eurobarometer Study, Sales Remedies, Conducted by TNS Qual+ at the request of Directorate General for Health and Consumers, December 2009, http://ec.europa.eu/consumers/archive/rights/docs/aggregate%20report_dec2009_en.pdf.

discovery of a defect, has to be construed in a very lenient way.[697] This means that the consumer will have more time to notify his seller, compared to a commercial buyer. A fixed period (of, for example, one or two months), without taking into account any reasonableness, is not preferred because of its rigid nature. The combination of a minimum period of time (e.g., two months) combined with an assessment of the reasonableness of the period of time if the consumer notifies after this fixed period of two months, will offer a judge the flexibility to take the particular circumstances into account.

4. The requirements, with regard *to the content* of the notification, should also be interpreted in a consumer-friendly manner. The consumer should merely be compelled to inform his seller that the transaction is troublesome. He does not have to describe the defects in detail or make clear that there is a breach of contract or that he wants to invoke a remedy.[698]
5. With regard to the *form* of such a notification, a mere informal complaint should be sufficient. An oral notice is allowed; but for reasons of proof it is wise to use a written notice (e-mail, SMS, letter, online chat).[699]
6. Finally, the most important measure to protect consumers with regard to the duty to notify of shortcomings deals with *its sanction.* The sanction of losing all remedies upon a lack of or late notification is too harsh towards a consumer.[700] Some authors propose that the buyer should not lose all his rights, but only certain remedies (such as termination and repair), thereby limiting the cut-off effect of the notification duty.[701] However, the correct approach is that the

697 Argues that a 'reasonable' period of time allows for more flexibility than a fixed 'straightjacket' period of time. A 'reasonable period of time' allows to take into account that the buyer is a consumer or to take into account extraordinary factors: Jeloschek, Christoph, *Examination and Notification Duties in Consumer Sales Law* (Munich: Sellier, 2006), p. 162.

698 With an exception for extrajudicial remedies, see *supra*, para. 92 *et seq.* and *infra*, para. 164. See also Jeloschek, Christoph, *Examination and Notification Duties in Consumer Sales Law* (Munich: Sellier, 2006), p. 181 (pleads at least for a clarification with regard to the content of a notification).

699 Depending on which means of proof are allowed.

700 The mitigation argument does not explain why the buyer will lose all his remedies when failing to notify and that the seller is exempt from any liability for the defect instead of a mere reduction thereof: Jeloschek, Christoph, *Examination and Notification Duties in Consumer Sales Law* (Munich: Sellier, 2006), p. 176.

701 Ibid., pp. 178 and 212 *et seq.*

consumer should just be responsible for the harm he has caused towards his seller by omitting to notify. This would mean that, for example, his right to damages will be reduced in so far he has damaged his seller by not notifying him (in a timely fashion). Hence, under some circumstances, some remedies will no longer be available (such as termination or specific performance) if the harm that has been caused to the seller by not notifying exceeds the additional damages upon which the buyer can rely. However, not all remedies will be lost. In any case the buyer will have the right to receive the remainder of his damages or a price reduction.

As already stated, getting rid of the notification duty altogether in order to strengthen consumer protection tilts the balance too far in the other direction. A compromise must be struck. A compromise that gives a consumer ample time to notify the seller (and does not require an extra *mise en demeure* in the systems that require one) of the shortcoming (not the breach of contract) in an informal fashion seems just. If the consumer does not notify (in time) he will not lose all his remedies; he will merely be responsible for direct damages that the lack of notification has caused the seller in the transaction with the consumer.[702]

3.2. NOTIFICATION REQUIRED FOR EXTRAJUDICIAL/ SELF-HELP REMEDIES

3.2.1. EU Consumer Sales Approach in the Case of Termination

163 *Notification only required in the case of termination.* The current Consumer Sales Directive does not prescribe anything with regard to the notification of remedies. This is left to national law. Most other EU Consumer Sales *acquis* instruments only prescribe a duty to notify the seller about the intention to invoke termination as a remedy. Moreover, those instruments do not require that the consumer has to notify the termination remedy *within a reasonable time*. The consumer is merely obliged to notify termination if *the consumer* intends to invoke it.

[702] No other implications or causation of damages (e.g. the seller could have mitigated damages in other transactions when knowing about the defect) will be taken into account.

Finally, it has to be mentioned that an extra notice of the remedy by the *buyer* (consumer) is logical in case of an *extrajudicial* termination. However, a *judicial* termination (or other remedies) implies that the buyer (consumer) requests termination in his writ of summons in his conclusions. This should be sufficient to count as a 'notice' of termination.

What about other remedies (such as price reduction or replacement)? Typically, they do not require such a notice, even if they are invoked extrajudicially. Nevertheless, a notification to invoke an extrajudicial remedy might benefit the creditor (buyer/consumer) as well as the debtor (seller).[703] First of all, this notification might be necessary for reasons of proof with regard to the question of which remedy the creditor has chosen (because a court can exercise an *a posteriori* control after the extrajudicial or unilateral use of a remedy). Such a notification enables, moreover, a judge to examine the conditions of application of the chosen remedy (e.g., by looking at the motivation in the notification). A notification also implies that the creditor (buyer/consumer) reflects upon the application of an extrajudicial remedy and that the debtor (buyer) is well informed about the creditor's intentions.

3.2.2. *Required for Self-Help Remedies under a Common Law Approach*

Notification of the self-help remedies rejection, revocation, and cure. 164
It is clear that the self-help remedies under UCC Article 2 – rejection and revocation of acceptance – require a notice within a reasonable time. For their counterpart under common contract law, namely the self-help remedy of termination, this is, however, fairly unclear. Moreover, UCC Article 2 foresees a right to cure for the seller in case of rejection. In this case, the seller has to notify his intention to cure to the buyer.

It is quite logical that the parties should have a duty to notify these extrajudicial remedies. It can be, for example, interesting for reasons of proof to know which remedy the buyer has chosen. If a buyer suddenly no longer wishes to pay it might be unclear whether the buyer wants to merely suspend his obligations or to terminate/cancel the contract by means of a rejection. Such a notification also informs the seller of the buyer's intention, which has to be applauded.

---

703 Jansen, Sanne, 'Notification, Non-performance, Remedies and Defenses: A Complex Relationship' in Loos, Marco B.M., and Ilse Samoy (eds.), *Information and notification duties* (Antwerp: Intersentia, 2015), n° 2.2.

Nevertheless, this 'notification' should perhaps not be bound to a strict timeframe when the buyer is a consumer. It has been argued that notice of termination (in case of rejection and revocation) has to be done *within a reasonable time* (see *supra*, paras. 131–132). A buyer may not be able to 'sit on his rights'. However, this reasoning disregards normal consumer behavior.[704] Often a consumer will 'wait and see' what happens before taking action because he is reluctant to take drastic steps such as immediately terminating the contract.[705]

The question arises whether the buyer's intention to invoke certain remedies must be notified (within a reasonable time) before he can *judicially* invoke a remedy. Or should the notification duty be reserved for the extrajudicial (self-help) variant of the remedy? This question arises in case of the remedies of revocation of acceptance and rejection. It would be harsh upon the consumer to require him to notify his intention to invoke, for example, termination remedies (such as rejection and revocation of acceptance) regardless of whether he wishes to invoke the remedy as a self-help remedy or in a courtroom. Nevertheless, the notification duty seems to be a condition without which rejection and revocation cannot be administered. In the case of rejection this is understandable. Rejection does not require a prior notification of a breach of contract (according to UCC §2-607(3)(1)). Thus, if the buyer has to give the seller a period of time *to cure* the defect, he should notify the seller of the rejection. In the case of revocation of acceptance, the seller will be often already be notified by the duty of the buyer to notify under UCC §2-607(3)(1) (notification of a breach of contract). In this case, it seems unnecessary to require notification of a judicial revocation of acceptance.

However, it has to be repeated, the notification duty within a reasonable period of time seems to be a condition without which rejection and revocation cannot be administered, *extrajudicially* and *judicially*. The common law system seems to start from a different rationale – not taking into account the judicial/extrajudicial character of the remedy – and tries to limit the use of the far-researching termination remedy if a certain period of time has elapsed.[706]

---

704 Phillips, Jerry J., 'Revocation of Acceptance and the Consumer Buyer', 75 *Com. L.J.* (1970), p. 356.

705 Ibid., p. 356.

706 Jeloschek, Christoph, *Examination and Notification Duties in Consumer Sales Law* (Munich: Sellier, 2006), pp. 193–94.

3.2.3. *Notifying Extrajudicial Remedies for Fair Balance*

Notification of extrajudicial (self-help) remedies. Under most instruments, the most drastic self-help remedy, termination, requires a notification. The consumer has to warn his seller of the fact that he intends to invoke this remedy. The instruments remain mostly silent about other remedies. 165

It is logical that *judicial remedies*[707] do *not require* any special or separate notification. The most well-known judicial remedies – such as damages – will indeed be preceded by a notification of a shortcoming (at least under the UCC, although not necessarily under EU consumer sales law), and will then require a judicial claim (summons). Indeed, the consumer will have to bring a judicial action to enforce his 'judicial remedies'. The consumer will specify the chosen remedy in his writ of summons or in his conclusion. Consequently, there is no need for any extra notification of the remedy. The claim for the remedy in the writ of summons or in the conclusion will suffice. As previously stated, remedies which can be invoked as self-help remedies, but are invoked judicially, will also follow the rule that there is no need for an extra notification of the remedy. It would be too harsh upon the consumer to require that he notifies his intention to invoke, for example, a termination remedy regardless of whether he wishes to invoke this remedy as a self-help remedy or in a courtroom. If the consumer invokes the remedy in a courtroom, he should not be automatically required to notify his intention to invoke it beforehand.

This is different for extrajudicial/self-help remedies (such as extrajudicial termination). Indeed, here, a notification of the unilateral application of the remedy should, in principle, be required. Unfortunately, none of the EU or US instruments explicitly prescribe a notice for invoking other self-help remedies (such as, e.g., price reduction or cover (*supra*, footnote 43)). It would be wise to require, for any self-help remedy, a notification duty, unless it would be totally useless because time is of the essence.

Moreover, a *right to cure* is often appropriate in case of the extrajudicial application of remedies (*supra*, paras. 87, 90, and 112). The buyer's notification will give the seller the chance to cure his shortcoming. This implies that the consumer will often have to *allow the seller a certain period*

[707] I.e., remedies that require a prior intervention of a judge, or that the consumer chooses to enforce before a judge.

of time in his notification before he can unilaterally apply the chosen extrajudicial remedy.[708]

What about the *form* and *content* of this notification? Well, similarly to the notification of a shortcoming, these requirements should be interpreted in a lenient way in the consumer context. With regard to the form of the notification, this implies that an informal (and even oral) notification suffices. Nevertheless, for reasons of proof, it is advised that the consumer uses a written notice (e.g., e-mail, online chat, SMS, or letter).[709] With regard to the content, it will often be required that the consumer sets a period of time within which the seller can cure. The consumer has to make clear that he intends to invoke an extrajudicial remedy and link it to an alleged shortcoming. This notification can also count as a notification of a shortcoming, but the shortcoming can also be already notified by a previous and separate notification.

With regard to the *timing* of the notice of an extrajudicial remedy, a consumer-friendly approach would be that this notification duty is *not bound to a time limit*. In commercial sales, notice of a remedy is often required within a reasonable period after discovery or delivery and this is probably justified. However, in consumer cases it should not be necessary to notify an extrajudicial remedy within as a 'reasonable period' after discovery or delivery. The harsh consequence would be that the consumer loses the remedy if he fails to comply with this requirement of timeliness.

---

708 See also Mak, Vanessa, *Performance-oriented Remedies in European Sale of Goods Law* (Oxford: Hart Publishing, 2009), p. 174 *et seq.*

709 Depending on which means of proof are allowed.

CHAPTER 5
CONCLUSION

The organization of remedies. The main discussion of this book took place over three chapters. Chapter 2 discussed the so-called '*hierarchy*' of remedies that is prescribed by consumer sales law in the US and the EU. Then, in Chapter 3 the (in)ability to invoke remedies *extrajudicially* was assessed. Finally, in Chapter 4, the role of *notification duties* was examined. When carrying out this analysis, the main question was: what is the best possible organization of remedies to protect consumers?[710] 166

Current state of affairs. With regard to the *hierarchy* of remedies (damages, specific performance, and termination), the US system basically favors damages over specific performance, while the European system mostly sticks with the promised contract,[711] favoring specific performance. At first sight, the starting points for the two systems are very different. Nevertheless, the exceptions to these basic rules in both systems are sometimes so important that it cannot be denied that both systems are converging.[712] When comparing the *termination remedy* (also called cancellation or rescission) in the different legal systems, it has to be concluded that often a certain degree of 'seriousness' of the breach is required, both in the EU and the US.[713] 167

With regard to the *extrajudicial application* of the remedies, it has been seen that under almost all of the EU instruments examined in this book, the termination remedy can be applied extrajudicially (except

710 See also for a clarification of this goal, *supra*, para. 4.

711 Of course, the preference for specific performance is not present to the same extend in civil law countries.

712 See also Haas, Daniel, et al., 'Introduction' in Smits, Jan, et al. (eds.), *Specific Performance in Contract Law: National and Other Perspectives* (Antwerp: Intersentia, 2008), p. 2 ('the practical difference between the civil law and the common law is not as great as the diverging principles suggest').

713 Llewellyn defends the argument that consumer should be permitted rescission (termination) for minor defects: Llewellyn, Karl N., 'On Warranty of Quality, and Society: II', *Colum. L. Rev.* (1937), p. 388.

for termination under the current Consumer Sales Directive in some EU countries). Similarly, in the US system, termination can be invoked extrajudicially. Concerning specific performance, the EU instruments do not explicitly provide or prescribe an extrajudicial application for this remedy (repair or replacement). However, in the opinion of the present author, those instruments allow the consumer to unilaterally invoke specific performance. In contrast, in the US system specific performance is certainly not considered a self-help right. As consumer, one has to go to a judge to enforce it. Finally, the damages remedy is typically, under both systems, applied judicially (and not extrajudicially) because of the necessary assessment of the amount of damages by a judge.

With regard to the *notification duty of shortcomings*, the EU consumer system currently tends towards abolishment. Indeed, the legislator is gradually shifting towards a notification-free system. Whereas the Consumer Sales Directive still gives the national legislator the opportunity to introduce such a notification duty within certain boundaries; the CESL and the newest Commission Proposal (ODSD Proposal/2017 Proposal) do away with such a notice. In the US, notification of a shortcoming is not typically required. Nevertheless, the UCC has introduced an important duty to notify a shortcoming in the case where the buyer has accepted the goods and wants to claim damages for a defect. Especially when consumers are involved, many authors do not believe that the benefits of a notification for the seller balance the disadvantages for the consumer.

The current Consumer Sales Directive does not prescribe anything with regard to the *notification of remedies*. This is left to national law. Most other EU Consumer Sales acquis instruments only prescribe a duty to notify the debtor about the intention to invoke termination as a remedy. What about other remedies (such as price reduction or replacement)? Typically, they do not require such a notice, even if invoked extrajudicially. Nevertheless, such a notification to invoke an extrajudicial remedy might benefit the creditor as well as the debtor. With regard to the US, it is clear that the self-help remedies under UCC Article 2 – rejection and revocation of acceptance – require notice within reasonable time. For their counterpart under common contract law, namely the self-help remedy of termination, this is unclear.

168 *The approaches to achieve the best possible organization of remedies.* Throughout the book the main question was: what is the best possible organization of remedies to protect consumers? At the beginning of this book, *economic* and *procedural* protection measures for consumers, related to the EU goals of consumer protection and the creation of an internal

market were highlighted (*supra*, para. 4). With regard to a remedial system, this should imply – in the present author's opinion – that this system can be fairly easily applied and that it would support fast and generous solutions for consumers. The interests of the sellers cannot be totally disregarded, implying safeguards to prevent consumers abusing the system (which is, in this author's opinion, mainly achieved by obliging the consumers to act in good faith). Throughout the book, answers have been provided for each element: the hierarchy of remedies, the (extra)judicial application of remedies, and the notification duties of the consumer. It should be remembered that the discussion here is incomplete. Indeed, not only does it omit to take into account other branches of the law and other contractual aspects, but it is also fails to treat each and every aspect of the organization of remedies (*supra*, para. 5 and *infra*, para. 174). Consequently, these results will have to be revisited after examination of other elements (such as the notion of non-conformity, limitation periods, examination duties, and other remedies). The provisional answers given here about the best possible ways to organize consumer sales remedies must be framed against the background of the methods used.

Indeed, it cannot be denied that this book has also implicitly (and sometimes unintentionally) used (or not used) certain methods to approach both legal systems to formulate recommendations for the 'best possible way to organize the consumer sales remedies'. Therefore, these methods and biases should be made more explicit.

In this book, the *law and economics* approach towards the damages/specific performance dilemma, stemming from a libertarian ideology (see e.g., para. 53), has been criticized as contradicting results have been reached by this method. Moreover, it is also dangerous to single out one approach – as classical law and economics scholarship does – merely focused upon reaching the most 'efficient' outcome.[714] This theory is also based upon the so-called rational choice theory; reflecting an unrealistic view on consumers. Consumers are thought to have fixed preferences and make rational choices in order to maximize their self-interested preferences. Sellers are trying to provide consumers with those products and services at the lowest possible cost.[715] However, research has suggested that consumers do not behave in this way.[716] This is not to say

[714] Be it pareto efficiency or Kaldor-Hicks-efficiency.

[715] For this description, see: White, Alan M., 'Behavior and Contract', 27 *Law & Inequality: A Journal of Theory and Practice* 1 (2009), pp. 138–39.

[716] See e.g. Camerer, Colin F., and Loewenstein, George, 'Behavioral Economics: Past, Present, Future' in Camerer, Colin F., et al. (eds.), *Advances in Behavioral Economics*

that the whole law and economics approach is useless altogether. Although efficiency is not the cornerstone of the discussion here, it does take into account – albeit as a secondary goal next to consumer protection – the idea of an EU internal market. This implies that the seller should not be too heavily burdened by consumer protection demands. Nevertheless, efficiency should not be the sole goal of legislation. White describes it correctly as: 'efficiency being one of the normative goals in a pluralistic value approach, also taking into account consumer autonomy, equity, and the prevention of consumer exploitation'.[717] This can also be reconnected with the approach of the EU towards consumers: sometimes the average, careful, and informed consumer is taken as the reference and sometimes the weakness of the consumer.[718] This pluralistic approach is indeed the way forward; a consumer cannot be seen as monolithic and invariable. A consumer is influenced by society and culture. The consumer's behavior differs in each given situation depending on the product or service.[719] Moreover, efficiency is not a goal in itself but is a means to achieve a goal. Thus, what is considered efficient for a given consumer or lawmaker will depend on the goals that are set by the consumer or the lawmaker.

It has to be stressed that the discussion in this book has not started from a certain ideology; however, it would not be fair to claim that the results are value-neutral.

First of all, the author has been *trained and educated as a European and Belgian* scholar with a strong preference for *dogmatic* research. Dogmatic research has to be understood as research trying to thoroughly describe a legal system as a coherent logical system, put in its historical context.

Also *legal comparison* is an important component in this book. The mere choice of a legal comparison with the US is also not void of any

(Princeton: Princeton University Press, 2004), pp. 3–51. See, for more references to research: White, Alan M., 'Behavior and Contract', 27 *Law & Inequality: A Journal of Theory and Practice* 1 (2009), p. 149 *et seq.* See, for the influence of neuroscience: Camerer, Colin, et al., 'Neuroeconomics: How Neuroscience Can Inform Economics', XLIII *Journal of Economic Literature* (2005), pp. 9–64.

717 White, Alan M., 'Behavior and Contract', 27 *Law & Inequality: A Journal of Theory and Practice* 1 (2009), pp. 171–72.

718 See Unberath, Hannes and Johnston, Agnus, 'The Double-Headed Approach of the ECJ Concerning Consumer Protection', 44 *CML Rev.* (2007), pp. 1237–84; Vannerom, Johan, *Consumentenbescherming bij de uitvoering en herziening van kredietovereenkomsten* (Antwerp: Intersentia, 2015), 699p. See also Incardona, Rossella, and Christina, Poncibò, 'The Average Consumer, the Unfair Commercial Practices Directive, and the Cognitive Revolution', 30 *J. Consum. Pol.* (2007), pp. 21–38.

719 Vannerom, Johan, *Consumentenbescherming bij de uitvoering en herziening van kredietovereenkomsten* (Antwerp: Intersentia, 2015), p. 98.

predestination. It goes without saying that legal comparison is quite an obvious choice if one originates from a small country, such as Belgium. Indeed, it is difficult to draw general conclusions when case law is limited and legal scholarship is too scarce to include all the newest innovative legal theories. Moreover, in Belgium, case law is published in a very partial and unsystematic way, which forces Belgian authors to look at other legal systems.

The previously described scarcity of availability of case law also influenced the choice to not conduct additional quantitative *empirical research*, since data would undeniably be incomplete. An added obstacle is the fact that in an EU context it is impossible to master all the languages of the local courts, and thus it is impracticable to conduct quantitative empirical research based upon case law without an EU-wide based research team. But what about the existing quantitative and qualitative empirical studies? For the US, that the limited empirical studies on remedies appeared to be inconclusive (see *supra*, para. 54). For the EU, answers were based mainly on the 2009 Qualitative Eurobarometer Study on sales remedies (see *supra*, paras. 81–82).[720]

White correctly pointed out that researchers should be explicit about their normative goals.[721] Therefore, it is important to make the goals and underlying values of this book more explicit. As previously stated, '*consumer protection*' has been chosen as being the most important pillar of this book. The interests of the sellers and the development of the internal market were also taken into account, but as a secondary goal. This is indeed a *normative and a value based* choice. This implies that the *main* criterion is – according the present author – not the most efficient outcome, implying the lowest or the most competitive price for consumers (which is closely connected to the internal market goal). Therefore it is clear, as stated before, that a single goal approach, such as the law and economics approach towards efficiency and welfare maximizing has to be rejected in so far it provides for '*the*' answer. It can only be a (secondary) part of the answer. In this author's view, the limits on unbridled consumer protectionism provide such an answer. Those limits are the consumers' notification duties and the duty of a consumer to act in good faith

720 Qualitative Eurobarometer Study, Sales Remedies, Conducted by TNS Qual+ at the request of Directorate General for Health and Consumers, December 2009, http://ec.europa.eu/consumers/archive/rights/docs/aggregate%20report_dec2009_en.pdf.

721 White, Alan M., 'Behavior and Contract', 27 *Law & Inequality: A Journal of Theory and Practice* 1 (2009), 171.

(see *supra*, paras. 85 *et seq.*, 162, and 165). These safeguards will protect the seller and will prevent him from being forced to raise his prices in a reaction to unrestricted consumer protection.

But how to further explain or to express this idea of consumer protection if not based on the most competitive prices? Whitman described this in an illuminating article as the difference between the consumer *economic* interest versus the consumer *protection* interest.[722] The economic interest is aiming at the most competitive prices, while the consumer protection interest implies, according to Whitman, what he pejoratively called 'paternalistic guarantees'. By describing these guarantees and their mechanisms, it is necessary to refer to the emotions of feelings of the consumer. Therefore, this book is indeed not free of an implicit behavioral approach. Indeed, reference is made to elements of psychology and the emotions of buyers and sellers. Consider, for example, references made to the *difficulty* for consumers to choose the 'right' remedy when there is a strict hierarchy to respect; the idea of *(dis)trust* between a consumer and the seller when a seller defaults; the concept of *simplicity* when it comes to the remedial system; the *ease* with which consumers can invoke extrajudicial remedies; *the emancipatory character* of extrajudicial remedies and the *bargaining power* of consumers when they have extrajudicial remedies at their disposal; the element of *good faith* obligations between consumers and sellers; and the idea of legal *certainty* and *clarity* for the seller when requiring a duty to notify.[723] All those elements have a connection to a certain feeling or emotion of sellers and buyers. At first sight, those elements seem trivial and even 'unscientific'. Nevertheless, they play an important role in consumer's well-being. Their protective value is – according the present author – underestimated.

Taking into account these pluralistic consumer protection interest values, the following answers have been formulated as to the best possible way to organize the remedies.

169 *Hierarchy of the remedies, providing a free, but tempered, choice.* In consumer sales contracts, the consumer should be granted a free choice between the different remedies (damages, specific performance, termination (and price reduction)). No strict hierarchy should prevail. This free choice will be tempered by the principle of good faith and proportionality (see also *supra*, para. 85). In case of, for example, termination, proportionality

---

[722] See also *supra*, para. 2. Whitman, James Q., 'Consumerism Versus Producerism: A Study in Comparative Law', 177 *Yale L.J.* (2007), p. 348.

[723] See *supra*, paras. 84, 85 *et seq.*, 112, 156, 161–62, and 165.

will often require that the consumer has to show that the breach of contract is not futile. Critics of this approach might say that the principle of good faith is too vague and heterogeneous to be a helpful guideline for judges to sort out the cases. However, a more strict approach of the good faith principle has been defended (see *supra*, paras. 85 and 87). Only if the seller chooses a remedy, and a reasonable and careful person would *manifestly* not ask for it in the same circumstances, would this lead to an intervention by the judge.[724] Critics may also suggest that more concrete rules, such as rules on a *Nachfrist*, a right to cure, or rules about fundamental non-performance[725] will lead to more legal clarity and certainty. Although these arguments cannot be denied, it seems to the present author that this legal certainty might lead to rigidity. In consumer cases the judge should be allowed to take into account all the circumstances of the case that might be in favor of the consumer. A good faith requirement leads to a flexible standard for a judge. The latter can intervene in the cases in which the seller's interests have been manifestly and disproportionally affected.

Extrajudicial remedies, but tempered. A consumer should be able to invoke most remedies, except for damages, without prior court intervention. We have seen that termination, for example, can in almost in all systems be applied extrajudicially. However, being one of the most invasive remedies, this possibility will be tempered by the principle of good faith and proportionality. Indeed, when invoking termination extrajudicially, the consumer should often leave the seller a reasonable time to cure the shortcoming (except in very urgent situations). Moreover, another boundary for extrajudicial (self-help) remedies, should be a notification duty of the intention to invoke such a remedy (see also *supra*, para. 165 and *infra*, para. 172). 170

'Light' version of notification of a shortcoming. As stated, getting rid of the notification duties all together to strengthen consumer protection tilts the balance too far in the directions of consumer protection, without taking into account the stakes for the seller. The consumer must take into account some mitigating principles, and therefore this book has proposed a compromise (see also *supra*, para. 160). This compromise would give a consumer enough time to notify (and would not require an extra *mise en demeure* in the systems that require one). A mere informal 171

---

724 I.e., the Belgian general criterion on which the abuse of rights is prohibited.

725 It can also be argued that rules about fundamental non-performance are also very vague.

notification of a shortcoming (not breach of contract) would be sufficient. If the consumer fails to notify (in time) he will not lose all his remedies. The consumer will merely be responsible for any direct damages that the lack of notification has caused the seller in the transaction with the consumer. These damages can be deducted from the consumer's remedies.

172 *Notification of extrajudicial remedies.* With regard to the notification of remedies, a distinction between judicial and extrajudicial (self-help) remedies has been made (see also *supra*, para. 165). It is logical that *judicial remedies* do not require – in principle – any special notification because the consumer will have to bring a judicial action to enforce those remedies. There is no need for a separate notification of the remedy, since the consumer will have specified the chosen remedy in his writ of summons or in his conclusion. However, in case of *extrajudicial/self-help remedies* a notification of the intention to unilaterally apply the remedy is required. Although US and EU instruments only prescribe this notification duty explicitly for the remedy of termination, it is wise to require a notification duty for every self-help remedy, unless notification would be totally useless because time is of the essence.

173 *Balanced system, including free choice, extrajudicial remedies, and notification duties.* Consumers are parties that have to be protected in case of a breach of a consumer sales contract. However, they may not be overprotected to the detriment of the sellers. Consumers must be able to choose the remedy they think fit for the shortcoming by the seller; they must be able to invoke extrajudicial remedies, such as extrajudicial termination, price reduction, and replacement. But this freedom has to be counterbalanced. A first boundary will be provided by the principle of good faith and fair dealing. In some circumstances the shortcoming has to be sufficiently serious (e.g., when deciding to terminate the contract completely) or the consumer has to give the seller a right to cure (when invoking a remedy extrajudicially). Another limit to the freedom and the protection of consumers is that a consumer has to complain in some way about the defect. He does not have to do it immediately; he does not have to respect any form; and he does not have to notify in a precise language. He will not lose his remedies if he fails to notify, but he will be responsible for the losses that the seller suffers in this transaction because of the lack of non-conformity. The whole idea of this proposal is to give a consumer freedom and boundaries at the same time.

The proposed system can be schematically represented as shown in Figure 1.

Figure 1. Organization of the consumer's sales remedies

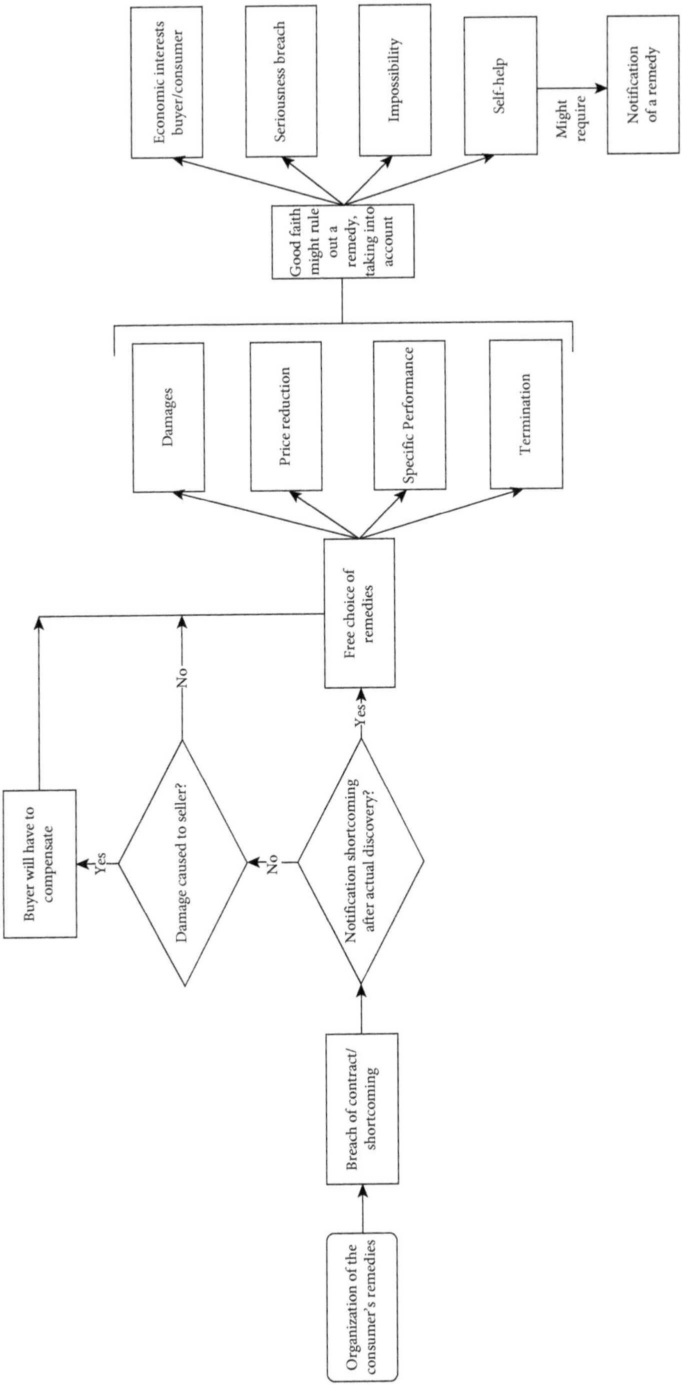

Source: Compiled by the author.

174 *Many elements un(der)explored.* As has been stated, this comparative study of the organization of consumer sales remedies is inevitably incomplete (see *supra*, para. 5). By merely taking into account the 'formal' hierarchy of remedies, the (extra)judicial application of remedies, and the notification duties (of shortcomings and of remedies) many important aspects have been left out, even with regard to the remedial systems. An important underexposed element is, for example, that some remedies are underexplored in this book, such as price reduction, cover/execution in kind by a third party or by the contracting party. Moreover, the duties to examine of the buyer, the limitation rules, and their relationship to the notification duties have not been sufficiently integrated in this book.[726] The influence of absolute limitation periods has also not been considered here. It is also useful to pay more attention to the question whether a remedy is only applicable if certain breaches of the contract occur (such as 'non-conformity' of the goods, hidden defects, and late delivery) or whether a remedy is applicable for all 'non-performances' or breaches of the contract. Therefore, this book has to be understood as a call for further research. It is vital to finally uncover the complex relationship between all those variable elements and to test their consumer-friendliness.

[726] See extensively Jeloschek, Christoph, *Examination and Notification Duties in Consumer Sales Law* (Munich: Sellier, 2006), pp. 40 *et seq.* and 50 *et seq.* and 194 *et seq.*

BIBLIOGRAPHY

Anenson, T. Leigh, 'Treating Equity Like Law: A Post-Merger Justification of Unclean Hands', 45 *Am. Bus. L.J.* (2008).

Arbel, Yonathan, A., 'Contract Remedies in Action: Specific Performance', *W. Va. L. Rev.* (2015).

Authenticated U.S. Government Information, 'Seventh Amendment', https://www.gpo.gov/fdsys/pkg/GPO-CONAN-REV-2014/pdf/GPO-CONAN-REV-2014-10-8.pdf (2014).

Averch, Craig H., et al., *Commercial Law and Practice Guide* (New York: Matthew Bender & Co., Inc., 2016).

Ayres, Ian, and Schwartz, Alan, 'The No-Reading Problem in Consumer Contract Law', 66 *Stan. L. Rev.* 3 (2014).

Badawi, Adam B., 'Self-Help and the Rules of Engagement', 29 *Yale J. On Reg.* (2012).

Bar-Gill, Oren, *Seduction by Contract: Law, Economics and Psychology in Consumer Markets* (Oxford: Oxford University Press, 2012).

Benfield, Marion W., and Greenfield, Michael M., *Sales: Cases and Materials* (New York: Foundation Press, 2015).

Berryman, Jeff, 'The Specific Performance Damage Continuum: An Historical Perspective', 17 *Ottawa L. Rev.* (1985).

Bianca, Cesare Massimo, 'Article 3. Droits et remèdes du consommateur' in Bianca, Cesare Massimo, et al. (ed.), *La directive communautaire sur la vente, Commentaire* (Brussels/Paris: Bruylant-LGDJ, 2004).

Bishop, William, 'The Choice of Remedy for Breach of Contract', 14 *J. Legal Stud.* (1985).

Bouckaert, Boudewijn, and De Geest, Gerrit, *Encyclopedia of Law and Economics*, http://reference.findlaw.com/lawandeconomics/contents.html: Elgar, 2000.

Braithwaite, John, *Regulation, Crime, Freedom* (Dartmouth: Ashgate, 2000).

Brandon, Douglas I., et al., 'Special Project: Self-Help: Extrajudicial Rights, Privileges and Remedies in Contemporary American Society', 37 *Vand. L. Rev.* (1984).

Bray, Samuel L., 'The Supreme Court and the New Equity', 68 *Vand. L. Rev.* 4 (2015).

——, 'The System of Equitable Remedies', 63 *UCLA L. Rev.* (2016).

Brès, A., *La résolution du contrat par dénonciation unilatérale* (Paris: Litec, 2009).

Büdenbender, Ulrich, '§441' in Dauner-Lieb, Barbara, et al. (eds.), *Schuldrecht* (Bonn: Deutscher Anwalt Verlag, 2002).

Cafaggi, Fabrizio, and Micklitz, Hans-Wofgang (eds.), *New Frontiers of Consumer Protection. The Interplay Between Private and Public Enforcement* (Cambridge: Intersentia, 2009).

Camerer, Colin, et al., 'Neuroeconomics: How Neuroscience Can Inform Economics', XLIII *Journal of Economic Literature* (2005).

Camerer, Colin, and Loewenstein, George, 'Behavioral Economics: Past, Present, Future' in Camerer, Colin, et al. (eds.), *Advances in Behavioral Economics* (Princeton: Princeton University Press, 2004).

Canaris, Claus-Wilhelm, *Schuldrechtsmodernisierung 2002* (Munich: Beck, 2002).

Carter, Caroline, et al., *Consumer Warranty Law* (Boston: National Consumer Law Center, 2010).

Cartwright, Peter, *Consumer Protection and the Criminal Law* (Cambridge: Cambridge University Press, 2001).

Cauffman, Caroline, 'The Principle of Proportionality and European Contract Law', Working Paper n° 2013/2, http://ssrn.com (2013).

——, 'The Principle of Proportionality and European Contract Law' in Rutgers, Jacobien, and Sirena, Pietro (eds.), *Rules and Principles in European Contract Law* (Cambridge: Intersentia, 2015).

Chafee, Zechariah, 'Foreword' in Re, Edward D. (ed.), *Selected Essays on Equity* (New York: Oceana, 1955).

Chavis, Marvin, 'Notice of Breach and the Uniform Commercial Code', 25 *U. Fla. L. Rev.* (1972–73).

Claeys, Ignace, and Vancoillie, Jonas, 'Remedies, Modification of Digital Content and Right to Terminate Long-Term Digital Content Contracts' in Claeys, Ignace, and Terryn, Evelyne (eds.), *Digital Content & Distance Sales* (Cambridge: Intersentia, 2017).

Clark, Barkley, 'The First Line of Defense in Warranty Suits: Failure to Give Notice of Breach', 15 *UCC Law Journal* (1982).

Cole, Tony, et al., 'Legal Instruments and Practice of Arbitration in the EU', *SSRN Working Paper* (2015).

Cooter, Robert, and Ulen, Thomas, S., *Law and Economics* (Boston: Addison-Wesley, 2016).

Corbin, Arthur Linton, et al., *Corbin on Contracts* (New Providence, San Francisco: Matthew Bender & Co., Inc., 2016).

Cosway, Richard, 'Sales – A Comparison of the Law in Washington and the Uniform Commercial Code', 36 *Wash. L. Rev.* (1961).

D'sa, Rose M., and Krummel, Thomas, 'Sale of Consumer Goods and Associated Guarantees: A Minimalist Approach to Harmonized European Union Consumer Protection', *E.L.Rev.* (2001).

Dang Vu, Tâm, 'Remedies in the European Harmonisation Projects: Enforced Performance, Termination and Damages' in Keirse, Anne L.M., and Loos, Marco B.M. (eds.), *Alternative Ways to Ius Commune* (Cambridge: Intersentia, 2012).

Davis, T., 'UCC Breach of Warranty and Contract Claims: Clarifying the Distinction', 61 *Baylor L. Rev.* (2009).

Dawson, John P., 'Specific Performance in France and Germany', 57 *Mich. L. Rev.* (1959).
Delahaye, Thierry, *Résiliation et résolution unilatérales en droit commercial belge* (Brussels: Bruylant, 1984).
Delforge, Catherine, 'Garantie des biens de consommation: primauté de l'exécution en nature par le vendeur' (note under Bree 2 October 2008, Tongeren 14 June 2010), *T. Vred.* (2012).
Delforge, Catherine, and Ninane, Yannick, 'La garantie de conformité des biens de consommation, Chronique de jurisprudence (2005–2015)' in Wéry, Patrick (ed.), *Théorie générale des obligations et contrats spéciaux* (Brussels: Larcier, 2016).
Delforge, Catherine, et al., 'De quelques délais emblématiques du contrat de vente' in X., *Contrats spéciaux* (Limal: Anthemis, 2013).
Demeyere, L. and Visser, M., 'Ingebrekestellingsclausules' in Ballon, G.-L., et al. (eds.), *Contractuele Clausules* (Antwerp: Intersentia, 2013).
Dobbs, Dan B., *Law of Remedies* (St. Paul: West Academic, 1993).
Driesen, David M. and Malloy, Robin Paul, 'Critiques of Law and Economics', *SSRN, Working Paper* (2015).
Duesenberg, Richard W., et al., *Sales & Bulk Transfers Under the UCC* (New York: Matthew Bender & Co., Inc., 2016).
Eisenberg, Melvin A., 'Actual and Virtual Specific Performance, the Theory of Efficient Breach, and the Indifference Principle in Contract Law', 93 *Calif. L. Rev.* (2005).
Eisenberg, Theodore, and Miller, Geoffrey P., 'Damages Versus Specific Performance: Lessons from Commercial Contracts', 12 *J. Empirical Legal Stud.* (2015).
Elster, Jon, *Explaining Social Behavior. More Nuts and Bolts for the Social Sciences* (Cambridge: Cambridge University Press, 2007).
Emmerglick, Leonard J., 'A Century of the New Equity' in Re, Edward D. (ed.), *Selected Essays on Equity* (New York: Oceana, 1955).
Engels, Martin, and Stark, Johanna, 'Buttons, Boxes, Ticks, and Trust' in Mathis, Klaus (ed.), *European Perspectives on Behavioural Law and Economics* (Heidelberg: Springer International Publishing Switzerland, 2015).
Farnsworth, E. Allan, 'Legal Remedies for Breach of Contract', 70 *Colum. L. Rev.* (1970).
——, *Farnsworth on Contracts* (New York: Kluwer, 2004).
Feltkamp, Regine, and Vanbossele, Frederic, 'The Optional Common European Sales Law: Better Buyer's Remedies for Seller's Non-Performance in Sales of Goods?', *ERPL* (2011).
——, 'Remedies Under the Optional Common European Sales Law – A Good Alternative for Belgian Sales Law?' in Claeys, Ignace, and Feltkamp, Regine (eds.), *The Draft Common European Sales Law: Towards an Alternative Sales Law?* (Antwerp: Intersentia, 2013).
Ferriell, Jeff, *Understanding Contracts* (New Providence, San Francisco: Matthew Bender & Co., Inc., 2009).

Fikentscher, Wolfgang, and Heinemann, Andreas, *Schuldrecht* (Berlijn: De Gruyter, 2006).

Fischer, James M., *Remedies* (New Providence, San Francisco: Matthew Bender & Co., Inc., 2014).

Flechtner, Harry M., 'Remedies Under the New International Sales Convention: The Perspective from Article 2 of the U.C.C.', *J. L. Commerce* (1988).

Fonseca, Patricia F., and Fonseca, John R., *Williston on Sales* (Eagan: West, 2006).

Foss, Howard, 'The Seller's Right to Cure when the Buyer Revokes Acceptance: Erase the Line in the Sand', 16 *S. Ill. U. L. J.* (1991–92).

Frank, John P., and Endicott, John, 'Defenses in Equity and "Legal Rights"', 14 *La. L. Rev.* (1954).

Freitheit, Jessica, 'The Breakdown of Hierarchy: Damages at Law versus Damages in Equity', 27 *Man. L.J.* (1999–00).

Fried, Charles, *Contract as Promise* (Cambridge: Harvard University Press, 1981).

——, 'Contract as Promise Thirty Years On', XLV *Suffolk U. L. Rev.* (2012).

Fuller, Lon L., and Perdue, William R., 'The Reliance Interest in Contract Damages: 1', *Yale L.J.* (1936).

——, 'The Reliance Interest in Contract Damages: 2', *Yale L.J.* (1936).

Gärtner, Anette, *Die Umsetzung der Verbrauchsgüterkaufrichtlinie in Deutschland und Grossbritannien* (Frankfurt am Main: Peter Lang, 2006).

Geis, Gilbert, and Edelhertz, Herbert, 'Criminal Law and Consumer Fraud: A Sociolegal View', 11 *Am. Crim. L. Rev.* (1973).

Gergen, Mark P., 'A Theory of Self-help Remedies in Contract' 89 *B.U. L. Rev.* (2009).

Gilbride, Gerard A., 'The Uniform Commercial Code: Impact on the Law of Contracts', 30 *Brook. L. Rev.* (1964).

Glenn, Garrard, and Redden, Kenneth R., 'Equity: A Visit to the Founding Fathers' in Re, Edward D. (ed.), *Selected Essays on Equity* (New York: Oceana, 1955).

Gold, Andrew S., 'A Moral Rights Theory of Private Law', 52 *Wm. & Mary L. Rev.* (2011).

Grädler, Thomas, and Köchel, Manuel, 'Das kaufrechtliche Abhilfenrecht nach dem Kommissionsentwurf für ein Gemeinsames Europäisches Kaufrecht' in Schmidt-Kessel, Martin (ed.), *Ein einheitliches europäisches Kaufrecht?* (Munich: Sellier, 2012).

Greenberg, Harold, 'Specific Performance Under Section 2-716 of the Uniform Commercial Code: "A More Liberal Attitude" in the "Grand Style"', 17 *New Eng. L. Rev.* (1981–82).

Grossfeld, Bernhard, 'Money Sanctions for Breach of Contract in a Communist Economy', *Yale L.J.* (1963).

Grundmann, Stefan, 'Consumer Law, Commercial Law, Private Law: How Can the Sales Directive and the Sales Convention Be So Similar?', 14 *EBLR* 3 (2003).

Haas, Daniel, et al., 'Introduction' in Smits, Jan, et al. (eds.), *Specific Performance in Contract Law: National and Other Perspectives* (Antwerp: Intersentia, 2008).

Hammond, George F., 'Notification of Breach Under Uniform Commercial Code Section 2-607(3)(a): A Conflict, a Resolution', 70 *Cornell L. Rev.* (1984–85).

Harris, D. R., 'Specific Performance – A Regular Remedy for Consumers?', 119 *L.Q.R.* (2003).

Hawes, Cynthia, and Twigg-Flesner, Christian, 'Sales and Guarantees' in Howells, Geraint, et al. (eds.), *Handbook of Research on International Consumer Law* (Cheltenham: Edward Elgar Publishing Ltd, 2010).

Hawkland, William D., *Sales & Bulk Sales* (Philadelphia: AliAba, 1958).

Henning, William H., and Lawrence, William H., 'A Unified Rationale for Section 2-607(3)(a)', 46 *San Diego L. Rev.* (2009).

Herman, Shael, 'Specific Performance: A Comparative Analysis', *Edin. L. Rev.* 7 (2003).

Herrestal, Carsten, 'Die Grenzen der richtlinienkonformen Rechtsfortbildung im Kaufrecht', *WM* (2007).

Heutger, Viola, and Oosterhuis, Janwillem, 'Specific Performance Within the Hierarchy of Remedies in European Contract Law' in Smits, Jan, et al. (eds.), *Specific Performance in Contract Law: National and Other Perspectives* (Antwerp: Intersentia, 2008).

Hillman, Robert A., 'Keeping the Deal Together After Material Breach – Common Law Mitigation Rules, the UCC, and the Restatement (Second) of Contracts', 47 *U. Colo. L. Rev.* (1976).

——, *Principles of Contract Law* (St. Paul: West Academic, 2014).

Hodges, Christopher, 'Collective Redress: A Breakthrough or a Damp Sqibb', 37 *J. Consum. Pol.* 1 (2013).

Hoffmann, Jan, 'Verbrauchsgüterkaufrechtsrichtlinie und Schuldrechtsmodernisierungsgesetz', *ZRP* (2001).

Holmes, Oliver W., 'The Path of the Law', *Harv. L. Rev.* (1897).

Incardona, Rossella, and Christina, Poncibò, 'The Average Consumer, the Unfair Commercial Practices Directive, and the Cognitive Revolution', 30 *J. Consum. Pol.* (2007).

Ionescu, Raluca Nicoleta, *L'abus de droit en droit de l'Union européenne* (Brussels: Bruylant, 2012).

Jansen, Sanne, 'Hiërarchie in de remedies bij consumentenkoop: bescherming van consumenten en verkopers?' (note under Gent 20 October 2010), *DCCR* (2012).

——, 'Notification, Non-performance, Remedies and Defenses: A Complex Relationship' in Loos, Marco B.M., and Samoy, Ilse (eds.), *Information and Notification Duties* (Antwerp: Intersentia, 2015).

——, 'Price Reduction as a Remedy in European Contract Law and the Consumer Acquis' in Keirse, Anne L.M., and Loos, Marco B.M. (eds.), *Alternative Ways to Ius Commune. The Europeanisation of Private Law* (Antwerp: Intersentia, 2012).

——, *Prijsvermindering: remedie tot bijsturing van contracten* (Antwerp: Intersentia, 2015).

Jansen, Sanne, and Stijns, Sophie, 'Proposal for a Directive on Certain Aspects Concerning Contracts for the Online and Other Distance Sale of Goods. Scope of Application, Definitions, and Conformity' in Claeys, Ignace, and Terryn, Evelyne (eds.), *Digital Content & Distance Sales* (Cambridge: Intersentia, 2017).

Jeloschek, Christoph, *Examination and Notification Duties in Consumer Sales Law* (Munich: Sellier, 2006).

Jolls, Christine, et al., 'A Behavioral Approach to Law and Economics', *Stan. L. Rev.* (1998).

Katz, Avery W., 'Remedies for breach of contract under the CISG', 25 *Int. Rev. Law Econ.* (2006).

Keeton, Page W., et al., *Prosser and Keeton on Torts* (St. Paul: West, 1984).

Kelman, Mark, 'Consumption Theory, Production Theory, and Ideology in the Coase Theorem', 52 *S. Cal. L. Rev.* (1979).

Kennedy, Duncan, 'Law-and-Economics from the Perspective of Critical Legal Studies' in Newman, Peter (ed.), *The New Palgrave Dictionary of Economics and the Law* (Macmillan).

Knapp, Charles L., *Commercial Damages: A Guide to Remedies in Business Litigation* (New York: Matthew Bender & Co., Inc., 2016).

Kötz, Hein, *Vertragsrecht* (Tübingen: Mohr Siebeck, 2012).

Krämer, Hannes, 'VW "Dieselgate" – eine juristisch saubere Sache?', *SVR* (2017).

Kronman, Anthony T., 'Specific Performance', 45 *U. Chi. L. Rev.* (1978).

Kruisinga, Sonja A., 'The Seller's Right to Cure in the CISG and the Common European Sales Law' in Keirse, Anne L.M., and Loos, Marco B.M. (eds.), *Alternative Ways to Ius Commune* (Cambridge: Intersentia, 2012).

Lagarde, Xavier, 'Remarques sur l'actualité de la mise en demeure', *JCP G* (1996).

Langbein, John H., 'What ERISA Means by "Equitable": The Supreme Court's Trail of Error in Russel, Mertens and Great-West', 103 *Colum. L. Rev.* (2003).

Langbein, John H., et al., *History of the Common Law. The Development of Anglo-American Legal Institutions* (New York: Kluwer, 2009).

Lawrence, William H., 'Cure After Breach of Contract Under the Restatement (Second) of Contracts: An Analytical Comparison with the Uniform Commercial Code', 70 *Minn. L. Rev.* (1986).

Laycock, Douglas, 'The Death of the Irreparable Injury Rule', 103 *Harv. L. Rev.* 3 (1990).

——, *The Death of the Irreparable Injury Rule* (New York: Oxford University Press, 1991).

——, 'The Triumph of Equity', 56 *Law & Contemp. Probs.* (1993).

Leete, Burt A., 'The Notice Booby-Trap of U.C.C. Section 2-607(3)(a)', 22 *Am. Bus. LJ* (1984).

Lenaerts, Annekatrien, 'The General Principle of the Prohibition of Abuse of Rights: A Critical Position on its Role in a Codified European Contract Law', *ERPL* (2010).

Lewinsohn-Zamir, Daphna, 'Do the Right Thing: Indirect Remedies in Private Law', 94 *B.U. L. Rev.* (2014).

Libchaber, Rémy, 'Demeure et mise en demeure en droit français' in Fontaine, Marcel, and Geneviève Viney (eds.), *Les sanctions de l'inexécution des obligations contractuelles* (Brussels: Bruylant, 2001).

Linzer, Peter, 'On the Amorality of Contract Remedies – Efficiency, Equity, and the Second *Restatement*', *Colum. L. Rev.* (1981).
Listokin, Yair, 'The Empirical Case for Specific Performance: Evidence from the IBP-Tyson Litigation', *Journal of Empirical Studies* (2005).
Llewellyn, Karl N., 'On Warranty of Quality, and Society: II', *Colum. L. Rev.* (1937).
Loos, Marco B.M., 'Consumer Sales Law in the Proposal for a Consumer Rights Directive', *ERPL* (2010).
——, 'Sales Law in the DCFR', *SSRN, Centre for the Study of European Contract Law Working Paper Series No. 2010/04* (2010).
——, 'Not Good But Certainly Content: The Proposals For European Harmonisation of Online and Distance Selling of Goods and the Supply of Digital Content' in Claeys, Ignace, and Terryn, Evelyne (eds.), *Digital Content & Distance Sales* (Cambridge: Intersentia, 2017).
Looschelders, Dirk, *Schuldrecht, Besonderer Teil* (Munich: Vahlen, 2011).
Lord, Richard A., *A Treatise on the Law of Contracts by Samuel Williston* (Westlaw, 2013).
Mackaay, Ejan, *Law and Economics for Civil Law Systems* (Cheltenham: Edward Elgar, 2013).
Mak, Vanessa, *Performance-oriented Remedies in European Sale of Goods Law* (Oxford: Hart Publishing, 2009).
Marysse, Steven, 'De Wet Consumentenkoop: enkele beschouwingen' (note under Gent 27 May 2009), *RW* (2010).
Matusche-Beckmann, A., '§441' in Martinek, M., *von Staudingers Kommentar zum BGB* (Berlijn: Sellier – de Gruyter, 2013).
Micklitz, Hans-W., and Wechsler, Andrea (eds.), *The Transformation of Enforcement. European Economic Law in a Global Perspective* (Oxford: Hart Publishing, 2016).
Milberger, Patrick A., 'Section 2-607(3)(a): Effective Notification of Breach under the Uniform Commercial Code', 44 *U. Pitt. L. Rev.* (1983).
Miller, Lucinda, 'Specific Performance in the Common and Civil Law: Some Lessons for Harmonisation' in Giliker, Paula (ed.), *Re-examining Contract and Unjust Enrichment* (Leiden: Martinus Nijhoff Publishers, 2007).
Minish, Robert A., 'The Uniform Commercial Code In Minnesota: Articles 2 and 6 – Sales and Bulk Transfers', 50 *Minn. L. Rev.* (1965–66).
Müller-Chen, Markus, 'Art. 50 CISG' in Schlechtriem, Peter, and Ingeborg Schwenzer (eds.), *Commentary on the CISG* (Oxford: Oxford University Press, 2005).
Muris, Timothy J., 'The Cost of Freely Granting Specific Performance', 1982 *Duke L.J.* (1982).
Murray, John E., *Murray on Contracts* (Durham: Carolina Academic Press, 2011).
Musgrave, Thomas D., 'Comparative Contractual Remedies', *U.W. Austl. L. Rev.* (2008–09).
Nadel, Andrea G., 'Specific Performance of Sale of Goods Under UCC §2-716', 26 *A.L.R.4th* 294 (*s.d.*).

Nader, Ralph, *Consumer and Corporate Accountability* (Boston: Houghton Mifflin Harcourt P, 1973).

Navarretta, Emanuela, 'Good Faith and Reasonableness in European Contract Law' in Rutgers, Jacobien, and Sirena, Pietro (eds.), *Rules and Principles in European Contract Law* (Cambridge: Intersentia, 2015).

Nordstrom, Robert J., *Law of Sales* (St. Paul: West Academic, 1970).

PEB Study Group 'Uniform Commercial Code, Article 2 Executive Summary', 46 *The Business Lawyer* (1991).

Perillo, Joseph M., *Contracts* (St. Paul: West Academic, 2014).

Pesando, Marie K., 'Election of Remedies', 25 *Am. Jur. 2d* (2017).

Phillips, Jerry J., 'Revocation of Acceptance and the Consumer Buyer', 75 *Com. L.J.* (1970).

——, 'Notice of Breach in Sales and Strict Tort Liability Law: Should There Be a Difference?', 47 *Ind. L.J.* (1971–72).

Poillot, Elise, 'The ECJ and General Principles Derived from the Acquis Communautaire' in Rutgers, Jacobien, and Sirena, Pietro (eds.), *Rules and Principles in European Contract Law* (Cambridge: Intersentia, 2015).

Popineau-Dehaullon, Catherine, *Les remèdes de justice privée à l'inexécution du contrat* (Paris: LGDJ, 2008).

Posner, Richard A., 'Law and Economics is Moral', 24 *Valparaiso U. L. Rev.* (1990).

——, *Economic Analysis of Law* (New York: Kluwer, 2011).

Pozen, David E., 'Self Help and the Separation of Powers', 124 *Yale L.J.* (2014).

Priest, George L., 'Breach and Remedy for the Tender of Nonconforming Goods Under the Uniform Commercial Code: An Economic Approach', 91 *Harv. L. Rev.* (1978).

Prince, Harry G., 'Overprotecting the Consumer? Section 2-607(3)(a) Notice of Breach in Nonprivity Contexts', 66 *N.C. L. Rev.* (1987–88).

Prosser, William L., 'The Assault upon the Citadel (Strict Liability to the Consumer)', 69 *Yale L.J.* (1960).

Purnhagen, Kai, 'Never the Twain Shall Meet? A Critical Perspective on Cultural Limits Between Internal Continental Dogmatism and Consequential US-style Law and Economics Theory', *Munich Risk and Insurance Center Working Paper 14* (2013).

Reich, N., 'Negotiation and Adjudication. Class Actions and Arbitration Clauses in Consumer Contracts' in Cafaggi, Fabrizio, and Micklitz, Hans-Wofgang (eds.), *New Frontiers of Consumer Protection* (Cambridge: Intersentia, 2009).

Reitz, John C., 'Against Notice: A Proposal to Restrict the Notice of Claims Rule in U.C.C. §2-607 (3) (a)', 73 *Cornell L. Rev.* (1987–88).

——, 'The Mysteries of the *mise en demeure*', 63 *Tul. L. Rev.* (1988–89).

Rendleman, Doug, 'Irreparability Irreparably Damaged', 90 *Mich. L. Rev.* (1991–92).

Riefa, Christine, 'Uncovering the Dangers Lurking Below the Surface of European Consumer Arbitration', *SSRN Working Paper* (2010).

Ring, Gerhard, 'Absgas-Manipulationssoftware und Gewährleistungsrechte der Käufer', *NJW* (2016).

Roberts, Caprice L., 'The Restitution Revival and the Ghosts of Equity', 68 *Wash. & Lee L. Rev.* (2011).
Samoy, Ilse, and Dang Vu, Tâm, 'Performance and Non-performance in the DCFR' in Sagaert, Vincent, et al. (eds.), *The Draft Common Frame of Reference: A National and Comparative Perspective* (Antwerp: Intersentia, 2012).
Schmidt-Kessel, Martin, 'Art. 120 GEK-E' in Schmidt-Kessel, Martin (ed.), *Der Entwurf für ein Gemeinsames Europäisches Kaufrecht* (Munich: Sellier, 2014).
Schmitt, Michael A., and Pasterczyk, M., 'Specific Performance under the Uniform Commercial Code – Will Liberalism Prevail?', 26 *DePaul L. Rev.* (1976).
Schopper, Alexander, 'Verpflichtungen und Abhilfen der Parteien eines Kaufvertrages oder eines Vertrages über die Bereit-stellung digitaler Inhalte (Teil IV CESL-Entwurf)' in Wendehorst, Christiane, and Brigitta Zöchling-Jud (eds.), *Am Vorabend eines Gemeinsamen Europäischen Kaufrechts* (Vienna: Manzsche Verlags- und Universitätsbuchhandlung, 2012).
Schulze, Reiner, and Zoll, Fryderyk, *European Contract Law* (Munich: Beck, 2016).
Schwartz, Alan, 'The Case for Specific Performance', *Yale L.J.* (1979).
——, 'Regulating for Rationality', 67 *Stan. L. Rev.* 6 (2015).
Schwartz, Alan, and Scott, E. Robert, *Sales Law and the Contracting Process* (New York: Foundation Press, 1991).
Sebert, John A., 'Legal Theory: Rejection, Revocation, and Cure under Article 2 of the UCC: Some Modest Proposals', 84 *Nw. U.L. Rev.* (1990).
Shavell, Steven, 'Specific Performance Versus Damages for Breach of Contract: An Economic Analysis', 84 *Tex. L. Rev.* (2006).
Shiffrin, Seana V., 'The Divergence of Contract and Promise', 120 *Harv. L. Rev.* (2007).
Shoben, Elaine W., 'Of Carts and Horses: Organizing Remedies for the Classroom', 57 *St. Louis U. L.J.* (2012–13).
Shreve, Gene R., 'Book Review. The Premature Burial of the Irreparable Injury Rule', 70 *Tex. L. Rev.* (1992).
Sibony, Anne-Lise, 'Can EU Consumer Law Benefit from Behavioural Insights?' in Mathis, Klaus (ed.), *European Perspectives on Behavioural Law and Economics* (Heidelberg: Springer International Publishing Switzerland, 2015).
Sibony, Anne-Lise, and Alemanno, Alberto, 'The Emergence of Behavioural Policy Making: A European Perspective' in Alemanno, Alberto, and Sibony, Anne-Lise (eds.), *Nudge and the Law: A European Perspective* (London: Hart Publishing, 2015).
Sibony, Anne-Lise, and Helleringer, Geneviève, 'EU Consumer Protection and Behavioural Sciences: Revolution or Reform?' in Alemanno, Alberto, and Sibony, Anne-Lise (eds.), *Nudge and the Law: A European Perspective* (Oxford: Hart Publishing, 2015).
Sievers, Alexander, 'Rechtsprechungsübersicht zur Abgasthematik (EA 189)', *DAR* (2016).
Simpson, Alfred W.B., *A History of the Common Law of Contract. The Rise of the Action of Assumpsit* (Oxford: Clarendon Press, 1987).
Sinel, Zoë, 'De-Ciphering Self-Help', 67 *U. Toronto L.J.* (2017).

Smiley, Michael S., 'Where Do We Start Professor? An Approach to Starting and Navigating Article 2 of the Uniform Commercial Code', 40 *Idaho L. Rev.* (2003).

Smits, Jan, 'The new proposal for harmonised rules for the online sales of tangible goods: conformity, lack of conformity and remedies, Policy Dept C in-depth analysis, PE 536.492', https://polcms.secure.europarl.europa.eu/cmsdata/upload/d0da0b4b-4afd-4ac1-8ed8-7a2ed8e1bb5d/Smits.pdf (2016).

Speidel, Richard E., 'Buyer's Remedies of Rejection and Cancellation under the UCC and the Convention', 6 *J. Contract L.* (1993).

Steennot, Reinhard, 'Garantietermijn tweedehandsgoederen' (note under Gent 27 May 2009), *NjW* (2010).

Steennot, Reinhard, and Dejonghe, Sofie, *Consumentenbescherming en Handelspraktijken* (Antwerp: Intersentia, 2007).

Stijns, Sophie, 'De remedies van de koper bij niet-conformiteit' in Stijns, Sophie, and Stuyck, Jules (eds.), *Het nieuwe kooprecht, De wet van 1 september 2004 betreffende de bescherming van de consumenten bij verkoop van consumptiegoederen* (Antwerp: Intersentia, 2005).

——, 'De consumentenkoop: actuele knelpunten' in Tilleman, Bernard, and Verbeke, Alain (eds.), *Knelpunten verkoop roerende goederen* (Antwerp: Intersentia, 2009).

Stijns, Sophie, and Swaenepoel, Elke, 'Consumentenkoop' in Tilleman, Bernard, and Terryn, Evelyne (eds.), *Beginselen van Belgisch Privaatrecht* (Brussels: die Keure, 2011).

Stolzenberg, Doreen, 'UCC Section 2-608: Reasonable Time for Revocation of Acceptance', 44 *Ford. L. Rev.* (1976).

Straetmans, Gert, and Meys, Shana, 'The New Proposals for Directives Concerning Digital Content and Online/Distance Sales' in Claeys, Ignace, and Terryn, Evelyne (eds.), *Digital Content & Distance Sales* (Cambridge: Intersentia, 2017).

Strong, S.I., 'Regulatory Litigation in the European Union: Does the U.S. Class Action Have a New Analogue?', *SSRN, University of Missouri School of Law Legal Studies Research Paper No. 2012–25* (2012).

Sutherland, Edwin H., *White Collar Crime: The Uncut Version* (New Haven: Yale University Press, 1985).

Szladits, Charles, 'The Concept of Specific Performance in Civil Law', 4 *Am. J. Comp. L.* (1955).

Taibleson, B., 'Forgiving Breach: Understanding the Preference for Damages over Specific Performance', 27 *Quinnipiac L. Rev.* (2009).

Taylor, Celia R., 'Self-help in Contract Law: An Exploration and Proposal', 33 *Wake Forest L. Rev.* (1998).

Tiefer, Charles, 'Forfeiture by Cancellation or Termination', 54 *Mercer L. Rev.* (2003).

Twigg-Flesner, Christian, and Meltcafle, D., 'The Proposed Consumer Rights Directive – Less Haste More Thought?', *ERCL* (2009).

Ulen, Thomas, S., 'The Efficiency of Specific Performance: Toward a Unified Theory of Contract Remedies', 83 *Mich. L. Rev.* (1984).

Unberath, Hannes, and Johnston, Agnus, 'The Double-Headed Approach of the ECJ Concerning Consumer Protection', 44 *CML Rev.* (2007).

Van Hecke, M.T., 'Changing Emphases in Specific Performance', 40 *N.C.L. Rev.* (1961–62).
Vandemaele, Sanne, 'Hiërarchie tussen de remedies bindt zowel de eindverkoper als de consument: focus op herstel en vervanging is en blijft essentieel', *DCCR* (2017).
Vannerom, Johan, *Consumentenbescherming bij de uitvoering en herziening van kredietovereenkomsten* (Antwerp: Intersentia, 2015).
Visscher, Louis, 'De rangorde van remedies voor wanprestatie: subsidiariteit en proportionaliteit versus efficiëntie', *NTBR* (2007).
Voet, Stefaan, 'European Collective Redress Developments: A Status Quaestionis', *SSRN, Working Paper*, https://ssrn.com/abstract=2318809 (2013).
Vogenauer, Stefan, 'The Prohibition of Abuse of Law: An Emerging General Principle of EU Law' in De La Feria, Rita, and Vogenauer, Stefan (eds.), *Prohibition of Abuse of Law. A New General Principle of EU Law?* (Oxford: Hart Publishing, 2011).
Von Bar, C., and Clive, E., *Draft Common Frame of Reference (DCFR)*, 6 V. (Munich: Sellier, 2009).
Weinrib, Ernest J., 'Corrective Justice in a Nutshell', *U. Toronto L.J.* (2002).
——, *Corrective Justice* (Oxford: Oxford University Press, 2012).
Weller, Marc-Philippe, *Die Vertragstreue: Vertragsbindung, Naturalerfüllungsgrundsatz, Leistungstreue* (Tübingen: Mohr Siebeck, 2009).
Wendehorst, Christiane, 'Rücktritt ("Beeindigung") im Entwurf für ein Gemeinsames Europäisches Kaufrecht' in Schmidt-Kessel, Martin (ed.), *Ein einheitliches europäisches Kaufrecht?* (Munich: Sellier, 2012).
——, 'Art. 114 GEK-E' in Schmidt-Kessel, Martin (ed.), *Der Entwurf für ein Gemeinsames Europäisches Kaufrecht* (Munich: Sellier, 2014).
Wéry, Patrick, 'Les droits légaux du consommateur en cas de défaut de conformité' in Biquet-Mathieu, Christine, and Wéry, Patrick (eds.), *La nouvelle garantie des biens de consommation et son environnement légal* (Brussels: die Keure, 2005).
Westermann, H.P., '§441' in Krüger, W., and Westermann, H.P. (eds.), *Münchener Kommentar BGB* (Munich: Beck, 2012).
White, Alan M., 'Behavior and Contract', 27 *Law & Inequality: A Journal of Theory and Practice* 1 (2009).
White, James J., and Summers, Robert S., *Uniform Commercial Code* (St. Paul: West Academic).
——, *Principles of Sales Law* (St. Paul: Thomson Reuters, 2009).
Whitman, James Q., 'Consumerism Versus Producerism: A Study in Comparative Law', 177 *Yale L.J.* (2007).
Whittaker, Simon, 'Unfair Contract Terms and Consumer Guarantees: The Proposal for a Directive on Consumer Rights and the Significance of "Full Harmonisation"', *ERCL* (2009).
Whittaker, Simon, and Zimmermann, Reinhard, 'Coming to Terms with Good Faith' in Zimmermann, Reinhard, and Whittaker, Simon (eds.), *Good Faith in European Contract Law* (Cambridge: Cambridge University Press, 2000).

——, 'Good Faith in European Contract Law: Surveying the Legal Landscape' in Zimmermann, Reinhard, and Whittaker, Simon (eds.), *Good Faith in European Contract Law* (Cambridge: Cambridge University Press, 2000).

Wittenberg, Jeffrey D., and Kaplan, Elizabeth, *Commercial Contracting: Sales Under the UCC* (New York: LJP, 2016).

Wright, Charles Alan, 'The Law of Remedies as a Social Institution', 18 *U. Det. L.J.* (1955).

Wright, David, 'Discretion with Common Law Remedies', 23 *Adel. L. Rev.* (2002).

Yorio, Edward, 'In Defense of Money Damages for Breach of Contract', 82 *Colum. L. Rev.* (1982).

——, 'A Defense of Equitable Defenses', 51 *Ohio St. L.J.* (1990).

Zimmermann, Reinhard, *The New German Law of Obligations* (Oxford: Oxford University Press 2004).

Zimmermann, Reinhard, and Simon, Whittaker (eds.), *Good Faith in European Contract Law* (Cambridge: Cambridge University Press, 2000).

Zöchling-Jud, Brigitta, 'Rechtsbehelfe des Käufers im Entwurf eines Gemeinsamen Europäischen Kaufrechts' in Schmidt-Kessel, Martin (ed.), *Ein einheitliches europäisches Kaufrecht?* (Munich: Sellier, 2012).

——, 'Art. 106 GEK-E' in Schmidt-Kessel, Martin (ed.), *Der Entwurf für ein Gemeinsames Europäisches Kaufrecht* (Munich: Sellier, 2014).

——, 'Art. 109 GEK-E' in Schmidt-Kessel, Martin (ed.), *Der Entwurf für ein Gemeinsames Europäisches Kaufrecht* (Munich: Sellier, 2014).

——, 'Art. 110 GEK-E' in Schmidt-Kessel, Martin (ed.), *Der Entwurf für ein Gemeinsames Europäisches Kaufrecht* (Munich: Sellier, 2014).

Zoll, Fryderyk, 'Article 106' in Schulze, Reiner (ed.), *Common European Sales Law (CESL)* (Munich: Beck, 2012).

——, 'Article 109' in Schulze, Reiner (ed.), *Common European Sales Law (CESL)* (Munich: Beck, 2012).

——, 'Article 110' in Schulze, Reiner (ed.), *Common European Sales Law (CESL)* (Munich: Beck, 2012).

——, 'Article 114' in Schulze, Reiner (ed.), *Common European Sales Law (CESL)* (Munich: Beck, 2012).

——, 'Article 115' in Schulze, Reiner (ed.), *Common European Sales Law (CESL)* (Munich: Beck, 2012).

——, 'Article 120' in Schulze, Reiner (ed.), *Common European Sales Law (CESL)* (Munich: Beck, 2012).

Zollers, Frances E., et al., 'Consumer Protection in the European Union: An Analysis of the Direction on the Sale of Consumer Goods and Associated Guarantees', *U. Pa. J. Int. Econ. L.* (1999).

INDEX*

* References are to paragraph numbers.

ABOUT THE AUTHOR

Sanne Jansen is a trainee judge and prosecutor in Antwerp, Belgium and a research fellow at the Institute for the Law of Obligations, KU Leuven.

Sanne obtained her Bachelor's degree at the University of Antwerp and her Master's degree at KU Leuven. She defended her PhD thesis, 'Price Reduction: A Remedy to Adjust Contracts', at KU Leuven in 2015, while holding a research assistant mandate (2010–2012) and a FWO predoctoral fellowship (2012–2016). She completed several research stays (Université Catholique de Louvain, University of Vienna, University of Oxford and Paris I Panthéon-Sorbonne University) as part of her PhD thesis. In 2016–2017, she was a postdoctoral BAEF fellow at the Yale Law School and Columbia Law School.

www.ingramcontent.com/pod-product-compliance
Ingram Content Group UK Ltd.
Pitfield, Milton Keynes, MK11 3LW, UK
UKHW021012120926
8556IPUK00039B/1039

9 781780 686516